A Storm Within

By Esther Vance

TEACH Services, Inc.
PUBLISHING
www.TEACHServices.com • (800) 367-1844

World rights reserved. This book or any portion thereof may not be copied or reproduced in any form or manner whatever, except as provided by law, without the written permission of the publisher, except by a reviewer who may quote brief passages in a review.

This book was written to provide truthful information in regard to the subject matter covered. The author assumes full responsibility for the accuracy of all facts and quotations as cited in this book. The opinions expressed in this book are the author's personal views and interpretation of the Bible, Spirit of Prophecy, and/or contemporary authors and do not necessarily reflect those of TEACH Services, Inc.

This book is sold with the understanding that the publisher is not engaged in giving spiritual, legal, medical, or other professional advice. If authoritative advice is needed, the reader should seek the counsel of a competent professional.

Copyright © 2013 TEACH Services, Inc.
ISBN-13: 978-1-4796-0084-7 (Paperback)
ISBN-13: 978-1-4796-0085-4 (ePub)
ISBN-13: 978-1-4796-0086-1 (Kindle/Mobi)
Library of Congress Control Number: 2001012345

Some names have been changed to protect privacy.

Published by

www.TEACHServices.com • (800) 367-1844

Acknowledgments

With much love and gratitude to some very special people who made a difference in my life. They showed me kindness and love when I was stranger in a new land.

To Dorothy Kotz, who took me under her wing and supported me through many of my trials.

To Betty Bizer, the principal who created a job for me.

And to Patty Moll, Kitty Getz, and Mary Bennett, dear friends I will never forget.

I want to express my many, many thanks to Dede Hammond. Without her, I would never have had the patience to compile this book. Her continued assistance was a godsend and to me, she is an angel from heaven.

Much gratitude also to Cynthia Dixon who gave me the push I needed to bring this book out into the open. She gave me a great deal of courage and support and I will always think of her as friend.

Prologue

I stood gazing at the majestic eagle perched on a high limb in a cage at the zoo. A throb of pain and sadness went through me as I thought of him confined and denied his freedom. He should be soaring proudly through the sky.

An attendant stopped nearby. "Will he ever fly free again?" I asked.

"No, he was badly injured during a storm. At first we didn't know if he would live. His wings will never be strong enough for him to survive in the wild."

I thought about the storm that had changed the eagle's life, and then I thought of the storms that raged within my life. At times I felt there was no escape, but it was only when I became so tired and weary that I remembered to call upon Jesus. Each time I talked to my Savior, He reached out and set me free. After weathering many storms over the years, I no longer hesitate to pick up the pieces of my life fearing the storm within.

This book is written in hopes that other women will find the peace and freedom I now have. While a partner isn't necessary for life to be fulfilling, beautiful relationships can develop between a husband and wife. My parents' marriage is one of the greatest examples. Many times, however, loyalty and dedication are missing in a union. My prayer is for each couple to allow God to be part of their marriage.

Chapter 1

Mama gave me away when I was seven years old. She gave me away because we didn't have enough food to eat and scarcely enough room to sleep in our thatch-roofed house on stilts. Ten children—Willie (Alson), Udeen, Carolyn, Corine, Esther (me), Francine, Avanel, Niome, Edney and Judyk—and two adults crammed into a house approximately twelve feet by twelve feet. Of the ten rapidly growing children, I was the one who cried the most because of hunger. It made my mama and daddy sad to hear me cry and beg for food.

A little mud hut store stood on a hill not far from our house on Savannah Bight, a small town in Guanaja, one of the bay islands of Honduras. Miss Luisa was a tiny Spanish lady who spoke very little English. She and her husband lived in a house beside their store. The store always had a funny odor from the chickens, pigs, fried beans, and tortillas. As a child, I visited often. If there were a lot of chickens in the store, Miss Luisa would tell me to shoo them out.

"Get out, chickens," I'd say. "Leave Miss Luisa and me alone."

When my dad came back from fishing, he would sell the fish and give each of us ten kids a penny to buy candy. Miss Luisa always gave me two candies for my penny. She liked me best.

Miss Luisa gave Mama a little white dress and specified that it was "just for Esther." It was the first ready-made dress I ever had. My mother sewed by hand all the other clothing the family wore. Occasionally we received secondhand clothing, but that was very seldom.

One Sunday Mama dressed me in the pretty white dress Miss Luisa had given me. At church I asked the lady in charge if I could go up front and sing.

"What are you going to sing?"

"*Row, row, row your boat.*"

"You sang that the last time. Do you know another song?" she asked.

The lady didn't know that it wasn't the song I cared about; I wanted everyone to see my pretty ready-made white dress.

"If you can think of another song, you can sing."

"I can sing the song about Jesus loving all of the children with all the colors."

The lady laughed and said, "Okay."

That day there were many people in church. I sang my song, and they clapped for me. When church was over, I saw Mama talking with an older lady.

"Come here, Esther. I want you to meet someone," Mama said.

All of my sisters and brothers came too, but the lady was only interested in me.

"Hello, Esther; my name is Miss Ethelle. I liked your singing. You are a brave little girl to get up in front of all those people and sing."

"Do you like my dress?" I asked her.

"Yes, it's very pretty."

"Miss Luisa gave it to me," I said.

She just smiled and went on talking. She probably didn't know Miss Luisa. "Your mother tells me you like pretty dresses and shoes. She said you like to dress up."

One of my sisters butted in, "She likes to show off. That's what she likes to do."

Miss Ethelle didn't pay any attention to her; she just kept talking to me.

"How would you like to come and live with me and be my little girl?"

I thought she was joking.

"I'll buy you pretty dresses and shoes, and lots of candy," she said.

My mom just stood there smiling at the woman. My sisters and brothers fell silent. Like me, they couldn't believe what they were hearing.

"I'll bring you to Sunday School here sometimes," Miss Ethelle said. "I have a big house, and only my son and I live there. I would like to have a little girl to keep me company and run errands for me."

"No!" I cried. "No, Mama. Give her Deen; she's the oldest."

"But the lady doesn't want Deen. She wants you." Mama caught my arm, pulled me aside, and whispered, "Esther, you know how you cry every day when you don't have any food to eat."

"Yes, Mama."

"Well, if you go with this nice lady, you will have good food to eat every day."

That sounded too good to be true. I wouldn't have to go to sleep hungry anymore. "Well, Mama," I said. "If I go, will you all come and see me every day?"

"Not every day, but we will come as often as we can," Mama promised.

Some of the people began leaving church, and Miss Ethelle had to leave to catch the boat back to her island. She seemed like a nice woman, and she spoke very kindly. I liked her a little.

"Will you come and give it a try?" Miss Ethelle asked. I said okay, and she gave Mama a few *lempiras* to pay our way to her island. Mama promised to bring me the next day. On the way home, my sisters and brothers teased me, saying I was only going to stay with the woman so I could have food every day. When we got home, we all talked at once, telling my dad about the woman. Later, I learned both my mom and dad had met Miss Ethelle before and knew she was a good Christian woman.

Morning came quickly, and all too soon Mama said, "It's time to get ready to go. Put your clothes in this." She handed me a white pillowcase. I stuffed my three little dresses and two panties inside.

"I'm leaving, Daddy," I said.

"Are you sure you want to leave me?" Daddy asked.

Then it hit me. School! I won't be able to go to school. "What about school? Who will walk with Desiree?" I asked.

"I'm sure the lady will send you to school," Daddy said. "And I'll explain to Desiree that you have gone to live with Miss Ethelle for a while."

Everyone said goodbye to me. Two of my sisters followed behind Mama and me to the dock. I think they were sad for me, but I wasn't sad. The lady had said my family could come and see me anytime, so I thought I would have the best of both worlds.

I can still recall how beautiful the day was as if it was today. Of course, then it seemed every day was beautiful to me. My brothers, sisters, and I were happy playing together, climbing trees, swimming, and building sand houses. There were so many of us we didn't need other kids to play with.

The day Mama took me to Miss Ethelle's house, the ocean was calm and the tide was out. When we reached the island where the lady lived, Mama asked a man for directions to Miss Ethelle's home.

"Which Ethelle? I know at least two of them." He reached for my mother's hand to help her from the dory onto the dock. My mother described Miss Ethelle, and right away the man knew whom she meant. He reached for my hand to help me.

"No, sir," I said. "You don't need to help me. I can get out all by myself." I hopped up on the dock as he told Mama how to find Miss Ethelle's house.

A boy in the dory said, "Hey, little girl, you're leaving your sack behind." My mother bent down, and the boy handed the pillowcase up to her.

"I want to carry my own sack," I said.

Mama gave it to me and then caught my other hand as we walked away from the dock.

"Why are we going so slow?" I asked Mama as other people passed us. "Why are you letting people ahead of us?" She didn't answer. I understand now why she walked so slow and didn't answer. Her heart was sad. She didn't want to leave me with Miss Ethelle.

We finally reached the house. It was painted red and white. I couldn't believe it. I was excited to think I was going to live in a painted house. I knew my brothers and sisters would be jealous when they came to see me. The door was wide open. No one locked their homes on the island. Mama knocked two or three times, but no one came.

"Maybe the lady forgot we were coming," I said.

"Perhaps she went to the store," Mama said.

"Let's go in and sit down and wait until she comes home."

"No, Esther," Mama said. "You know I taught you better than that. You don't walk into anyone's house just because the door is open. We'll wait here for a little while. If she doesn't come, we will find a bench down the street and wait. We can return when we think she is home."

We walked up the boardwalk. Just before we reached the end, we saw a lady step off the main road onto the boardwalk. She came toward us.

"Here she comes," Mama said.

I looked up as the lady drew near. "Mama," I said. "That is not the same lady."

She was so close Mama could not answer me. She cleared her throat, indicating I should hush. "Well, this lady looks much older," I said.

"Hello, hello," the lady said. "I'm so sorry I was not at home. I need to bake bread today, and I went to the store for yeast. I didn't know what time you would arrive, so I left the door open hoping you would realize I wasn't too far away. You could have gone inside and sat down. I was hoping you would."

"My mama doesn't go in people's house if they are not home," I said.

The lady looked at me and smiled. I could see Mama wanted me to hush. I was still thinking she didn't look like the church lady. She had the same kind voice, and when she smiled, she looked like the same lady, but I was unsure.

"I'm so happy you came. I kept thinking the little girl wouldn't come after I left on Sunday. I'm surprised to see her with you today," she told my mother. "Do sit down."

She turned to me. "Welcome to my home, Esther. I think you are going to like it here."

I sat down on Mama's lap, and she put her arms around my waist and pulled me close. Miss Ethelle and Mama began talking about the things I could do to help around the house. I looked around, checking out everything. She had a big, white stove in her kitchen. I had never seen anything like it before, nor the chairs and table that were all polished and shiny. Our stove was a mud stove that Mama had made. My dad or mom had made our table and stools from driftwood picked up from the beach. We had never purchased a piece of furniture. In fact, I had never seen a store that sold furniture. I was fascinated by so many pieces of furniture in the house, especially the rocking chair that I saw as we came in the front door. Oh, I couldn't wait to sit in that chair if she would let me.

All too soon Mama told Miss Ethelle she had to leave because she needed to buy some thread and some worm medicine.

"It's time for your medicine, too, Esther," Mama said.

She gave us medicine every six months because we got worms in our intestines. Sometimes children died when their parents didn't give them the medicine. I guess they didn't have the money to buy it. My parents always sacrificed to save money for the medicine, even if we had to do without salt or sugar for a couple days. Mama knew how important it was for us to have the medicine. After taking the medicine, I would often pass fifty to sixty worms at one time. All of us kids used to be afraid to use the bathroom after we took the medicine. My parents reminded us that we would die if we didn't take the medicine. I'm glad they loved us enough to sacrifice other things so we could have the medicine.

As Mama neared the door, she said, "Be a good girl, Esther, and remember, I'll come to see you often."

I didn't even cry when she left. I stood and watched her walk out of sight. I stood by the door for a long time just looking at the bridge and wondering what the lady was going to do with me now that my mom was gone.

"Come back to the kitchen, Esther," the lady called to me. I didn't want to go. I didn't feel the same now as when my mom was there. I didn't want to stay anymore, but it was too late. My mom was gone.

Miss Ethelle came toward me. "Come into the kitchen, Esther, so we can talk while I cook supper for my son."

I was beginning to be frightened, but her voice was soft and gentle, so I walked with her to the kitchen. She told me I could sit in the chair, but I stood and watched her. She kept talking, but I don't remember anything she said. I just stood there, wondering how far away my mom had walked. I wanted to run and catch her, but I was afraid I would get lost. I wanted to tell her I'd changed my mind. I didn't care if she didn't have food every day for me, I wouldn't cry anymore.

"Would you like something to eat?" Miss Ethelle asked.

"No," I said. I couldn't believe I was saying "no" to food. Food was the reason I had wanted to come here, but now I didn't care about food. I wanted to go back home. It was too late. Mama was gone, but I still didn't cry.

"Tell me when you're hungry," Miss Ethelle said. "And I'll get you something to eat."

I had just turned seven years old, and I suddenly realized that physical food was no longer important. My mother's words came back to me. "Children, there are more important things in this world than food, even though we need it to survive."

How true her words were. At that moment, I would have given anything to be back home with my mom, my brothers and sisters, and especially my dad. I knew I would miss him more than anyone in my family.

Miss Ethelle asked me to help fold some laundry. I had no problem folding clothes. We all helped my mother at home with our clothes. While we worked, she talked. "The house only has two bedrooms," she explained. "My son has one, and you will sleep with me in the other bedroom on a cot until I can find a bed small enough to fit in the room."

The whole time she was talking, I was thinking, *I'm not going to stay here with you. I'm going back home with Mama when she comes to see me tomorrow.* Miss Ethelle tried very hard to make me feel at home, but nothing she did or said made me feel any better. All I could think of was *my* home and *my* family. The day passed. When night came, it brought a surprise. Instead of Miss Ethelle lighting kerosene lamps, lights came on all over her house. I was fascinated because I had never seen a house lit up like this at night. I liked the brightness. Now, I had something to tell my siblings. Something I had seen that they hadn't.

Soon it was time to go to bed. Miss Ethelle got out the cot and showed me how to open it. She gave me a blanket, a pillow, and another sheet to cover up with.

"Does your mother say your prayers with you at night?" she asked.

"Mama and Daddy have worship with us children every night," I said.

"That's great," she smiled. "Would you like me to pray with you, or do you want to pray by yourself?"

"You can pray with me."

She prayed, and then waited for me to pray. I just knelt there. I did not want her to hear me pray, so I got off my knees and climbed onto my cot.

She got up. "It's all right if you don't feel like praying out loud. You can pray alone if you want to."

So I did. I lay on the cot and prayed, *Dear Jesus, I love You with all my heart. Please make Mama come and get me tomorrow. I want to go home. I promise I will not cry for food or anything else anymore. Amen.*

When I woke the next morning, the house was quiet. Miss Ethelle was not in her bed. There was not a sound in the house. I quickly put on my clothes and went out of the bedroom. There was no one in the house. I didn't even think about being scared. I went into the living room and sat in the rocking chair by the window and rocked and rocked. I was finally able to rock in a rocking chair, and no one was around to tell me not to rock too fast. I did not rock hard because I was afraid it would break, but I had fun just being able to sit and rock.

Finally Miss Ethelle came back. She knocked on the door. When I opened it, she asked, "Were you scared to be alone?" Before I could answer, she said, "I always get up early to go to the meat market. They only kill one cow at a time, and if I am not early the best meat will be gone. There was a large crowd at the market this morning, that's why I was so long. I'm sorry you were left alone, but I thought I would be back before you woke up."

I followed Miss Ethelle to the kitchen. "Do you know how to pick beans?" she asked. She took a bag of red beans from her shelf and poured some on the table. There were lots of little pieces of mud and little black bugs among the beans. I finished cleaning the beans and went to the living room to wait for my mom. I waited and waited, but my mom didn't come. My heart grew sadder and sadder. As it began to get dark, I began to cry. Miss Ethelle didn't get angry with me for crying.

"I'm going to fix you something to eat," she said. I wasn't hungry. I just wanted my mom, but she took my hand and asked me to come and sit. I had been standing by the front door most of the day.

"I know you must be tired of standing," she said. "I'm sorry your mom did not make it back to see you today. Maybe she didn't have enough money to pay the dory. I'm pretty sure she will come to visit in a few days."

"My mama is coming tomorrow to get me," I said. "You wait and see."

Miss Ethelle didn't comment. I think she knew my mom wasn't coming, but she didn't have the heart to tell me. The next morning I was up early looking out the front door toward the bridge. I wanted to see my mom step off that main bridge onto the boardwalk that led to Miss Ethelle's house. Another long day passed, and Mama didn't come. I sat in the front door with my legs hanging outside on the boardwalk and cried and cried. I couldn't believe two days had passed and my parents hadn't come for me. I told myself, *I know why they didn't come. I bet the ocean is rough, and my Daddy couldn't go fishing, so he didn't have any money to give Mama to come and get me. Tomorrow they'll come.*

But as the days passed, no one came. I knew my family loved me, but I couldn't understand why they didn't miss me enough to come and get me. I didn't think they should leave me here just because I cried for food all the time.

Miss Ethelle was kind to me, but she never offered to send for my mom. I don't know how many days or weeks passed. It seemed like a long time that I had not seen my family. One day a lady came to visit Miss Ethelle. They must have been friends as they talked for a long time. I heard Miss Ethelle telling her about my mom.

"She has so many children. I felt sorry for her." Then Miss Ethelle told her about me. "I'm so proud of Esther for being so good. I think she is settling down and getting used to being here with me."

That's not true. I'm never going to get used to being here, I wanted to tell her, but my mom had told me not to be disrespectful to adults. Mama had said that when two adults were talking we should never interrupt unless something really bad was happening.

When the lady left, Miss Ethelle said, "Esther, the lady I was talking to is going to ask your mom and dad if they will let her have one of your sisters to come and live with her."

Before she could finish speaking, I burst out, "No! No! Jesus, please don't let her go see my mom. I don't want my sister to come. She will be sad and cry, too."

Miss Ethelle kept talking, telling me how I would have my sister nearby to play with. I didn't say anything more to her. I knew when Mama came to see me I was going to tell her not to give my sister away to that lady. I sat by the window in the living room looking out on the main street. There were a lot of people passing by, more than I used to see at home. I saw a bunch of children dressed in blue and white, and I ran out of the house to the end of the boardwalk so I could watch them march by. I was shocked to recognize some of the children I used to go to school with on my island. Then I saw my brother.

"Hey, Alson!" I hollered. "Where is Mama?"

He was marching so fast he didn't see me. My heart was pounding, and I ran back to the house and told Miss Ethelle I had seen my brother. I don't remember what she said. I just know I was so happy, I did not know what to do with myself. Oh, how I wished I could march with the children. Then I remembered they all had on a uniform. Perhaps, if Miss Ethelle would ask the teacher if I could march with them, I could march even if I didn't have a uniform.

"Let's follow them," I wanted to say to Miss Ethelle, but she didn't look happy when I told her about my brother. I was afraid to ask her to follow the children. I didn't think Miss Ethelle wanted to talk to me about my family, so I walked away from her. I sat by the window again with tears pouring down my face. I felt as if my family was never coming to see me.

A few minutes later a lady stopped in front of the boardwalk leading to Miss Ethelle's house and pointed at it. A little girl stood beside her. I got up from the window and went to the front door. The little girl was my sister Udeen.

"It's my sister!" I screamed to Miss Ethelle. "My sister is coming to get me." I ran out the front door to meet her. Udeen was so happy to see me.

"Is the lady treating you okay?" she asked.

"Where are Mama and Daddy? How come they didn't come to get me?"

"Miss Ethelle wrote a note telling Mama you were doing good," my sister said. "The note said it was better for them not to come for a while until you had gotten used to being away from them."

I couldn't believe what Deen, our family's nickname for Udeen, was telling me. How could my parents believe I was okay without them? How could they not come to see me if they loved me?

Chapter 2

Miss Ethelle met Udeen and me at the door. "Did your mother come, too?" she asked Udeen.

"No, only my brother and I came. I don't know why Mama didn't come. It's the fifteenth of September, Independence Day," Udeen explained.

To celebrate Independence Day, it was the custom for the school children to dress in uniforms and march on the cay. When I had started school with my brother, I had looked forward to the event. Now, I was here, and I only caught a glimpse of the children passing by. I wanted to see Desiree and Jenny and my brother dressed in their uniforms marching with all the other children. Thinking back, I don't believe my sister was supposed to come and see me.

"Could I go with my sister to watch the program the children are going to put on after they finish marching?" I asked Miss Ethelle.

"No, I don't think that is a good idea."

I started to cry, and I begged Udeen to take me anyway. My poor sister—I can't imagine what she must have been going through.

"Couldn't Esther please come with me to see our brother?" Deen asked.

"I'm planning to take Esther to prayer meeting this evening," Miss Ethelle said.

"I don't want to go with you," I cried. "I want to go with my sister." I could see Udeen was scared because I had talked back to Miss Ethelle. If my mom had been there, I know I wouldn't have talked to Miss Ethelle like that, but I was mad because she said I couldn't go with my sister.

Udeen stayed as long as she could, then she said she had to leave. She started to cry and that made me cry even more. I didn't want her to leave me. Miss Ethelle must have felt sorry for both of us because she suddenly decided to let me go to the program. Udeen and I took off running, asking people for the location of the schoolhouse. People kept directing us until we found it. The place was packed by the time we arrived, and the program had already started. We pushed our way through the crowd until we were almost in front of the stage. I saw all of my friends, some were on the stage, and some were sitting in the front rows. I wanted to be a part of them. I started crying again.

"Take me back home with you tonight," I begged Udeen.

"Esther, you know I can't do that. I wasn't even supposed to let you know I was here on the cay."

"Please, please, Deen. Take me home with you."

The crowd was beginning to become upset with my crying as it was disturbing the program. Udeen looked scared and confused, but she finally grabbed my hand and pulled me to where my brother was sitting with the other kids. She bent down and whispered something to him. I don't know what she said. I saw Alson shake his head. Then she turned and pulled me through the crowd.

When we got to the door, Udeen said, "Do you think we can find that lady's house?"

"What lady? What lady do you mean?"

"Miss Ethelle," she said. "Esther, don't play dumb with me. What other lady would I be talking about?"

I started to cry again. "Udeen, don't take me there. Let me stay with you until you are ready to leave."

She caught my hand and started running back the way we had come. While we were running, Udeen was talking. "I'm taking you home with me. Do you know where your clothes are?"

"Yes. I've kept them folded in my pillowcase waiting for Mama to come and take me home."

We ran all the way to Miss Ethelle's house.

"Praise the Lord," Udeen said. "She's not home from prayer meeting yet." The house was dark. I pushed the door wide open, but we were afraid to go inside.

"You know you need your dresses," Udeen said. "Come on, we have to go get them."

We both made a dash inside the house. I went straight to the bedroom where I kept my bag. My fingers closed on the pillowcase. "I've got it," I exclaimed.

"Let's get out of here," Udeen said, and we took off running again.

Two old men were sitting at the end of the boardwalk. We were frightened and stopped running. Neither of us had any idea which way to go.

"Could you please tell us where the dock is?" Udeen asked.

The men looked at us, then at each other. One had a wad of tobacco in his jaw. He spit some nasty stuff right down in front of him.

"Lost, huh, little girls?"

"No sir," Udeen said quickly. "Could you please tell us where the Nidy is docked?"

The old man with the tobacco stood up. "I'm going to show these little girls where the boat is," he said to the other man.

"Little girls," he said. "Why are you going to the boat at this time of the night?"

"We are from Savannah Bight," my sister said, "and we need to get to the boat before it leaves us."

When we got to the boat, my sister jumped to the deck of the boat, and I jumped down behind her. We were both scared. We sat on the deck until the crowd of school children came. Everyone got on board, and the boat took off. When my brother Alson found us, we were in a room with bunk beds. I was laying on the bottom bunk bed, and Udeen was on top.

"Girl," he said to Udeen, "you are going to be in bad trouble when you get home."

"I don't care," Udeen said. But I knew she was scared of what my mother was going to do or say. But praise God, Mama was asleep when we got home.

Daddy heard us come in. "Udeen, your mother is going to be angry with you when she wakes up."

"Don't make any noise, Daddy. I don't want to wake Mama. I'll tell her what happened in the morning."

"All right, child," Daddy said. "There are two pieces of roast corn and a piece of coconut under the bowl on the table. It's your supper. You and Alson will have to share with Esther."

"Udeen can give Esther half of her corn. She was the one who brought her back home. I'm going to tell Mama in the morning, too," Alson said. "I'm not going to take the blame."

Deen shared her corn and coconut with me.

"Turn down the lamp and go to bed, children," Daddy said.

When we woke up the next morning, my dear father had already explained to my mom what Udeen had told him had happened. To our surprise, Mama was not angry with us.

"It was wrong for you to bring her home that way, Udeen," Mama said. "Miss Ethelle must be worried. We need to get word to her that Esther is back home."

I was so happy to be back home and thankful it was all right with my mother. I promised not to complain about food or cause any problems. I was just so thankful to be back with those I loved.

I knew my mother loved me, but I felt separated from her because she hadn't come for me. Weeks slipped by, and I fell into my old habits, playing, and having fun with my sisters and brothers, but they never let me forget my experience and the fact that I had run away.

Chapter 3

I grew up in Guanaja, a small island off the coast of Honduras in Central America. There was a government school on the island. It was a small building with simple benches and a blackboard. Children were rarely able to attend, as the families didn't have money for the necessary paper and pencils. Once every year, my parents could scrape together enough money for the paper and pencils so one or two of us children could go to school.

Neither of my parents had an education, yet my mother taught us to read the Bible. That was the only thing she read. She refused to read anything else. I don't know if she couldn't read anything else or if the Lord just inspired her to stay with the Bible. To this day, the only other book my mother ever picked up was a hymnal. She took time to tell each of us children about God and His wonderful love. She prayed with us every chance she got.

"You pray too much," we would tell her.

She would reply, "Children, I could never pray too much for you."

I had the most precious dad in the whole entire world. He was a hero to every single one of us. Whenever we were scared at night, Daddy would come into our room to comfort us. He didn't have material things to offer, but he gave of himself.

The only job I can recall my father having was when the government built a small airstrip on the island. That was the biggest thing that had ever happened there. Everyone was excited. Planes were going to be landing on our island. When dad heard they were hiring men, he applied and was hired. The boss called the workers together and explained their jobs to them. Daddy told us all about his job when he came home.

With my dad working at the airstrip, we were responsible for working in the bush. That's what we called our little farm where my dad planted bananas, plantains, cassava, coco, pineapples, corn, sweet potatoes, pumpkins, and everything else we ate.

Daddy sold some of what he raised. He grew corn every year. He would run a stick from one end of the house to the other. Two ears of corn were tied together and thrown over the stick. The bad thing about this was that rats came in to eat the corn, and huge snakes came in to eat the rats. The snakes were harmless, but it was startling to wake in the night and see a huge snake eating a rat.

It was hard work helping with the farm because we were so young, but we were all good workers, and we knew how to survive. It was just part of our life living in such poor conditions. But God knew of our circumstances, and He had pity on us. I used to walk on the beach and pick up ketchup bottles the ships had thrown overboard. I would drain the contents into my hand and eat whatever was left in the bottle. We ate anything we could find to survive.

In addition to working our small farm, my dad fished often. In this third world country you were either rich or poor. There were no middle class, and we were the poorest of all. We boiled bananas or whatever we had while we waited for my dad to come home and add fish to our pot. We ate a lot of seafood.

Everything from the garden went into our cooking pot, including yucca, malanga, and whatever fish, conch, or meat we had. It was delicious. When we cooked on the mud stove, we always coated the pots with mud. Whenever the pot got a hole, my mom would plug the hole with cloth and then the cloth was coated with mud so it wouldn't burn. The pot could then withstand the fire. When we had enough flour, we mixed it with grated coconut or bananas to make a cake. It could then be cut into pieces and sold. We also made corn rice to sell.

Life was hard for our family. We never had enough food from the garden, so we hunted iguanas, pigeons, rabbits, turtles, and other small game we could find. My brother Alson liked to hunt iguanas, and sometimes, when I begged him, he would let me go hunting with him. I had to promise not to talk too loud, and not to cry if I fell down, which I did a lot trying to keep up with him. I would beg him to let me use a machete to help chop our way through the woods. At times he let me take one if it wasn't too sharp. I liked chopping through the woods behind Alson. We had two dogs he often took with us to chase down the iguanas when he shook them out of the trees. If the iguana ran into a hole, we had to dig it out. It wasn't an easy job, but when it was your only meal for the day, you did it.

Sometimes we found an iguana lying on the ground bathing in the hot sun laying its eggs. It was an easy prey for the dogs to catch then. The ones on the ground were a different species, which we called "Wushie Willie." The only difference I could see was the color of their skin. They tasted the same to me, and they were delicious. I used to love iguana eggs. They were in a plastic-like sack. Mama would wash the eggs, and just before the iguana meat was completely cooked, she would put the eggs in. That plastic-like bag became like soft rubber. The yolks of the egg would get hard inside, rather like a soft shell.

Most of the time Alson would climb a tree holding a dogwood stick with a snare at the end of it. He would whistle and the iguana would lift his head to see where the whistle was coming from. Then Alson would slip the snare around its neck. With a quick jerk the snare would tighten around the iguana's neck, and another quick jerk brought it out of the tree. Some of the iguanas were huge—we called them *hache-iguanas*.

My dad sometimes hunted with us, but he did not like to kill any kind of animal. In fact, he was a vegetarian all of his life, but he brought us meat so that we could survive. I used to wish I felt the same way about food my dad did.

The beach on which we lived did not belong to us, but to an elderly gentleman named Mr. Willie. Mr. Willie allowed people to build houses out in the water and gave them permission to build a bridge to the shore. Our little house was built slightly better than others in that our kitchen was on the beach. It had a dirt floor and a thatch roof. Like our neighbors, we did not have a bathroom in our house, which was built on stilts in the ocean. Mama cut a hole in the floor under the edge of our bed. We used it to go to the bathroom when the tide was in. It was called a "scuttle hole." I remember sitting over that hole at night and hanging onto Daddy's legs. He never complained about us waking him at night to help us.

There were many coconut trees loaded with coconuts on the beach. There were also mangoes, wild plums, and a few other fruits along his property on the beach. We were not allowed to touch any of them, and my mother tried her best to see we obeyed. However, some days when we were so hungry, the temptation would be too much for us. We would find ourselves up in a coconut tree, mango tree, or under the hog plum tree, knowing we would get a whipping if we were caught. If my mom or dad didn't catch us, someone passing by might tell on us. Sometimes we told on one another.

"We are lucky to live on Mr. Willie's land," Mama would tell us. "When you take his fruits and coconuts, you are stealing." Mom always called sin by its full name. It sounded ugly to me. My poor mother tried to teach us right from wrong, but we found ways of manipulating and pretending what we did wasn't bad.

One of our tricks was to walk on the beach until we were out of Mother's sight. Then one of us would watch to see if anyone was coming while the others climbed the coconut tree. We could climb like monkeys, and in no time we would have those coconuts on the ground. Most of the time we would throw them in the water from the tree. If one fell on the ground, we would kick it into the water since there was a law that anything drifting in the ocean belonged to the person who found it. Afterwards, we would run home as fast as we could and pretend we hadn't left the yard. We hoped our parents hadn't missed us.

One of us would get close to Mama and say, "I see something drifting toward our house. It looks like a coconut. Can we go see?"

Most of the time she would say, "No, wait until it drifts by the house."

Every so often someone else would spot the coconut and get it. If we cried, Mama would say, "There's no reason to cry. That person has just as much right to those coconuts as you do."

She didn't know the trouble we had gone through to get the coconut in the water, but we didn't dare let her suspect what we had done. We knew our mother. She would have made us apologize to Mr. Willie and tell him exactly how we managed to get his coconuts in the water. We tried to convince ourselves that kicking coconuts in the water was not stealing. We told ourselves Jesus knew we were hungry, but deep in my heart, I knew Mama was right, and we were wrong.

Every morning when Mama had worship with us, she made us repeat the Ten Commandments. I hated it when we got to "Thou shall not steal" and "Thou shall not bear false witness." I could recite the Ten Commandments by the time I was seven years old—I knew every one by heart.

Food wasn't the only thing that was hard to come by. Clothing was scarce, too. Mama sewed everything we wore by hand. Sometimes she could buy material, but mostly she used the hundred pound brown cotton bags the flour, sugar, beans, and rice came in. She bleached the brown color and writing from the bags with lemon juice, and then laid the bags in the sun on the beach. When they dried, she wet them again and laid them on the white sand again and again until the dye was gone. Bras, panties, and slips were also made from the bleached bags. A string around the waist kept them on.

Chapter 4

One day after I'd been home several months, a speedboat pulled up on the beach beside our house. I did not recognize the lady who got out, but I soon learned that it was Mrs. Camille, the lady who had talked to Miss Ethelle about having one of my sisters come live with her. Later I learned that she found out I'd run away from Miss Ethelle and decided to ask my mom if she could have me. She was not interested in my sisters; she came especially for me.

I was still only seven years old, and I cried, "No, no, Mama. Don't give me away. I want to stay at home with you. I don't care if we do not have food to eat. I won't cry when I have to share."

But Momma didn't listen to me. She was talking to Mrs. Camille.

"She's a good little girl. Esther is brave and a good little worker."

I think the lady only wanted to hear that I could work.

"Please take her to church sometimes." I heard Mama tell her.

I wanted to hear Mama say, *Baby, you do not have to go. I love you, and I'll never let anyone take you away from me.*

Then the saddest moment came as Mama gave me a hug. She squeezed me and whispered, "I love you. Pray to Jesus at night before you go to sleep." I could see that my brothers and sisters were sad. Two of my sisters had tears pouring down their faces, and then I saw my dad turn his face away. He had tears in his eyes. I kept hoping he would say, "Don't let her go. She is our little girl. She is too young to go to work."

I wanted to scream and say, "Daddy, don't let her take me." But I was afraid, and my mom had said I was brave. I kept thinking that if I cried, the lady would think I wasn't brave and that my mom was lying. I knew Mama felt bad letting me go. I realize now how hard it must have been for her to make the decision. It must have broken her heart, but she knew I would have food that she and my dad couldn't provide.

And that was that. I left that day to go live with Mrs. Camille. "We're just going to the next island. It's not far away," Mrs. Camille said. "You'll get to see your Mama often." Then in the next breath she said, "Little girl, I don't want to hear any crying. Your mother has so many children. She needs help. You will be one less mouth for her to feed."

Even though I was old enough to know the islands were close to one another, I was overwhelmed with the feeling I would never see my family again.

"All right, little girl," Mrs. Camille said when we reached her island. "I'm going to take you to meet my mother."

I followed behind her up an alley until we came to the main road. She walked fast, and I could hardly keep up with her. She kept looking back and saying, "Hurry, girl."

When we finally reached our destination and I hesitated at the door, she said, "Come in, girl, there is no one here that is going to eat you."

Before I could walk inside, she said, "This is my mother, and you will be sleeping with her tonight. Come over here so she can see you."

My heart pounded as I walked over to the hammock where her mother was laying. She was the biggest woman I had ever seen. I was frightened and wanted to go home.

"Tell her your name," Mrs. Camille said.

"Esther," I said, but the word was only a whisper.

"You have to speak louder. She didn't hear you." She turned to her mother. "Mama, her name is Esther."

"Esther? Oh, she has a Bible name. How old is she?"

"Tell her how old you are, Esther."

"Seven."

"What are you going to do with a seven-year-old girl?" her mother asked. "I thought you wanted someone to work for you."

"I do, but it is not easy to find people who want to work today. I am going to teach this girl how to work."

"Good luck," her mother said.

"Mama, do you have any old hammocks, or any kind of bedding that Esther can sleep on until I can make her a bed?"

"I'll see what I can find when I get up," she said. "But I still would like to know what you are going to do with a seven-year-old girl around? "

"Mama, let me worry about that. Now you will have someone to sleep with you at night. You know how I worry about you being alone at night."

"Yeah, well, I would like to know what good a seven-year-old girl can be to me at night. I don't need anyone with me."

"Mama, I want the girl to sleep with you at night. I don't have any place for her to sleep. Why can't she sleep at your house? I want her here with you."

"Well, then she will have to sleep out in the hallway. You know that other old bedroom has too much junk in it. No one can get in there."

"She can't sleep in the hallway, Mama. You know how drunk Campo is when he comes home some nights. He doesn't even know where he is. He will fall over her."

"Well, then I don't know what you are going to do with her?"

"How about out here in the living room on the floor?"

No! No! I wanted to cry. *I don't want to sleep in the living room. I want to go home.* I could feel the coldness in their hearts. I didn't want to be there, but I didn't have a choice. I began to sob quietly. I tried not to let them know I was crying, but the sound came out.

"What are you crying for, girl?"

By this time, I was crying so hard I couldn't speak. I could see I was getting on Mrs. Camille's nerves, and I began to think maybe if I kept crying she would get angry and send me back home.

Her mother finally said, "I guess she can sleep in the corner of my bedroom on the floor until you figure out what you are going to do with her. I think you should send her back to her family. She is too young."

I prayed in my heart, *Dear Jesus, please let her listen to what her mama is telling her.*

"I need to get home," Mrs. Camille said. "I'll bring the girl back later. Try and find bedding for her for tonight. Let's go, girl," she said, turning to me.

We started back to her house. I followed, staying as far back as I could. She didn't even look to see if I was coming. I thought, *If I run away, she won't even miss me until she gets home*, but there was no place for me to run. Then I told myself, *I are not a little girl anymore. Mama said I was brave and a good little worker.* Mama would be very angry with me if I ran away again. On that short walk to Mrs. Camille's house, I changed from a seven-year-old to a twelve-year-old girl.

"All right, Esther," the lady said when we got to her house. "You see this belt hanging on this nail? I hope I never have to use it on you."

I couldn't believe what I was hearing. Would she really whip me with a belt? I thought only moms and dads were allowed to do that. My mom used to whip us with a belt sometimes, but that was okay. She was our mom and she loved us. She would tell us how much it broke her heart to whip us. My mom had a Bible scripture for everything. She repeated Proverbs 23:13 to us, which says, "Withhold not correction from the child; for if thou beatest him with the rod, he shall not die. Punish him with a rod and save his soul from death." All of us children got whippings once in a while, but not until we were warned several times.

The physical and verbal abuse began the second day I was at Mrs. Camille's home. I believe she wanted a slave for she treated me like a slave. She whipped me every day.

She would wait until she was ready to cook before sending me to the store for a missing ingredient. She always expected me back with the onion, salt, or whatever the item was in time for it to be added to what she was cooking. Sometimes, I had to wait in line, but mostly I was able to make it back in time because the people in the little store on the island knew me and felt sorry for me. They dreaded selling anything to Mrs. Camille because she was so fussy. Nothing pleased her—either the garlic heads were too small, the sugar too brown, or she wanted red onions instead of white ones.

My mom and dad did come to see me at Mr. Camille's home. Often one of my brothers or sisters came with them. But this made me cry even more when they had to leave. Before she left, Mama always prayed with me and reassured me that she loved me. But there was a little voice inside me saying, *Mama, why do I have to stay here? Why can't I go home with you if you love me?*

I told Mama I was being treated badly, but I don't think she believed me. Whenever Mama came, Mrs. Camille was nice, but as soon as Mama left, the abuse began again. Mrs. Camille did not have any children of her own, but she treated her husband like a child. The day I arrived her husband spoke kindly to me, and I liked him right away. But I was afraid of Mrs. Camille from the first time I saw her. She was very stern and often used words I did not understand.

In spite of my difficult circumstances, I kept believing that God had a purpose for everything that was happening to me

My bed was made from two large burlap bags sewed together. It was stuffed with *polock*—that's what we called the pods that grew on a large tree. I slept on the floor in a corner of Miss Camille's mother's bedroom. The old lady gave me two old, raggedy hammocks. I spread one of them over the bed, and covered up with the other one. When it was very hot and I didn't need a cover, I would fold one of the hammocks and use it as a pillow. I was promised a pillow, but I never received one. Every morning when I awoke, I rolled up the hammock bed and put it in an old closet. I slept on and covered myself with those old hammocks for five or six years without them being washed. They smelled so badly that I hated to open the closet. I remember turning my face away from the closet door when I opened it at night because of the smell. Clothes were washed in a big washtub using a washboard. I didn't know hammocks could be washed. The hammocks were too heavy for me to wash, and no one else cared that they were not washed.

Each week Miss Gozel came to wash Mrs. Camille's clothes, and she taught me how to rub my clothes on the washboard. She would ring the water out of my clothes for me and help me hang them on the clotheslines. When I was twelve, I told her how awful the hammocks smelled, and she helped me wash them. I really liked Miss Gozel. She talked to me whenever she had a chance if Mrs. Camille wasn't around.

"One day you will grow up and be able to take care of yourself. Then no one will be able to treat you mean." She would whisper to me. "Someday everything will be better."

At times it seemed as if things got worse instead of better. My mom told us we had no control of our circumstances and that we needed to trust in the Lord because He is in complete control. She said because we live in a sinful world none of us are exempt from the results of sin.

I was happy when Miss Gozel came to wash. Even though I was not supposed to talk to her or disturb her, her presence brought a level of comfort to me. Occasionally she brought homemade candy for me. She worked hard. It would take her three or four days to complete the washing for each of the three families she worked for. All the washing, ironing, and starching of the clothes was done by hand.

I felt sorry for Miss Gozel. She had a huge lump on her throat. I watched it grow and grow. It got so big her chin rested on it, and she started to lose her voice. Every so often I overheard people say if they had money they would give it to her to go to the doctor to have the lump removed. If I had money, I would have given it to her because I liked her so much. She had many little children and grandchildren and no husband to help her. Her daughter and grandchildren often came looking for her. They would stand outside the fence and tell her they were hungry and wanted her to come home with them.

"Go home," she would tell them. "You are going to make Grandma lose her job if you stay there." Her daughter was lame and limped when she walked. I can still see her hanging onto that fence calling for her mother to come home. I knew how they felt when they said they were hungry. I had been there, but praise the Lord, I had three meals a day every day now. (It's a good feeling knowing you can eat every day.)

I was not allowed to eat at Mrs. Camille's dinner table. There was a little table in the corner of the kitchen that had been made especially for me. My food was left in the pots on the stove, so I did not have to eat what was left over on the table. But I had to sit outside on the steps until everyone was through eating before I could eat.

When Miss Gozel was there, she was allowed to sit at my little table with me. She always said a blessing with me, but she never ate. She saved the food for her grandchildren. Often, I would share some of my food.

"Give this to your little crippled girl," I would tell her. She didn't want to take it, but I knew I would have food the next meal.

Every so often Mrs. Camille would give Miss Gozel some leftovers and tell her to go home and take it to her children. Sometimes when Mrs. Camille baked bread, she would bake two extra loaves for Miss Gozel to take home to her children. I used to think that was so nice of her. Mrs. Camille really did like Miss Gozel. That was the side of her I liked. She was constantly sharing with someone. I wanted to tell her if she let Jesus come into her heart He would help her not to say bad words or be mean to me. I did not like her when she was mean to me. I asked Miss Gozel to send word to my mom about how I was being treated, but she was afraid she would lose her washing job.

"I feel really, really sorry for you, baby, but you are going to have to grow up fast," Miss Gozel would say. I saw her cry for me many times because of the harsh whippings I received. She tried to tell me what to do so I could avoid being punished.

"When you are sent on an errand, start running the moment you close the gate. Run until you reach the store, then run all the way back home."

I would do it sometimes, but if I saw the other kids playing, I would forget. As I got a little older, I was better about hurrying. But playing was the only thing on my mind until I was about twelve years old.

After a while one of my sisters arrived on the island. When Corine was ten, Mama brought her to the cay to work for Miss Lilly. Of all us children, she had always been the closest to our mother. She missed my mother so much that she became sick and cried most of the time. Corine had been there for two or three days when I went to visit her. She was sitting on the porch crying when I arrived. Miss Lilly was inside by the sink.

"I want to go home," she sobbed.

I remembered how I had felt when I was given away the first time, and I knew it was worse for Corine—she was devoted to our mom. I had to do something to help her.

"Sneak in and get your bag. Be very quiet," I told Corine.

She made it in and out without being seen. I grabbed her hand, and we took off running toward the dock. I found a dory that was going to Savannah Bight, and I talked the man into taking Corine home.

Later, when Mrs. Camille found out what I had done, she gave me a whipping. But I didn't care because I knew that Corine was home where she belonged. I knew I'd do it again if the need arose.

Chapter 5

I wanted to go to school like the other kids. When I asked Mrs. Camille why I was not going to school, she said she needed me to run errands and help around the house. As the years passed, I learned to clean, cook, and keep house, but I longed to go to school, especially since I was not allowed to have a friend over to the house.

I had been with Mrs. Camille three or four years the day I told my mother to tell Mrs. Camille I wanted to go to school to learn to read and write. My mother was afraid to tell her, so I told her if she would come with me, I would tell Mrs. Camille. Mama hesitated, but she could see I was determined. Mrs. Camille was lying in her hammock reading a book. I walked right up to her. It startled her, and she looked right in my face.

"I want to go to school," I blurted out.

She looked up and saw my mother, than she looked back at me. "You do? Well, I was thinking about that, and I talked to Miss Cassie about it. She is willing to help you."

"No," I said. "I want to go to a real school like the other kids do. I don't want to go to Miss Cassie's house." I had never talked to her this way before, and my mom was getting nervous. I didn't care. I wanted to go to school.

Then, Mrs. Camille said, "Miss Leila, you know Esther is here to help me around the house, not to go to school."

"Esther wants to go to school so much. She always did," my mother said. "Please try to send her."

"I need to think about it," Mrs. Camille said.

I knew she would be angry because I had asked in front of my mother, but I didn't care. I was angry inside for the way I was treated. I didn't think there was much more she could do to me. I was whipped every day, cursed at, and called names. My mother had no idea what my life was like there.

I waited for Mrs. Camille to say something to me after my mother left, but she didn't. Then, a couple weeks later, she told me she had talked to a teacher friend of hers. "You can go to school from ten o'clock until eleven-thirty. After that, I need you to be home to set the table and help with lunch."

I was so happy, but I had no idea an hour and a half was such a short time, especially when I was doing something I had always dreamed of doing.

The other children at school couldn't understand why I was allowed to come to school late and leave early. The teacher, Miss Elaine, told them I was just coming to see if I liked it, and then next year maybe I would come full time. I knew she felt sorry for me. She told me every day that I was a smart girl. I did all the homework she gave me. I wanted to learn to read better and do math. Math and spelling were the only two subjects I had time for.

It was a big responsibility for Miss Elaine to stop right in the middle of teaching to tell me when it was time to leave. I had attended school for about two months the day she forgot to tell me it was time to leave. There was no clock in the classroom, so none of us knew what time it was. The teacher wore a watch, which meant she was "high class." I dreamed about wearing a watch, but thought it could never happen.

"Oh, my, Esther!" The teacher suddenly said in a near panic. "Your time is up; you have to leave. Don't worry about your book, just run all the way home. Tell the lady it was my fault as I forgot to tell you what time it was."

I had no idea it was so late. When I got home, they had already eaten lunch, and the kitchen was closed. I tried in vain to explain what had happened.

"I don't want to hear your excuses," Mrs. Camille snapped. "I've made my decision. You are not going to school anymore."

I burst out crying and begged her to give me another chance.

"No, it isn't working out anyway. I need you here all morning," she said. "You can go to Miss Cassie's home in the afternoon from two o'clock until three thirty for school."

I think that was the day I started to hate Mrs. Camille. I told myself I would never go to Miss Cassie's house. I didn't care if I learned to read or write. I was too angry to realize that something was better than nothing and going to Miss Cassie's house was better than not going to school at all.

A couple weeks later, Mrs. Camille told me I could start going to Miss Cassie's for school. That first day Miss Cassie was waiting for me on her front porch. She welcomed me with a smile. She had everything ready and explained what she expected of me. I didn't want to be there, so I didn't pay attention to what she was saying. I wanted to be with the other kids and go to a normal school. But it wasn't my choice, so I went to Miss Cassie's school. In fact, I attended for a long time, and I learned to read a lot better, and do a little bit of math.

I had started to mature some now, and everything embarrassed me. All of my friends knew I got whippings. Whenever they saw marks on my arms or legs, they would pity me, which made me angry. I think everyone on the island knew I was whipped every day. The lady's husband was an iron welder, and he worked right in the yard. People brought their engines to him, or whatever they needed welded. The yard was always full of people. I hated that they could hear me getting whipped. When I saw them on the street or in the stores, I would overhear them say, "I feel sorry for that poor girl." I didn't want people to say that. I didn't want anyone to know I was being mistreated by Mrs. Camille.

Unfortunately, it didn't get any better as I got older, but somehow I got used to the treatment. As the years went by, I would often think about the happy times of my early childhood when I lived with my mom and dad and siblings. I thought about the lessons of faith that Mama had taught me. My mom and dad had enough trust in God for all of us. Even though my dad didn't have much to say, we all knew in his heart he felt the same way Mama did.

"Worship! Worship!" Mama was always saying. "It is time to give God thanks."

My brother Alson would cry sometimes and say, "Why are we giving so much thanks? All we had for supper last night was a piece of coconut."

"How many children went to bed last night without even a piece of coconut?" my dad would respond. He didn't speak often, but he would ask us this question whenever we said anything about not having enough to eat.

"Huh! We're the poorest people on the face of the earth," Alson would say.

I thought we were too, but now I know we were rich in comparison to some of the people around the world because we had love.

One thing that was hard for me to understand while living at home was tithing. Every time my dad sold a few *lempiras*' worth of fish, he would come in and lay the money on the table for my mom. Many times there would be only three *lempiras* for the whole week. My mother would count it out and say, "Thirty cents for tithe." My mom was a faithful steward. She gave ten percent of every *lempira* she had. I could not understand it for the life of me. Why? Why did God need our few dimes and nickels when we were so poor? My mom tried to explain that God did not need our few dimes or nickels, but we needed the blessings that came from being faithful in giving back to God what belongs to Him.

We'd ask, "How do you know what belongs to God?"

Mama would back up her answer with verses from the Bible. Her favorite was Malachi 3:6-12. She knew it by heart, but she always got the Bible out and read it to us. She said if we were faithful to God, He would always be faithful to us. Then she'd remind us of the many blessings we received each day. The air we breathed, the sunshine, the rain, and the ability to move and do things. I often wondered how my mom knew so much since she had never been to school. One day we asked her how come people who didn't pay tithe still received blessings.

"God is love," she explained. "It rains on the just and the unjust, and He loves each one of us the same whether we are faithful to him or not. God desires in His heart that everyone love and serve Him, but He never forces anyone against their will."

"Boy!" Alson said. "People better be glad I'm not God."

"Why, son?" Mama asked.

"I would make people like Mr. Willie and all of the rich people buy food for the poor children every day."

"That would be forcing someone to do something they did not want to do, son. Whenever we do something good for someone, it should always come from the heart. God loves a happy and cheerful giver."

"Did that come from the Bible, too, Mama?"

"You know it did," I said, "Mama doesn't ever tell us anything unless it comes from the Bible."

Mama smiled. "I want you children to know that when you are faithful and obedient to God you have the assurance He will never forsake you."

Mama always spoke to us as if we understood every word she said. That is why when she said she would come often to see me, I believed her. I knew she was telling me the truth.

Another happy memory I would think about was the special times I would spend with my dad. I remember lying in bed listening to him getting ready to go fishing and wishing I could go with him. Most of the time he would tell us he was going too far out in the ocean in the dory and it would be too dangerous for us. However, there were times he would let me go with him. Fishing with my dad was one of the highlights of my life. It meant spending the whole day together—just him and me. Daddy let me look through his "looking glass." It was a square box with glass in the bottom that he would use when the ocean water was not clear, when the wind was blowing, or after a storm. It was used to find lobster holes, but I just liked to look in it to see the beautiful coral and colorful fish at the bottom of the ocean. The reason my dad didn't like taking me with him was because I was constantly telling him I was thirsty or needed to go to the bathroom. Then Daddy would have to pull up anchor and paddle to one of the little nearby islands. While I was gone doing my business, Daddy would find a coconut and crack it so that I would have something to drink. I loved drinking the water from the coconut.

Chapter 6

I remember the day I went to the store for Mrs. Camille and overheard people saying there had been was a bad fire in the East End, which was where my family was living. People were talking about the fire and pitying the poor people who had lost their home.

"I heard they lost everything they had," one man said.

I listened to see if someone would say whose house had burned down, but no one seemed to know. I ran all the way home and told Mrs. Camille what I had heard. Then I begged her to let me go to the dock to see if there was a dory from the East End. She agreed, and I took off running.

On my way to the dock, I met Miss Velda and another lady who had come to the island to shop. They recognized me and told me it was my parents' house that burned down. "Your brother was badly burned saving one of your sisters," Miss Velda said. "Praise God, everyone made it out alive with just burns."

"Oh, God, why did You let this happen to my family? Where are they going to live now? What are they going to do? There is no place for them to go! Oh God, Oh God."

Miss Velda put her arms around me and held me. "Cry if you need to," she said.

I didn't have time to cry. I pulled away from her and started running back to Mrs. Camille's house. When she saw me, she knew right away it was my family's home that had burned. I could see she felt bad for me. At that moment I felt like grabbing her and holding on to her and crying. Between sobs, I said, "What are they doing to do now?"

She started to cry with me. "Your parents are great believers in God. He will help them."

"But He shouldn't have let their house burn down. Please let me go to my family," I begged.

"It wouldn't help them to have you there now." I knew she was telling the truth, but I wanted to see for myself that they were okay.

"Where are they going to sleep?" I cried. I knew there was no one who could take them in. No one on the island had a large house; most houses were not even big enough for the family living in it.

"What about their clothes? Miss Velda said they were just sitting on the grass on the beach in their nightgowns." I knew I had to do something to help my family. But what could I do? I cried for a long time. Then I knew what I had to do. I had to talk to Miss Edna, my Sabbath School teacher. She was a kind, loving teacher, and I looked forward to seeing her every Sabbath. I ran all the way to her house and told her about the fire.

"I want to pray for you and your family," she said. We bowed our heads and she told Jesus all about my family.

"I need to talk to the church members. I know they will try to help," Miss Edna said. "First, I'll write a note for you to take back to Mrs. Camille. I'll ask her to please let you take a note to every house on the island. You won't have to say anything to the people, just knock on the door and pass the note to whoever opens the door. If it's a kid, ask them to please give it to his or her mom or dad. Ask them to read the note and then give it back to you. Take it to as many houses as you can."

I took the note from her hand. She patted me on my back and said, "Don't worry. Everything is going to be all right."

I was still worried, but I felt a lot better than when I got there. I thanked Miss Edna and took off for Mrs. Camille's house as fast as I could. I was not even scared that she would be mad at me for staying away so long. Miss Gozel, the wash lady, was talking to Mrs. Camille when I reached home and handed her Mrs. Edna's note. Mrs. Camille read the note out loud. "Esther's family has lost everything in the fire. Any and everything you can give will be appreciated. Bring the things to Esther, and I will help see that the family receives them."

"That's a good idea," Mrs. Camille said. "Run along with the note."

Then my dear friend, Miss Gozel, said, "I'll stay and do your work around the house until you get back." I couldn't believe she would do that for me, but she did. I took off and went from door to door as fast as I could. Every person who read the note was very sympathetic and said, "Yes, I will help." It was amazing the way people helped my family. I was so thankful to the good Lord for touching people's hearts so they were willing to share from the little they had. I know each person who helped my family in their desperate need received a special blessing because Jesus said, "Whosoever helps one of the least of my children, is helping Me."

People brought everything from pots and pans to food and dishes. Some people even brought old lumber they were willing to donate. I remember thinking, *Jesus, where are they going to put all of this stuff?* In my heart, I knew if Mama heard me she would say, "Esther, how many times do I have to tell you? God says He will supply all of our needs according to His riches in glory."

Before I knew it, someone came with Miss Edna to help take the donated items to my family. I wanted to go with them, but Mrs. Camille would not allow it. The next day my mom sent a little note letting me know how good God was to them. They were all alive, and my brother was doing fine. She praised God he was not burned as badly as they first thought.

"Tell everyone how thankful we are for their love and concern. Aunt Hilda is letting us sleep in her water house until we can make other plans," Mama wrote.

A water house is the island name for a warehouse. Coconuts, bananas, and cowhides are stored in bins in the water house to await shipping. I was so sorry for my family. I cried and cried because I knew how terrible the water house smelled.

Not long after the fire I saw my mom on Mrs. Camille's island with Corine. Corine was a year older than me, and she had a pillowcase in her hand. Right away I knew what was happening. She was going to someone's house to work, just like I had been doing. She was going to be a slave, too.

"No, Mama! Take Corine back home with you. Don't give her to anyone. Please, Mama," I begged.

Corine was quiet. She just stood staring at me, as if she was in another world.

"Esther, child," Mama said. "You don't understand. Things are so bad at home. It is getting worse day by day. Your father cannot find any work. There is hardly enough food. We're living in the water house, and you know how it is there. It's better for Corine not to be there."

I knew my mom spoke the truth, but I was still worried about Corine.

"I know this woman Corine will be living with," Mama said. "She is a Christian woman and all alone. She just wants some company."

I could see that my sister was sad.

"If for any reason Corine decides she does not want to stay, she can send for me."

"Where does this woman live?" I asked.

Mama kind of hung her head. Then she said, "She does not live here on the island."

"Where does she live then, Mama?"

"She lives in La Ceiba."

I was shocked. "Mama, you are not going to let Corine go all the way to La Ceiba? That is too far away. We'll never see her."

"Yes, we will," Mama said. "I talked to Corine about it already, and she is willing to give it a try."

I couldn't understand how she could send us out to work at such a young age. I didn't realize how hard it was for my parents when we cried because we were hungry. My mother and father did everything in their power to take care of us, but when there were no resources, there was absolutely nothing more they could have done. Because they loved us unconditionally, they gave us away in hopes we would have a better life. Of course, this was extremely hard to understand as a child, and I questioned God as to the fairness of life.

I was often discouraged when I saw others prospering. I would ask God, "Why did You allow my family to even be born in this world?" The thing that kept me going was my mother's faith and loyalty to God. I loved my mom and dad so much that I did not want to disappoint them. Sometimes I wanted to tell God how unfair He was to us and how I felt He loved some people more than He loved my family. It didn't seem fair, especially since my mom loved Him so much and taught us all about Him. Why couldn't He honor her for that?

Now, as an adult, I realize how wrong I was about God. He has always been there for my family through all of our difficulties. He never left us, not for one second. We are the ones who stray from Him and misinterpret His promises.

As I got older I often complained about how unfair life was to me. One day I said to myself, *Girl, if you don't like it, then do something about it!* So I began to get "fresh," as my mother called it. "You had no right to give me away. How dare you still try to boss me? You didn't raise me," I'd say under my breath when my mom came to visit. "You have no right to tell me what to do. I'll do as I please, regardless of the consequences."

I wanted to be like my friends. They had freedom and no responsibilities. They acted as if no one told them what to do. They always seemed to be having fun. Why did I have to stay home all the time and work for some old lady who beat on me? I was sick and tired of my life. I often cried myself to sleep at night; I was so frustrated. I felt trapped without any hope of ever being free. I knew deep in my heart I shouldn't listen to my friends. I knew what they were doing was wrong. My mom taught me right from wrong, but I was tired of being a slave, and I was determined to do something about it.

It scared my mom when I talked that way. "Esther," she would say, "don't say things like that, child. One day something good is going to happen for us."

I couldn't see anything good happening. For people like us, it would take a miracle from God. I felt we were doomed for life. I didn't see any way out of our situation. Trapped on that island, my future looked dim.

Udeen was the next to be given out to work. After the fire, my mother came to see me. She had Udeen with her. Mama was taking her to work for another family. Udeen was sixteen at the time, and I figured if the people were mean to her she wouldn't have to stay. I could see she was scared.

"It's going to be okay," I told her. "You'll be on this island, and I will come to see you."

I asked Mrs. Camille if I could go with my mom to take my sister to the family. She gave me permission to go. I wanted Udeen's family to know that if they were mean she would tell me, and I would try to do something about it. I wasn't scared anymore, or at least I thought I wasn't. I felt I could watch over my sister now.

I started getting more whippings than I had before because whenever I was sent on an errand I stopped to check on Udeen. I don't think there was another girl anywhere who did more laundry in her entire life than she did. It seemed Udeen washed for those people twelve hours a day, three hundred and sixty-five days a year. Every time I went to see her, Udeen was bent over that washboard. She washed, starched, and ironed clothes constantly.

Sometimes, if I didn't think Mrs. Camille was waiting for whatever I was sent after, I would stay to help Udeen. Most of the time, I knew I would get a whipping anyway, but I didn't care anymore. I don't know which one of us felt worse for the other. Udeen thought my treatment was worse than hers, and perhaps it was because she wasn't physically abused. She did receive verbal abuse and was treated like a servant, but she was paid six *lempiras* a month. Of course, they made sure they got their money's worth.

My whippings increased as I got older. Mrs. Camille no longer whipped me with the blue plastic belt now. Instead, she used one of her husband's leather belts. I showed Udeen the marks on my body, but I told her not to worry. Udeen told my mom that she needed to take me away from Mrs. Camille because she was abusing me. Mama came, but I wouldn't leave. I hated the beatings, but I didn't want to live in the smelly old water house where they were living since the fire. I was still a child and my reasoning was not the best.

"Don't tell Mama anything else about me," I told Udeen. "She doesn't need more children than she has."

Still, I was getting tired of Mrs. Camille's constant cussing and beatings. I started going to my sister crying, "I hate Mrs. Camille. One day I'm going to hit her back." Udeen made me promise not to.

On my way home from an errand one day, I met Mr. Charliemer, my teacher in Savannah Bight when I lived with my parents. He recognized me.

"How are you doing?" he asked.

"I'm not able to go to a real school. I'm going to grow up to be a real dummy."

"I don't think that will happen," he said. "You're a smart girl, and there is no reason for you to feel that way about yourself. I'll help you learn to read and do math if you come to my house in the evenings three days a week. It will only cost one *lempira* a month."

I was excited. Mrs. Camille often gave me money to go to the movies on Saturday nights. I was able to save the money and put it toward the lessons. Mr. Charliemer was a good teacher, and in no time I became a good reader. Math came harder for me, but I didn't give up. I felt better about myself because of the schooling I was receiving, and I also became a more responsible worker.

It wasn't easy, but I tried very hard to please Mrs. Camille. It was important to keep everything on schedule, as that meant a great deal to her. There was no room for mistakes in her life, and whenever I messed up, she would go all to pieces. Mrs. Camille felt like she needed to curse me to get her point across. I often wished she would whip me instead of curse me and call me names. But this was my life, and it only seemed to get worse.

One day I accidentally ruining one of her good knives while trying to peel a pumpkin. Mrs. Camille came into the kitchen and saw the damaged knife. Without thinking, she grabbed the knife and started hitting me with it. I was scared and began to scream. There were a few small cuts and one large one on my arm. When I saw the blood, I screamed even louder until she stopped beating me. I know she didn't mean to cut me, but Mrs. Camille was so angry she lost control of herself. When she realized I was bleeding, she panicked. She grabbed my hand and pulled me over to the sink and started washing my arm.

"You should have had better sense than to peel the pumpkin with my good knife," she said as she began to calm down. After she got me cleaned up, she said, "I hope you don't tell your sister any lies about me."

I said to myself, *I will tell her you beat me with a knife. That is a fact. My sister will see the cuts for herself.* I couldn't wait until that afternoon to show Udeen what Mrs. Camille had done to me. I don't know why I was so anxious to tell her about it, as there was absolutely nothing she could do except to cry with me. Still, I don't know what I would have done without Udeen. She always tried to be brave for me.

That very next afternoon, Udeen came to visit me, and she confronted Mrs. Camille. "What did Esther do that was so bad you beat her with a knife?"

Mrs. Camille was so surprised and shocked that my sister had the nerve to speak to her that she was silent for a moment. Then she said, "I didn't mean to hit her with the knife. Esther was jumping around and would not stand still." She made it sound like it was my fault I had been cut. Right then and there, I hated her, and I knew in my heart that I would hate her for the rest of my life. That day I started to make plans to kill her. I know how awful this sounds, but I swore to God I was going to kill that woman. I started to think of ways to do it. We lived over the water, so I thought of hitting her in the head and pushing her overboard so she would drown. I knew these were evil thoughts, but I was sick and tired of being mistreated. I began having nightmares about these evil thoughts.

I didn't mention my thoughts to Udeen. It was something I needed to keep secret. I knew if I told her, she would tell my mother. Only God in heaven knew what I was going through. Every time Mrs. Camille and I were alone, I would tell myself, *This is your chance! Do whatever you have to do!* My heart would pound so hard that sometimes I thought it would beat right out of my chest. I'll never understand why I wanted to do that evil thing, but I guess it happens when one allows hate to develop in his or her heart.

Fortunately, as Satan was battling for me to do evil, God was battling for me to make good choices. I have to praise Him for my wonderful mother. She taught me the Ten Commandments, and as I thought of killing Mrs. Camille, the sixth commandment—"Thou shalt not kill"—ran in my ears and kept me from doing evil.

The Bible speaks truth when it says our hearts are naturally evil. As I write this, I shudder to think I could have had such evil thoughts that involved taking someone's life. I am so glad my mom taught me about Jesus. He is my very best friend. I tell Him everything, and I thank Him for helping me not to commit that evil crime. I still don't know how He kept me from doing it. I harbored that thought in my heart for many years. Hate is like a vicious worm that eats a hole in your inner soul. It keeps getting bigger as you pile hate upon hate. The devil grows stronger because he thrives on any sin we commit. Eventually evil thoughts turn into action if we continue to harbor them in our hearts. Fortunately for me, I never raised my hand against Mrs. Camille.

The abuse continued, and then Mrs. Camille gave me another assignment. She had a good friend with three children. The girls all went to school, but when the mother had a new baby, Mrs. Camille told me, "You won't be going to Miss Cassie's school anymore, Esther. I need you to help my friend in the afternoon."

I cried and cried to Udeen, but there was nothing she could do to help me. It was a difficult schedule to keep up with, and I had no time to rest. With the added work, I was very tired and began to make clumsy mistakes, such as dropping and breaking dishes, that only further unleashed Mrs. Camille's wrath upon me.

Then one day when Mama came to see Udeen and me, the lady I was helping in the afternoon asked if my sister Carolyn could come and work for her. I was relieved because I was so tired working for two families, but I hated to think of my sister having to work. At least the lady she would be working for didn't beat children or cuss at them. She made them work hard, but she wasn't mean. She promised to pay Carolyn five *lempiras* a month, the same amount that Udeen was receiving. Neither she nor Mrs. Camille paid me—I guess they thought I was too young—which didn't help my morale that I was being mistreated and was not even receiving compensation for my hard work and the abuse I endured.

Now I had two sisters on the cay with me, which made me feel better. But I also felt a sense of responsibility to check on them and make sure they were being treated with respect and kindness. After working for Mrs. Camille for five years, when I turned twelve, she decided to pay me five *lempiras* a month. At that time, this amount was equivalent to two dollars and fifty cents in U.S. dollars. I was so happy. At last I was getting paid for working. I decided to give my mom three *lempiras* a month, which was a great help to the family. I was proud to think I was getting paid for my work.

With the remaining two *lempiras*, I planned to tell my mother to let my younger brother Edney go to school. I would be responsible for his composition books and pencils. My two sisters decided to do the same thing for our younger sisters, Francine and Avanel (Nelly). Between us we were able to put three of our siblings in school at the same time. Composition books cost about twenty-five cents in U.S. money. A pencil was a nickel. Those three children never stopped thanking us for helping them go to school. They were the only ones from our family who were able to graduate from the sixth grade, which was the highest grade taught in public schools on the island at that time. If you finished sixth grade, you were "one of the lucky kids."

Chapter 7

The four oldest girls—Udeen, Carolyn, Corine, and me—worked for other families to bring in a little money to help support our parents and siblings. Even though I was the youngest, I always felt as if I was the oldest. Udeen and Carolyn were quiet and well mannered, and they often tried to mother me.

My sisters were allowed to visit our family one Sunday a month for about seven hours. I begged to go with them and was allowed if I wasn't in trouble. I tried to stay out of trouble so that I could visit my family. Those were the best Sundays for us girls.

"We'll never live all together again," I told my dad when we visited.

"Don't say that, Esther. You can't give up hope," my dad said. "Nothing is impossible with God." Then he added, "Maybe we won't live together here on earth, children, but we can plan to live together in heaven with Jesus when He comes."

Even with the lumber some people had given my parents, I doubted they would ever be able to live in a house of their own.

The years passed. I turned sixteen, then seventeen. Nothing changed. I still got slapped around and cussed at every day.

Then one day Mrs. Camille caught me washing the glasses with the wrong dishrag—she was extremely particular about how things had to be washed and with what rag. She grabbed it from my hand and hit me in the face with it. I was so angry; I wanted to slap her back. If she knew how badly I wanted to kill her, she never would have come near me.

"Never, never touch me again!" I yelled at her. I was almost eighteen now. "You are not my mother. I am sick and tired of you abusing me." I was scared to death, but I knew the time had come for me to stand up for myself. I believe she would have continued abusing me as long as I worked for her. She was shocked. I had never stood up to her before, and it frightened her. I'd tried to be respectful to her, but that day she had pushed me to my limit. I couldn't take another moment of her abuse.

The next day when Miss Gozel, the wash lady, came, I told her what happened. She couldn't believe I had talked back and not been sent away.

"I'm sure she cares for you. She just doesn't know how to show it," she said.

I knew why she didn't run me out of her house. She had trained me to take care and be responsible for all the chores around the house.

After that, things were a little better. Mrs. Camille stopped hitting me, but the cursing got worse. When I was very young, Mama often sang a little song to us: "Shun evil companions, bad language disdain. God's name hold in reverence; not taken in vain. Be thoughtful and honest, kind hearted and true. Look ever to Jesus, He will carry you through." I hated the cursing and bad language that she hurled at me, but I was powerless to stop it.

At eighteen I was still running errands like a ten-year-old, barefooted with no everyday shoes to wear. The money Mrs. Camille paid me didn't last long, and I was never able to save enough for shoes. However, the desire to have shoes increased when I fell in love at first sight with a soldier who was stationed next door to Mrs. Camille's house at the Commandant Station.

One day when I was sweeping the sidewalk, a new group of soldiers arrived. I glanced up and saw the cutest soldier I had ever seen. He was standing by the fence talking to another soldier. I looked right at him and our eyes met. I swear something exploded inside me. He stared at me for a few seconds. I felt paralyzed. I was embarrassed and didn't know what to do with myself. I didn't want to turn and walk away because I was barefooted. My heart pounded in my chest, and I knew from the moment the feelings came to me I was in for trouble. I knew the soldiers came and went weekly, so it was foolish to fall in love with one of them.

The next day on my way back from the store, I met him on the street. We both smiled. I wanted to talk to him, but if someone saw us, they would tell Mrs. Camille, and she had forbid me from dating anyone, especially the soldiers. I saw him two or three times that day. Every time I looked over to the Commandant building, he was looking back at me. I wanted to talk to him so badly that I could hardly stand myself.

One evening after supper, I decided to go swimming. I waited until Mrs. Camille left to visit her friend, then I took a pair of old tight pants and cut them off as short as I could. I cut my shirt so it would show my belly button. I weighed about one hundred and thirty pounds, and when I looked at myself, I knew I looked good. If Mrs. Camille had been around, I would have been out of that outfit faster than I got in it. My mother would have scolded, too, saying I was putting the whole family to shame. But right then, I didn't care what anyone thought of me. I had a feeling inside me that I had never had before. It felt good, but a little scary. I was determined to talk to that boy.

I planned to walk down the boardwalk right in front of the Commandant building and attract his attention. I hoped he was not on duty so that I could invite him to go swimming with me. I walked over to the chain link fence and opened the gate, making as much noise as I could. I could only hope he would look out and see me as I walked down the boardwalk. A couple of other soldiers looked out and whistled. I kept walking, pretending I didn't hear them.

He must have told the other soldiers he liked me, and when I passed by, they told him. Before I made it to the end of the bridge, I looked back and saw him walking toward me.

He was so handsome dressed in his uniform, and when he got closer to me, he was smiling. His hair was jet black, and his eyes were green. He held out his hand and introduced himself. He didn't speak English, but I spoke Spanish, so there was no problem. His name was Rolando Escalante. I told him my name. "That's a pretty name for a pretty girl," he said.

I blushed. I was in high heaven. At that moment, I came to my senses and felt embarrassed about my attire, but I shoved those feelings aside and invited him to go swimming. I was disappointed when he said he couldn't go. We stood and talked. He told me where he was from, and that he was twenty-two years old. I thought he looked about sixteen.

"Do you live with your parents?" he asked.

"No, I work for these people."

"Can I take you to the movies tonight?"

I had to say no, which was the hardest thing because I wanted to go with him. I knew if I were seen going to the movies with him, I would be in serious trouble.

"When can I see you again?"

I didn't know what to say. "I'm going to babysit for the lady next door on Saturday night. You can come to the gate, and I can talk to you there."

"Okay, but I would rather take you dancing," he said.

I thought, *Oh my—me—dancing with a boy!* I couldn't imagine that happening to me.

On Saturday evening, I asked the lady I was babysitting for if this boy could come and sit on the porch with me after her two little boys were in bed. She said she had no problem with that as long as we stayed and talked on the porch.

He arrived dressed in uniform with two guns buckled around his waist. I have always been afraid of guns, so I was nervous and did not enjoy my time as much as I could have. Before I knew it, he said he had to go to relieve another soldier who was on duty.

Before he left he moved toward me. My heart beat rapidly, and I thought it was going to fall out. He reached for my hand. When he touched me, I wanted to fall in his arms, but he leaned over and kissed me on the side of my cheek. I could not believe a boy had held my hand and kissed me. I was sad when he left, and I didn't sleep much that night.

The next day when I saw him, I was embarrassed because I had let him kiss me. Still, I kept imagining him doing it again. When we saw each other again, I told him a little bit about Mrs. Camille. "She doesn't want me to have a boyfriend, and I can't have a real date," I said.

So every time he saw me leave the house, we would meet on the road to walk and talk. That way we weren't going on a real date. However, I wanted more than that. I wanted to do fun things with him, like going to the beach and dancing. I knew Mrs. Camille would never let me—in hindsight I am thankful she didn't allow me to.

I had one pair of shoes, and I started wearing them every day because I didn't want him to see me barefooted.

"Why are you wearing your shoes?" Mrs. Camille asked.

"I'm tired of walking barefooted."

"Those shoes are for church, not for wearing every day," she said.

I pursued my friendship with Rolando as often as I could, and one day everything came to a head with Mrs. Camille inadvertently because of my secret crush.

I had worked for Mrs. Camille for almost twelve years when early one morning, about 6:30 a.m., she sent me to the store to buy soda crackers for her breakfast. Everyone on the island knew how she treated me. People pitied me.

That fateful morning, Mrs. Camille sent me to purchase a nickel's worth of soda crackers. The crackers were in a red can on the store counter. They were a penny apiece. Bins of sugar, flour, etc., which was shipped from the mainland, sat behind the counter. Everything was weighed separately for each customer.

Mrs. Camille constantly sent me back to the store because she objected to what I had purchased. The store owners were so upset by this that they allowed me to serve myself, hoping that Mrs. Camille would accept what I selected. If the item was damp or a little discolored, I would have to take the item back. "You pick it out," they would tell me. Even though they knew I'd still probably have to bring it back, it was worth a shot. She always reminded me not to bring crackers that were browned dark, and I had to check each cracker before leaving the store.

I'll never forget that morning. The store had a bar in the back. You could see all the way to the back where the bar was, and the minute I walked in, Rolando spotted me. I was shocked. I never dreamed I would meet him there at that time of the morning. I was wearing a green flowered dress with puffed sleeves and a big sash that tied in the back, and I was barefoot. He was the last person I wanted to see looking as I did. He did not move from where he was sitting, and I felt he probably had been there all night and was drunk. It made me sick to my stomach to think of anyone drinking so early in the morning. Still, I was ashamed for him to see me without shoes.

I asked the clerk for a nickel's worth of soda crackers. She put them in a little brown bag and I turned and walked out of the store.

When I got home, Mrs. Camille was sitting with her cup of coffee waiting for her crackers. She looked in the bag and screamed.

"Why would you bring me crackers like this? They are too brown! Take them back!"

I had forgotten to remind the clerk not to put dark brown crackers in the bag. I was so taken with Rolando, I didn't think about the crackers.

"Take them back, and get me some decent ones!"

My heart sank. There was no way I was going to take those crackers back. I had always taken things back, but no more. I couldn't bear to let Rolando see me returning five crackers.

I turned around and looked her right in the face. "I do not want to take those crackers back," I said. I knew better than to be disrespectful. My mother never allowed any of us to be disrespectful, so I quickly added, "Please, don't make me take those crackers back."

"What? You are talking back to me!" Before I could say another word, she doubled up her fist and struck me in the mouth, busting my lip. I was so angry that the hatred welled up inside me, and I wanted to kill her. I tried to hit her in the mouth, but my fist caught her in the chest. I wanted to bust her lip, too. We both began crying. I was ashamed of what I had done, but it was too late to feel sorry. I had warned her not to touch me again, but in her anger she had lashed out at me. I knew she wouldn't allow me to live there anymore.

"I'm going home to my mother today," I said. I didn't want to go home. I wasn't close to my family having been away all these years, but I didn't know what else to do. Subconsciously, I resented my parents, feeling that they had abandoned me by sending me off to work. In my heart I knew they loved me and had tried to do their best for me, but all the years of abuse had added up, and I just felt defeated and alone.

Mrs. Camille didn't let things end that easily. "You are not going anywhere. Your mother brought you here, and your mother needs to come and get you."

"So you can tell her a bunch of lies about me? You and my mother are just alike. You can send for her, but I'll be long gone." I told her. "I'm going home."

I walked out of the house without a backwards glance. I went to her mother's house and packed my few clothes. Then I found the first dory that was going to the island where my mother lived. The dory belonged to my cousin Simon.

"Will you please take me home?" I asked him. "I don't have the *lempiras* to pay you." I had already spent what was left of my wages from the previous month after sending most of it to my parents.

"I can, but you'll have to wait. It'll be about two hours before I can leave."

I didn't care how long I had to wait. I sat on the end of the wharf where the dory was tied and waited and thought about my life. At the appointed time, my cousin called me to get on board. Everyone piled into the dory, and we headed for Savannah Bight. I was so sad; I don't think I said a word to anyone the whole trip. When we reached Savannah Bight, I wanted to run and run and never stop running. But how can one run when there is no place to go? No one paid any attention to me. I thanked my cousin, took my bag, and started walking toward our house. I made it all the way there without anyone seeing me coming.

When I appeared in front of the door, my mother saw me, and I think she went into shock. Before she could say anything, I burst out crying and told her the whole story. "I'll never go back to work for that lady again, so don't try to tell me I have to go back," I sobbed.

My poor mother did not know what to say to me.

"Are you angry with me, Mama?"

"No, Esther, and I won't try to make you go back."

I couldn't wait for my dad to get home from fishing that evening. I knew he would be happy I was home, in spite of what had happened. My brothers and sisters were happy I was home, but as I looked around, I knew I could not live in this place for long. Night was beginning to fall. There was no electricity or running water as I had been used to at Mrs. Camille's house. I have always been afraid of the dark, so I dreaded nighttime. My dad came home just before dark, and I told him what happened.

"Sweetheart, I am happy you are home," he said. "We will do the best we can for you."

I knew my dad would say the right words to me. I loved him so much.

"If you want to bathe," one of my younger sisters said to me, "you need to get water from the gully before it gets too dark."

For me, it was already too dark. "That's all right," I said. "I'll skip the bath tonight, and go to the gully tomorrow when it's daytime."

Depression settled over me. The darker it got, the worse I felt. A lantern was lit in the kitchen along with two kerosene lamps. I was scared to go the short distance from the house to the kitchen. I overheard my two little sisters talking about where I was going to sleep.

"She can sleep with me on the floor in the hallway," my little brother Edney piped up and said.

"So you can float her away with pee?" they teased, embarrassing him because he knew I heard them.

"I would be happy to sleep with you, Edney," I told him. My mother gave me some bedding, and I slept with my little brother in the hallway that first night.

Early the next morning, my mother's singing awakened me. I had forgotten about my mom's morning worship. I listened for a while, and then one by one I heard everyone joining in. It sounded like a regular song service.

Old memories came back. *This is the way it used to be when I lived here as a little girl*, I thought. It sounded so good to hear my mom singing instead of someone cussing at me. I sat up and edged myself against the wall close to my dad. I did not participate; I was a little embarrassed that first morning. Worship was a daily custom at our home, and everyone participated with great respect. That was how all of us children learned about Jesus—from the wonderful mother He gave us.

It was such a relief to know Mrs. Camille wasn't standing over me with a belt, telling me I had overslept and would pay with a beating. I decided that maybe mornings weren't so bad, waking up with the sun and listening to the waves slap against the shore. However, my early morning revere didn't last long. As the days went by, I became restless, and I didn't know what to do with myself. I helped with the chores around the house, but strangely, I missed taking orders and being on a schedule. However, I did not miss the cruel punishments. Living with Mrs. Camille, I had become accustomed to responsibility and discipline. I was having a hard time adjusting to freedom.

One day Mrs. Camille arrived on our doorstep. She brought some groceries and tried to persuade my mother to let me return with her. I stayed in the bedroom and refused to see her.

"It's up to Esther," my mother told her.

I don't know why, but I felt sorry for Mrs. Camille, and somehow I felt she cared a little for me. I was still upset, so I refused to come out until she left.

Every day I dreamed of leaving home, but weeks turned into months, and I stayed on. I tried to fit into the routine, but my younger sisters refused to let me in their little circle. I was lonesome living in a house full of people—people who cared about me but with whom it seemed I had nothing in common with.

"The world is too beautiful for me to sit on one island and waste away," I told my dad. "I dream of something better."

"You're not wasting away. You're young. You have your whole life before you," he said. "If you put your trust in God, set high standards, and wait patiently, He will fulfill your dreams."

I wanted to believe my dad, but I was impatient. I wanted things to happen right then. One day while I was sitting on the boardwalk, a boy passed by with a wheelbarrow full of suitcases.

"Whose suitcases are those?" I asked. No one living on the island had suitcases like that.

"Mr. Mejia's son just came home from the United States," he said.

"How old is he?"

"I don't know. He looks like a man to me," the boy replied.

I waited and waited. I wanted to see the man when he walked by. His parents lived only about a half-mile up the road from us. I walked up and down the beach, hoping to catch a glimpse of him, but he never came.

Later on my brother told us that everyone was partying and drinking in town to celebrate Mr. Mejia's son's homecoming. I wanted to go to see what was happening, so I grabbed a bucket and ran to the gully for water. I decided I was going to bathe and dress up and then go check things out. While I was getting ready, my little sisters ran and told my mom what I was planning. Mama was ready for me when I emerged all dressed and ready to leave. I was planning on asking her to let me go, but before I could say anything, she said, "Esther, I hope you are not planning on going downtown near those bars where people are partying. No daughter of mine will ever go near a bar as long as she lives under my roof."

I looked over to my dad to see if he would defend me, but the look on his face told me he stood firmly behind Mama. I was angry. I wanted to tell both of them off. I wanted to say, "You did not raise me. You have no right to tell me whether I can go or not." But I knew better than to open my mouth. My mother did not tolerate any kind of disrespect.

Several days later I saw the young man. He was in his twenties. He stopped in the yard and shook hands with my dad and spoke with him for a few minutes. However, he didn't pay any attention to me, much to my distress. I was so lonesome, and I desperately craved male attention in the wrong way.

Then one day when I was playing kickball with my little brother, Edney saw the young man coming up the road and ran up to him and told him his sister wanted to talk to him. The man knew I was embarrassed, but a little while later he stopped and talked to me.

"I'm only home for a short time; then I'll be leaving again," he said.

"I'm eighteen, and someday I'm leaving home, too," I told him. I wanted him to know how old I was. I was glad he didn't ask where I was going because I had no idea. For the next couple weeks, I spent most of my time outside waiting for him to pass by. He always stopped and talked with me for a few minutes.

Whenever my little sisters got mad at me, they would say, "You should be ashamed of yourself. We saw you throwing yourself at that man." I didn't care what they said. I was lonesome and needed someone to talk to. They did not understand me; no one in my home did.

One evening my two sisters asked Mama if they could go downtown to the government pipe to get water, instead of going to the gully. I heard her say yes, so I grabbed a bucket and went along even though I knew they did not want me to come with them. I knew the young man was downtown, so this was a perfect opportunity for me to see him after dark. I knew if he weren't inside the bar, I would see him on the street. There was only one main street. Sure enough, he was standing on the side of the road talking to a bunch of other guys. I was so happy when I saw him.

I was the first to fill my bucket and start on my way again. My sisters knew what I was up to. "If you are afraid of the dark, why are you running ahead of us?" they asked.

I ignored them. I wanted to get back before he left that spot. I think he knew what I was doing because as I went by he left the group and followed me. He caught up with me, reached down for my bucket of water, and began walking beside me. I hoped my sisters wouldn't catch up with us. I was walking with a man, not a boy, and I didn't want them around. I felt like a woman walking on an enchanted island with a handsome prince. As we walked along the road beside the ocean, I could hear the waves as they broke against the shore, and I felt the wind blow in our faces. I smelled his sweet cologne. I closed my eyes for a moment and imagined him holding me in his arms. A man, a real man, and I was alone with him.

I looked up to the heavens and saw a half moon. It seemed as if there were millions and millions of stars. I know they were shining just for me that night. In that short walk, I allowed my imagination to take me on a journey of fantasy. I wanted so much for it to be real. We reached a little bridge, and as I started to step up, he put the bucket down, took me in his arms, and kissed me. It was a kiss I will never forget. He held me in his strong arms for a few minutes. I wanted it to last forever.

My sisters were approaching. I didn't dare let them know he had held my hand, never mind kissed me. As they passed, they both cleared their throats as if to say, *You better come on, girl, or we are going to tell on you.* He walked me all the way to my house.

"I'll be leaving in about a week and a half," he said. "You are very young and need to be very careful. One day you will leave this island, and your dreams will come true."

When we reached my house, he kissed me again, squeezed my hand, and told me good night. Surprisingly, my sisters didn't tell on me.

I saw him a few times during his last week on the island. I walked along the road with him the day before he left, and he told me goodbye. But that is where that dream ended. I was still stuck with no plan for the future.

Chapter 8

I became more restless and lonesome as the days passed. A couple boys on the island stopped by my house wanting to talk with me, but I had no interest in boys my age. One night, out of the blue, I told my family that I was leaving the next day.

They looked at me as if I had lost my mind. I know my mom wanted to tell me I couldn't leave, but I think she knew the time had come for me to go.

"Where are you going?" they all asked.

But I had no idea where I was going, so I didn't answer them. I barely slept that night. I was scared, but I wanted to be on my own. I am a very strong-willed person, so even though I was scared, I felt I had to stand by whatever decision I made, even if it was not the best.

I heard my mother praying for me that night. She told God how sorry she was that she had not had the opportunity to raise me and teach me more about Him. Of course, what my precious mother didn't realize is that it was her prayers that had brought me through those years and would continue to sustain me. I was up at daybreak getting ready. My dad begged me not to leave. I promised him that if I didn't find work I would return home. He gave me seventy-five cents. I did not want to take it. I knew it was probably the only money he had. If my sisters knew I had taken my dad's seventy-five cents, they would have been angry. I knew my dad would have given it to them, too, if he thought they needed it.

Everyone was sad when I left home that Wednesday morning. I knew my life would be forever changed. With the seventy-five cents my dad gave me, I caught a dory going to the cay where I was raised. I was scared, but in my mind it was too late to turn around. After paying my passage on the dory, I had only twenty-five cents left.

It helped that I knew almost everyone on the cay. I had several girlfriends whom I could talk to. I usually saw them at church or when I was running errands, but I figured they might help me get settled on my own. I first visited my girlfriend Vivian, hoping her parents would let me stay with them for a few days. Her mother was bending over a washtub as I approached the house. I walked up to the porch, but with each passing minute, I became more apprehensive. I didn't know what I would do if they said no. I startled her when I spoke.

She was a very pleasant soft-spoken woman. She stopped washing to talk to me. Before I could ask for Vivian, she said, "She's gone on an errand but will be back soon."

A little baby girl hung onto her dress, and a little boy, about five or six, played nearby. I sat on the top step of the porch, and both children came over to me. I played with them for a long time before Vivian came home. She was surprised when she saw me since we had not seen each other for a long time.

I briefly filled her in on my life. She invited me into the house and went straight to the kitchen where she started kneading the dough she had in a pan on the dinner table. "I help mom make bread to sell to help feed the family," Vivian explained. Then she asked me where I was going.

"I have no idea."

"Why don't you spend the night with me?"

All I could say was *Thank you, Jesus* in my heart. "Are you sure it will be all right with your mother and father?"

"I'll tell mom I asked you. Dad gets home late and probably won't even know you are here. I'm going to the dance Saturday night. Do you want to come?"

"Yes, I'd love to," I said. She didn't know I had never been to a real dance before. I didn't want her to know. Then I confessed, "But I don't have anything to wear."

"You can wear one of my dresses," Vivian offered. But every one of her dresses was too tight or too short. My heart sank every time one wouldn't fit. I had a chance to go to a dance without anyone stopping me, and I didn't have anything to wear. I began to cry. Vivian felt sad for me. She seemed to understand how much I wanted to go to the dance.

"Can you sew?" she asked.

"Not really. I can sew a patch on or fix a rip, but I don't know how to sew a dress. Even if I did, I don't have money to buy material."

Vivian bent over and pulled a box from under her bed and took out a piece of lavender material. She placed it on the bed beside me.

"You can have this to make a dress for the dance." She gave me a spool of thread, and an old catalog. "See if you can find a style you like in here."

I was astonished to think Vivian would give me a piece of material. I was so happy. I knew by Saturday night I would have something made from that piece of cloth, even if I had to wrap it around me and pin it. I was going to that dance.

I looked through the catalog and found the exact dress I wanted. It had spaghetti straps and a flared skirt. It looked simple to make, but I had no idea how to begin. I lay in bed that night trying to think who could help me make a dress on such short notice. Then I remembered the lady I had babysat for had a sister-in-law who sewed. The next day I helped Vivian with her morning work and then headed for the lady's house who I hoped would help me sew a dress.

When I arrived at the home, a little boy came to the door.

"Where is your mother?" I asked him.

"She's in the bedroom with the baby," he said.

I called to her, and she told me to come in. I walked to the bedroom door. She was lying in bed with a newborn baby. The baby had been born the day before. My heart sank. Instead of greeting her and congratulating her, I wanted to cry. All I could think was, *There is no way she can help me make my dress by Saturday night*. I had heard you were supposed to stay in bed and do nothing for nine days after having a baby.

I didn't know what to do. I couldn't think of anyone else who could help me. I stood in the bedroom and talked with her. I didn't mention the dress.

"Why did you come, Esther? What brought you here today?" she finally asked.

"I want to go to a dance Saturday night. It's the first real dance I've ever been able to go to, and I really want to attend."

"What's the problem?"

"My friend gave me some material to make a dress, but I don't know how," I confessed.

"Do you know anything about sewing at all?" She kept talking before I could answer. "If you have your material and know the style of dress you want, spread it out here on the floor. I'll give you instructions on how to cut out your dress."

I could hardly believe what I was hearing. In no time, I had that piece of material laid on the floor in front of her bed. I did exactly as she told me, and I soon had the dress cut out without a pattern.

"You can use my sewing machine, Esther. It's a simple dress to sew, and I know you can do it."

It took me two days. Whenever I sewed a crooked seam, I had to tear it out and sew it over. I tried it on a number of times before it was finished. The hem was the last thing to sew, and it was the hardest as it had to be done by hand.

I was so excited. It was my very first dance dress, and I had made it myself. I could hardly wait to try on the finished dress. I was so proud as I slipped the dress on and stood in front of a mirror. I twirled around, pretending I was at the dance.

As excited as I was about going, you would think I knew how to dance. When I was little, my sister used to dance with me when our mother wasn't around. We would step on one another's feet every move we made. Now I worried about stepping on the feet of the boys who asked me to dance. I was embarrassed just thinking about it. Then I thought, *I bet everyone steps on the other person's feet the first time they dance*. And with that, I tried to stop worrying.

Saturday morning finally came, but this Saturday was unlike any others. For almost all my life, every Saturday I woke up and got ready for church, because it was the Sabbath. This was my first Saturday on my own, and no one was there to tell me what to do. That's when it hit me that whatever decision I made from then on I would be responsible for it. My first deliberate decision was that I was not going to church. I told myself I was tired of people making me go to church, and not letting me go other places and have fun. I knew I loved Jesus, but I was tired of being good. A battle was raging inside me, and I was determined to have my own way.

Even though I didn't want to go to church, I was uneasy. I spent most of the day in Vivian's bedroom. Her mother even came to check on me to see if I was okay. Vivian asked me to go with her to visit another friend to see if she was going to the dance. I said no. Vivian was puzzled but went off by herself. I was depressed, so I laid down on the bed and fell asleep. I slept for about three hours. When I woke, it was quiet. Everyone was gone. I was the only person in the house.

I had an awful headache, and I told myself it was because I had not eaten anything all day. But I was not hungry. In fact, my stomach was upset. I wanted to drink something, but I was in someone's house and was afraid to touch anything without permission. I did have some pills for headaches. After taking two, I sat on the front porch hoping my friend would come home. After a while I realized that if I was going to go the dance, I needed to take a bath, so I did. Then I went to sit on the porch again. My headache was getting worse, so I took several more pills.

It began to get dark. My friend's family did not have electricity in their home. I stayed on the steps because the light from the public light pole was shining. Vivian finally came home around eight o'clock. I was so thankful to see her.

"What have you been doing all day, girl?" she asked.

"Nothing."

"Let's get ready for the dance."

I had been waiting for this moment for four days. It had finally come, but my head was hurting so bad I didn't think I would be able to walk to the dance. I didn't want Vivian to know I was feeling sick, so I took some more headache pills. I told myself that once I got to the dance I would feel better.

"We'll stay at one dance hall a while, then go to another, and another," Vivian told me as we dressed. I was not excited about going anymore because I felt so sick. I wanted to beg her to stay home with me, but I knew she wouldn't want to do that. Vivian was so excited about going that she didn't pay much attention to how I looked or acted.

The dance hall was about five or six blocks away, and it was ten o'clock when we arrived. The place was packed with people. Everyone looked like they were having fun. I had walked by this place many times wishing I could go inside, but now that I was here, I felt miserable. I went inside with Vivian. Many of her friends were there, and she went to talk with them. I sat on one of the benches just inside the door. The benches ran along the sides of the dance hall. The music was so loud it made my head hurt even worse. And the cigarette smell made me feel sicker. I thought I was going to die. At least three boys asked me to dance as I sat there. All I could do was shake my head no. I felt worse by the minute. I began to get the chills and started to shake. People stared at me. Finally a lady came over and asked me what was wrong.

"I don't know," I managed to say.

"You look like you need to see a doctor, child."

A kind lady went home and brought a blanket and put it around my shoulders saying, "You need to go home."

I wanted to tell Vivian I was sick and had to leave, but she was lost in the crowd. I knew she wouldn't want to leave, and I didn't have the strength to push through the crowd. I decided to try to make it back to her house. I forgot that the government lights turned off at ten o'clock. All the nearby bars had private lights. When I walked a little further away from the dance hall it was pitch dark. I panicked, my fear of the dark threatened to overpower me. But I knew I needed to go to bed, so I prayed, "Dear God, please help me get to Vivian's home safely."

I stepped off the boardwalk near the dance hall, and walked almost three blocks before I reached the boardwalk leading to Vivian's home. I can't remember anything about that walk. When I tried to step up onto the boardwalk, I had no strength left. I could not take another step. I sat down on the end of the boardwalk. I was so sick and scared I thought I was going to die right there. The house was about three quarters of a block away. I don't know how long I stayed there curled up with the blanket the lady had given me, but I'm guessing it must have been about one thirty in the morning before I began crawling toward the house. The water under the boardwalk was about six to eight feet deep in some places. If I fell off the boardwalk, I knew I would drown. I was a good swimmer, but as sick as I was I didn't have the strength to swim.

I believe God saved my life. I don't remember getting to the house, or how I got inside, but the door to the house was open so I crawled to my friend's bedroom. When Vivian got home, it was very late. I was burning up with fever. My head hurt so bad I was crying.

"What's wrong?" she asked.

"I'm sick."

"I missed you at the dance, but I thought you had gone along to another dance hall." That was all she said. She was asleep as soon as her head hit the pillow.

I didn't think I was going to make it through the night. I prayed for daylight to come. I didn't know what I was going to do. I thought if I didn't get help, I was going to die. Morning finally came, but I didn't have the strength to get out of bed. I began to cry. Vivian hadn't been asleep very long. She wasn't happy with me for waking her, but when she saw how sick I was, she felt bad for me. She took the sheet off her bed and put it around my shoulders. I was shaking with chills.

"What do you want me to do?" She asked.

I didn't have any money, and there were no doctors on the island, only a few nurses. Vivian got her mother, and she brought me a cup of tea. Then she gave me some pills for my headache.

"Child," she said, "you need to get home to your family."

A part of me wanted to return to the safety of my parents' home, but would my family want me back? They had begged me not to leave, but I had gone anyways. I didn't have much choice. Vivian went to see if there was a dory going to my island. One was leaving in a few hours. She got my clothes together, and told me I could keep the sheet around me. I was so cold I could not stop shaking. Vivian and I were both afraid I would not be able to walk on the bridge without falling. She took my arm and helped me to the dory. Two of the boat crew helped get me on board and laid me in a bunk. I thanked her and apologized for being so much trouble.

"I'm sorry you got sick. I want you to come back to visit when you are well again," Vivian said.

Five minutes after the dory left the dock, I vomited in the bunk all over myself. I could not get up, and there was no one to help me. It was only a fifteen-minute trip to my island, but it seemed like forever. Someone sent for my family and told them I was on the dory and was very sick and couldn't walk. It took four men to carry me on a cot the mile home. The moment I got home my mom and dad went to work on me with herbs, teas, and hot water. It took three days before they could get my fever to break. My family thought I was going to die. On the fourth day, I began to feel a little better. Then my oldest brother, Alson, fell sick. By the third day, he was sicker than I was. Everyone who heard we were sick brought medicine and gave my parents advice. My brother was so ill my family could only pray and ask God to heal him. God heard our prayers.

I felt so bad that I had brought sickness into my family's home. Within a few weeks, it was like a wind blew the sickness all over the island. People on the island got sick, and everyone in our house was sick. My dad, my brother, and I were the sickest. Many children and elderly people on the island died. Later we learned it was the Hong Kong flu, but my brothers and sisters blamed me for bringing it to our home.

Chapter 9

After a few weeks, I was ready to take off again, but I was more afraid than before. I began going to the cay every chance I could. I went from door to door asking people if they needed a maid. Finally one lady asked if I would babysit her two boys while she worked nights. I was so happy to get the job; I told her I could start the next day. She offered to pay me twenty *lempiras* a month, plus she promised to give me food and a place to live. I was so excited; I couldn't wait to tell my family the good news. As the dory glided through the smooth blue ocean, I felt this was the beginning of my freedom. I was eighteen and ready to make my own decisions. Like most eighteen year olds, I thought I knew everything, and no one could tell me what to do.

When I got home and told my family, everyone was quiet. Then my mom broke the silence. "Is that what you really want?"

"Yes," I said. "It's what I want." I knew they were happy for me, but fear gripped their hearts. I promised I would make good choices.

Early the next morning, I was up before the sun could peep through the cracks in the house. Before I knew it, it was ten o'clock and time to leave. Everyone had tears in their eyes. My little brother sobbed. I told Edney how much I loved him and that I would still try to take care of him. Then out of the door I ran, waving goodbye to everyone.

I arrived at my destination feeling a little scared, but the welcome I received quickly took the fear away. The lady was a beautiful person. She was so thankful that I was there to take care of her boys, and I felt comfortable in no time. She treated me well and let me sleep in a nice bedroom on a real bed. I was allowed to eat at the table with her. I was also able to visit my family whenever I wanted to.

Things were going well, but the devil tempted me to make poor choices and ruin the good thing I had going for me. Friends I knew from when I lived on the cay started visiting me. They often attended the dances that were held in town. The girls dressed in low-neck tight dresses and wore high-heeled shoes. I became so jealous I would cry. The lady I worked for went to the dances. She was so beautiful when she dressed up. I wanted to be beautiful, too, but I didn't have any clothes or shoes nice enough for the dances. And I didn't know how to dance. But that didn't stop me from wanting to go and have fun.

I didn't believe I would get caught in the devil's trap, but I underestimated the power of the enemy to trap me in his lair.

One evening friends of the lady I was babysitting for came to visit her. They were managers of the most prestigious bar on the island. I was always allowed in the company of her friends, so I was not out of place to converse with them.

As we talked, the manager turned to me and said, "Would you like to work in the nightclub, Esther?" Then he teased the lady I babysat for. "We're going to take Esther away from you. She'll make more money working at the club."

I was not about to let the opportunity slip away. "If I worked at the night club, could I still live here?" I asked the lady. "I could help with the housework."

She was a very kind lady, so she said, "Of course you can stay."

"I'll wait until you find someone to take over my babysitting responsibilities first," I promised her.

In no time at all, she found a babysitter, and I started my new job. The first night I was scared to death. The bartender was very patient, and luckily business was slow that night and the next couple nights. Saturday night was a whole different story. By ten o'clock the bar was packed. Girls I knew arrived with their boyfriends. The girls wore beautiful dresses and high-heeled shoes. It was hard for me to pay attention to my job; I wanted to watch everything that was happening. The boys would select a beautiful love song on the jukebox, take their girl in their arms, and dance. They seemed to float across the dance floor. I was jealous. I wanted to be on that dance floor, and yet I didn't know how to dance. I tried to watch the dancers' feet to see how they managed to dance without tripping one another, but they were moving too fast, and I had to do my job of keeping drinks on their tables.

I loved my job at the bar. It was the most fun I had ever had. I loved every moment of it. My pay was thirty-five *lempiras* a month, which was very good for that time. *With my first paycheck, I'm going to buy a pair of high-heeled shoes, some perfume, and a dance dress,* I told myself. I could hardly wait to go to work every night.

It didn't take long for someone to tell my parents where I was working. Mama came right away to see me. "You need to get out of that place!" she told me.

"It's not a bad place, Mama. I'm not doing anything wrong."

She disapproved, but there was nothing she could do. I had turned nineteen, and I felt I was responsible for my life. I became a very good bartender and made lots of friends.

I began wearing low-necked dresses and tight pants. Deep inside I knew I was heading down the wrong road, but I liked what I was doing. It felt good. I wanted to be with my friends and have fun like they did. Boys began asking me to dance, and I ventured out on the dance floor on the nights we were not busy. The first few times I tried dancing I stepped on the boy's feet. I apologized again and again, but none of them seemed to mind as they kept asking me to dance. Soon I was floating across the dance floor just like everyone else. I was beginning to fit in with the crowd.

The boys asked if they could buy me a drink. I always said, "No, I don't drink." Even strangers buying drinks from the bar offered to buy me drinks. Whenever I thought about trying a drink, I would remember my mother quoting something from the Bible about strong drink being a mocker, and whoever drinks it is a fool.

Luckily, I had to work and wasn't allowed to drink even if I wanted to. Today, I thank God for that. I truly believe it kept me from doing even more wrong things. I was already making some bad choices. Even knowing I was doing wrong, didn't stop me from doing it. Finally, I began accepting drinks from customers when I worked behind the bar. I pretended to mix a drink for myself, but it was actually coke with ice or tomato juice instead of a Bloody Mary. My girlfriends would ask me how I could drink and still carry trays of drink without spilling anything or falling.

Then one night one of my drunk friends told everyone sitting around the table that I was lying and wasn't really drinking anything. "I can handle my booze," I snapped. "You mind your own business!"

When my bar closed, I bar-hopped with my friends. We went from bar to bar dancing and partying. I had fun without drinking. Every one of my friends drank, and most of them smoked. I was still a little jealous of my girlfriends. They seemed carefree and happy. They didn't have to support themselves since they lived at home with their parents and didn't have to earn a living.

Since most of my friends knew my secret that I wasn't really drinking, they kept pressuring me to drink. Finally, one night I tried a beer. The bottle came out of my mouth faster than it went in! There was no way I could drink that stuff. I couldn't imagine how they could drink something so nasty and have it make them happy. Another time, I tried rum with Coke. That was even worse. But my friends were determined for me to learn to drink. They said I could drink gin or vodka with orange juice and it wouldn't have a bad taste. They were right. I tried gin first. The orange juice tasted heavier and a little bitter, but I thought, *I can handle this.* Before I could finish the third drink, my head was spinning, and I was unsteady on my feet. I told my friends how I was feeling. They started laughing, and I laughed, too. I didn't know what I was laughing about. But then I realized I still had to do my job. Somehow I managed to get through the night without the manager discovering that I was drunk.

Now that I had steady work, I was able to rent a place of my own for thirteen *lempiras* a month. I felt in complete control of my life. I had my own place, and my friends could come visit me anytime they wanted.

One of my friends, Cassie, got a job working in a saloon not too far from where I lived. My best friend, Dahlia, stopped by the saloon to visit Cassie one day. Then she came to my place and told me Cassie would steal a bottle of vodka from the saloon if I would drink some with her. I agreed. We took a small bucket and a kitchen towel and went to the saloon. Cassie put the bottle of vodka in the bucket and covered it with the towel. Dahlia brought it to my place. We squeezed some oranges in a pot and dumped the whole bottle of vodka in. We got two glasses and started drinking. I couldn't taste anything but the orange juice, so I drank way more than I should have. Before I knew it, my head was spinning and my legs were unsteady.

I was drunk, and I was sick to my stomach because of it. I threw up a number of times, and I felt as if I were going to die. To make matters worse, I had to go to work at eight o'clock that night. I was still very sick when I went to work that night.

As I worked, I thought about the choice I had made to put that substance in my body, and the way I felt afterwards. While standing in the bar, I prayed, *Lord, this was the last time I'll ever drink. Please help me never to do this to my body again.*

God answered my prayer. I never had the desire to drink alcohol again.

Although He took that vice away, I continued partying. And because I had become such a good waitress and bartender, another bar that was only open during the day offered me a position, which I accepted. Although that didn't leave me much time to rest, I was earning quite a bit of money.

I also started flirting with men, especially older men. All my friends had boyfriends or were dating different boys. I couldn't seem to meet anyone I liked enough to consider him my boyfriend, but I definitely wanted the male attention.

One day a tall, lanky American walked into the bar and sat down. He started drinking one beer after another. Two other Americans joined him, and they drank heavily, too. They were drunk in no time. All three flirted with me. The tall guy told me they were shrimpers. They had approached the Niagara border and been picked up by the Coast Guard. Their boat had been seized, and their passports confiscated. Now the three Americans were stuck on the island until the government decided what to do with them.

The tall fellow came to the club every morning to talk to me. His name was Dewy. Although I kept most of my life a secret from my family, I told Udeen about him.

"I hope you don't get involved with him, Esther," she said. "He will be gone as quick as the government can get him out of here."

I wanted to listen to my sister, but Dewy started telling me about America.

"One day, I'm going to America," I told him. "That's my dream."

Right out of the blue, he said, "If you marry me, I'll take you to America."

"What did you say?"

He repeated it. "If you marry me, I'll take you to America."

I couldn't believe what I was hearing. "How can we get married? We don't even know each other."

"We can get to know each other," he said.

"You are not even legal in this country. How can you marry me?"

"My family and the company I work for are working on getting me home."

Was this the way to fulfill my dream of moving to America? I wondered. I was excited at the thought. "Will you come with me to meet my family?" I asked Dewy.

He agreed, and we caught a boat to Savannah Bight where my family lived. We spent the day with them.

"He seems to be a nice guy," my parents said. "But you don't know him well enough to marry him and go all the way to America."

"Why do you keep getting involved with guys you know are only going to be around for a short time?" my sisters asked. They were right, but of course, I told them to mind their own business.

Dewy began telling everyone who came into the club that he was going to marry me and take me to America. I wanted to go to America, but I didn't want to marry Dewy. Marriage was the last thing on my mind. I had too much freedom that I didn't want to give up.

Still, I wondered if I would ever get another chance to go to America if I passed up this opportunity. One day when Dewy walked in, I said, "Okay, I will marry you."

He came around the counter, picked me up and swung me around, and kissed me. But I wasn't happy; I was more scared than anything.

"I'll go over to the courthouse and see how quick they can marry us." He said and took off. He was sad when he came back a couple hours later. "They said I need my birth certificate and my passport."

I knew they were going to tell him that, but he needed to hear it from them. Communication was limited to writing letters and sending telegrams. He sent telegrams to his family and the company. Weeks and weeks went by with no response. He cried every day. Dewy made countless trips to the courthouse trying to get the immigration department involved so we could get married, but they gave him the same answer every time. He needed proof of who he was. I don't think I ever saw a man cry so much. It looked hopeless for us.

I was losing the little bit of interest I had in him. I felt sorry for him because the only reason I wanted to marry him was to go to America. He wasn't the husband I dreamed of, but I figured if he treated me right, I could learn to love him. If he didn't treat me right, I would be in America legally and could gain my freedom.

It was five months before he received word he was going to be sent back to America. He was very sad and tried to get me to go to another part of Honduras with him. "I'll live here with you and never go back to America," he said.

But I refused to leave my island and go anywhere with him but to America. The day he left, we both cried. I still didn't love him, but I wished I was on my way to America with him.

Chapter 10

Life went on as usual, but I couldn't stop thinking that I had lost a chance to go to America. A year slipped by, and the tourist season began. The first night the tourists descended on the town a man who had flirted with me and had taken me out on a few dates the year before arrived at the bar again. Raul entered and sat in the same seat where I had met him the year before. He began telling me how happy he was to see me again, and I was foolish enough to believe him. He sweet talked to me and told me I was more beautiful than before. Those must have been the same words Satan used with Eve in the Garden of Eden. When you are young and your self-esteem is low, those words sound good.

Raul came every night to see me. When I got off work, we would go to other clubs. He would hold me in his arms and dance with me. I felt like Cinderella wearing glass slippers, but all the time that little voice would whisper, *This is wrong. He is way too old for you.* I ignored the voice and had fun. In the two short weeks he was there, things happened that changed my life forever. Raul left again, promising he would return next year.

The people who ran the nightclub where I worked were offered a job on the mainland to run a nightclub there. They asked me to go with them, and I was happy to leave the island for a while. Everything was going well. I loved the place, and I loved meeting new people. I did miss running with my friends, but I was so busy that I didn't have time for fun.

After I was there a couple weeks, I didn't feel well. One morning while I was standing at the sink washing glasses from the night before, my head began to spin, and the next thing I knew the manager was picking me up off the floor. He joked with me, asking why I was drinking so early in the morning. He knew I didn't drink; he just didn't know what else to say to me. In the days that followed I felt sick every morning. Sometimes I threw up, but most of the time I just had a horrible sensation of nausea. Then one morning the manager asked me if I was pregnant.

I was shocked, and naïve. "No, why would you say something like that?"

"I'm just asking because you sure act like a pregnant woman."

I gasped, as I realized it could be true. My mother's words echoed through my mind,

"Esther, you can go out and wallow in the pigpen all night and come home to wash off the dirty mud, but every once in a while it sticks to you, and it won't wash away." Mama's words wouldn't stop ringing in my ears: "Your sins will find you out."

"Dear God, I don't want anyone to know I am going to have a baby. I cannot take care of a baby. Who is going to help me? I will be so ashamed. I can't let anyone see me. What am I going to say to my mom and dad and to my sisters and brothers? They are going to be mad at me. None of my friends have babies. They won't want to be my friend anymore."

I cried constantly. Every chance I got I stood in front of the mirror looking at my stomach and praying it wouldn't get big. I kept thinking, *Maybe if I pick up a wash tub full of water, I will hurt myself and the baby will come out.* I started filling the tub to the top and picking it up and swinging it to dash the water out. One day, hoping to have a miscarriage, I jumped from a high stair. I ended up hurting my feet so badly I couldn't walk for three days, but nothing worked. I told a strange lady who came to the nightclub about the baby. I said I wished I knew how to get rid of the baby before my family found out.

She listened and then said, "Someone told me that if you take two quinine tablets with one small pack of Epsom salt mixed with a bottle of castor oil the baby will come out the next morning."

I went to the drug store and bought the stuff, mixed it, and drank the concoction. It was the most awful tasting stuff. It kept me busy in the bathroom for two days, but it looked like I was stuck with a baby. When I was about four months pregnant, I knew I had no other choice but to go home to my family. That was the hardest thing I had ever done in my whole life. There was no other place to go. Words cannot express how shattered my life was. It was bad enough before, but now I would have a baby to take care of.

Going home to Savannah Bight would be the greatest punishment of all. Everyone on the island would know of my mistake. I would be the talk of the whole island. I did not let anyone know I was coming home. I caught a boat and went home to Savannah Bight. As I walked toward our house, I wished I could walk off the face of the earth and be swallowed up.

My clothes had gotten too tight for me. I looked like a stuffed duck. I felt like I was pregnant from the top of my head to the soles of my feet. The family was shocked when they saw me. Everyone blurted out, "Where did you come from?"

I began crying, and everyone asked if I was sick. Then my mom said, "You look like you are swollen from head to toe. Esther, are you pregnant?"

I wanted to sink through the earth at that moment. Everyone fell silent. My dad was so hurt that he turned and walked away. My mom was hurt, but I don't think she was surprised. She had told me many times the places I was working would bring temptations I wouldn't be able to handle. Along with pity, there was an "I told you so" expression on the faces of my sisters and brothers.

I didn't have any money and no idea where I was going to get clothes or diapers for the baby. My little brother Edney had given me a hen for buying him paper and pencils when he was in school a few years ago. Every time I visited, he would tell me he had chickens for me. I guess he overheard the family wondering how I was going to take care of a baby. One day Edney whispered to me, "You can sell the chickens, and buy clothes for the baby." I looked at him and thought how precious he was to be thinking of something like that for me.

I became depressed. I cried constantly and isolated myself from everyone. Mama told me crying wasn't going to change me being pregnant. I would sit by the window all day looking at the ocean. The pelicans and even the sharks looked so free and happy. I felt trapped and sad, and I had a little baby growing inside me. I was scared because I didn't know what I was going to do with it when it arrived. I did nothing to help around the house; I just sat on a stool and stared.

When my sisters would pick on me for not helping or talk bad about me, my dad would stick up for me and take me on walks along the beach in the evening, assuring me it would be okay. The Bible says that God loves us more than anyone else. If He loves me more than my earthly daddy, I know for sure I want to go to heaven where He is.

Shortly after my arrival, my oldest sister, Udeen, came to visit. She was married, but she often visited the family, staying for a week or more at a time. She had the cutest little red-headed baby boy.

"Talk to her, Udeen," Mama said. "Make her understand she can't just sit around feeling sorry for herself."

Udeen started joking with me about how I looked, and how she looked when she was pregnant. Udeen and I had always been very close. She made me laugh. She showed me a couple of baby outfits she brought for me, but I wasn't really interested in looking at them.

"You're not the first girl who has made a mistake, Esther," Udeen said. "And you won't be the last. Cheer up. I brought two white sheets; we can use them to make a few more outfits for that little baby. The way you look, it's not going to be long before that baby will be coming out."

I wanted to ask her about having a baby, but I was embarrassed. It was strange how I used to think I was so smart and knew everything. Now I realized I didn't know anything.

One of my other sisters asked, "What are you going to put on its bottom when it starts to pee?"

Every time anyone spoke to me about the baby, I got embarrassed. I didn't want them talking to me about the baby or asking me questions. When we were alone, I told Udeen what Edney had whispered to me about selling the hen.

"Why should you sell the hen?" Udeen said. "Just sell the eggs, and buy some flour, sugar, and coconut. We can make some coconut cakes to sell so you can earn enough money to buy a bolt of diaper cloth. One bolt will make fourteen diapers."

She told Edney to sell the eggs and give me the money. He was so happy. Every time the hens laid an egg, he ran downtown and sold it. He gave me the nickel or dime. When I had enough money, I gave it to Mama and asked her to show me how to make cakes. Mama was so happy I was finally getting off the stool. She taught me how to make the coconut cake and then how to slice the cake so that each piece was the same size.

Mama and Edney took the cake pieces downtown to my cousin's small grocery store where the cake was placed on the counter for customers to buy. Everyone in town sold their baked goods in this manner.

I continued baking coconut cakes to earn more money. Then I purchased one bolt of diaper material, safety pins, soap, baby powder, and a few pair of socks.

Udeen came to help me cut and hem the diapers. Mama and Udeen made four little baby dresses all by hand from an old sheet. The whole time they spent helping me, I was so embarrassed I couldn't even talk to them. Udeen tried to show me how to do a little fancy work on the dresses.

"They won't be so plain then, Esther," Udeen explained.

"I don't care how they look," I said. "You can wrap the baby in a piece of cloth for all I care." All I wanted was for that baby to be out of me.

Mama decided to make two different styles of little dresses, two for a boy and two for a girl. I had never thought what the baby was going to be, boy or girl, and I really didn't care. In my heart, I did not want the baby.

I think Mama finally got tired of my negative attitude. One day she spoke very frankly with me: "Esther, this was your choice. You are about to bring a real baby into this world. It's not the baby's fault. It had no choice. You made that choice. Now you need to take full responsibility and start making plans on how you are going to take care of your baby."

I knew it was hard for her to talk to me that way, but she knew it was time for me to face reality. The more I thought about what Mama said, the more scared I got.

The first thing I thought was, *What was the baby going to eat?*

"I need to buy some oatmeal and milk." I told Udeen, handing her the few lempiras left from selling cake.

"What are you going to do with milk and oatmeal?" Udeen asked.

"Feed the little old baby when it comes."

"Esther," Udeen said. "It's not going to be a little old baby. It's going to be your beautiful baby. When it is born, you are going to have to nurse it."

"Yuck! No way," I said. "It will starve to death before I let anyone see me pulling my breast out to feed any baby."

Deen just looked at me. "We'll see what happens when it gets here, and when it starts screaming and hollering. It's not going to be my breast going into its mouth."

Deen always had a way of trying to make me laugh. I did not feel so embarrassed when Udeen and I were alone and she talked to me.

It was December, and Christmas was only a few weeks away. I could feel the baby was going to come soon. I was so restless and could not sit in one place. I used to wonder who felt more trapped, the baby or me. I often pitied the poor little baby and wondered if it could feel how I felt about it.

Christmas Eve arrived and everyone went downtown for a special program. I was, of course, not up to going out, so Daddy stayed home with me. It was the first time since I was a little girl that we had been home alone together. I felt horrible. I was so embarrassed as I thought of what had brought me to this night. Daddy tried to talk to me, but I was so ashamed of myself I didn't know what to say to him.

"I love you very much, Esther," Daddy said. "I was never mad at you. I'm so sorry for you, but I know everything is going to be okay. God will take care of you and your little baby, Esther. You have nothing to be ashamed of."

I listened to his gentle words and was so thankful he was my dad. "Mother and I have never stopped loving you for one moment, and we are going to love your little baby, too."

"Thank you, Daddy," I said. I didn't know what else to say to him. "I don't feel good, Daddy. I'm going to lie down for a while." I went inside the bedroom and cried and cried.

Daddy turned the lamp up and sat at the little table reading his Bible. The house was quiet. I pulled the curtain to see what Daddy was doing. His head was bowed and his hands folded. I knew he was talking to Jesus about me. Daddy knew and loved Jesus so much that whenever he prayed, I knew Jesus heard him.

The family came home later that evening, and the following weeks went by without much fanfare. On New Year's Eve everyone was once again going to go downtown. This time I told my dad to go with the others. I didn't want him to miss out on the activities, but the thought also scared me to death because I still hated the dark. However, I resolved to survive on my own until everyone returned.

While everyone was gone I began to experience a shooting pain that wrapped around my abdomen. I assumed it was time for the baby to come. The pains came and went, and I earnestly hoped everyone would return before the baby came.

When the family arrived back home, I was too embarrassed to tell them what was going on, and since everyone was tired, they all went to bed and were asleep in no time. The labor pains continued, and I tried not to let anyone hear me crying. My pains grew worse during the night. It was getting harder for me not to cry out loud.

Once Daddy stuck his head in the door asking, "Is someone crying?"

I spoke up right away, "No, Daddy, someone is snoring."

I cried and prayed, *God, please let morning light begin to break through.* I felt as if my breath was going to leave my body. I tossed and turned all night; I was in so much pain. Finally, I felt if I didn't scream, I was going to choke to death.

My daddy heard the scream and jumped out of bed.

"Is everything okay?" Daddy asked. "Should I go get Grandma?" My grandma was the midwife who helped my mother deliver all ten of us.

"No, don't let Daddy bring Grandma," I cried to Udeen, who was right beside me.

"It's okay, Daddy," Udeen told him. "Esther doesn't need Grandma to come yet."

Daddy knew I would need her soon. "Let me know when you want me to get her."

Morning finally came, and everyone got out of bed saying, "Good Morning! Happy New Year!" and "How are you feeling this morning, Esther?"

"Esther doesn't feel very good this morning," Udeen said.

Mama came into the bedroom. "Do you think it's time for the baby to come? Are the pains coming fast or slow?" she asked.

"Sometimes fast, sometimes slow." I was embarrassed to talk to her about the pain.

"Udeen," I looked at my sister, "please open the east door for me. I need to get some fresh air." I felt as if I was going to smother.

Mama went back to the others and called everyone to gather for worship. They sang songs of praise, and I heard each one praying, thanking God for another New Year. I prayed, too, but I simply asked God to help me through the day.

I don't think there is a sunrise more beautiful in any other part of the world than on the island of Guanaja. When Udeen opened that door New Year's morning, the sun looked like a huge ball of fire coming right out of the ocean. I felt if I closed my eyes I could reach out and touch the sun. I stood there, gazing at the sun and felt as if God was looking down from heaven on me. At that moment, He spoke to my heart. I felt His presence. I knew in my heart I was forgiven and everything was going to be all right for the baby and me.

Everyone walked out of the house and across the boardwalk to the little kitchen shack for breakfast. I was alone again with the contractions coming even closer together. Nelly came back to check on me.

"Would you do me a favor?" I asked her. "I have a couple dimes. Would you go to the store and buy me a bottle of castor oil and a Coke?" At her nod, I handed her the money, saying, "Please don't tell anyone."

She didn't. In no time she was back from the store. I poured some of the coke in a cup, followed by the contents of the bottle of castor oil, then more coke, so the castor oil would kind of stay in the middle. I held my nose and gulped down every drop. I never dreamed I would take castor oil on my own again after the last time, but I was desperate for relief from the pain and that was the only thing I could think of to speed up the baby's arrival.

Soon Udeen came to check on me. I was so tired I felt I didn't have enough strength to stand up, but I was in too much pain to lie down. I really needed to go to the bathroom and was about to sit over the scuttle hole when Udeen said, "Esther, you better not do that. Your baby might come out and fall in the water and drown."

She got the bedpan and sat it on the bed. "Try to get in bed and sit on it."

I was getting on the bed when I felt warm water pouring down my legs.

"Udeen, I just wet myself!" I cried.

"No you didn't. Your water just busted," she told me.

I'd never heard anyone say such a thing before. "What does that mean?"

"It means the baby is coming."

The pains were now taking my breath away; they were so severe.

"I'm going to get Mama," Udeen said. "Something is wrong with you and that baby."

I was crying so hard that she became frightened.

"No, don't tell her. Don't tell her." I grabbed onto her and wouldn't let her go. I did not want Mama to see me looking like this. Udeen got me to lie down on the bed, with my legs up.

"Something is happening!" I cried.

"The baby is coming out! I don't know what to do!" Udeen was in a panic. She took off and was back in a second with Mama.

"Tell Daddy to go for Grandma right away," Mama told Udeen. Grandma was eighty-three years old and lived about two miles from our house.

Mama stayed with me, telling me to push and breathe, again and again. It seemed forever before the baby was all the way out. I was exhausted. All I wanted to do was sleep.

"Esther," Udeen said, "you have a little girl baby, and she is beautiful."

"It's not over yet, Esther," Mama said. "The afterbirth has to come."

That was foreign to me, too. I had never heard of "afterbirth," but all of a sudden I began having pains worse than before the baby came.

"You need to sit on the bedpan," Mama said.

I tried, but my legs wouldn't move. Mama and Udeen rolled me and pushed it under me, then they struggled to get me to sit up. I couldn't even sit up on my own. Udeen had wrapped the baby in a towel. When I looked down, there was a long cord coming out of me that was attached to the baby's belly button. "What's happening to the baby? Why is that string hanging onto her and coming out of me?"

"That's how the baby was fed inside of you," Mama explained. I learned many things that day, things Mama and Udeen would have told me if I hadn't been too ashamed and embarrassed to ask questions during my pregnancy.

"You can't lie down, Esther," Mama said. "You have to get up." Mama kept pushing on my stomach, saying, "Push, Esther, push."

I was very tired and in so much pain, I couldn't even sit up without being held. It seemed like eternity before my grandmother came. She knew exactly what to do, and when to tell me to push. Mama and Udeen were tired from trying to hold me in a sitting position and pushing on my stomach. It seemed like two or three hours before the afterbirth came. I thought I was going to die if it didn't come out when it did. After that, I went to sleep. I don't know how long Grandma and Mama let me sleep, but I know they had a hard time waking me. When they felt I was alert enough, they told me to sit up, but I couldn't move my legs.

"I'm paralyzed," I cried. "I can't move my legs."

The whole family gathered around the bed. Everyone was crying. They, too, thought I was going to be a cripple.

My sister and my Mom had the baby cleaned up and dressed. They brought her to me. She was a very big baby, and so beautiful. I don't know how much she weighed, as we didn't have a scale.

She started to cry. "She's hungry," Udeen said. "You need to nurse her."

"Not me," I said.

"If you don't nurse her, what are you going to feed her?" Mama asked.

"I don't know. I don't want people looking at me nursing a baby."

I could hear my other sisters in the hallway talking. They were upset with me because I did not want to feed the baby.

"She should have thought about that before she went and got pregnant," Francine said. "It's not the poor little baby's fault. Esther needs to stop being stupid and feed that baby."

I knew I needed to feed the baby. I was just having a hard time accepting everything.

"Mama, can I make some oatmeal and mix it with a little bit of coconut milk and strain it to feed the baby?"

"No, Esther," Mama said. "The baby is too young to eat oatmeal, especially with coconut milk in it. You need to nurse your baby." I could tell by the tone of her voice she was mad at me. She walked out of the bedroom.

Udeen was standing beside the bed holding the baby. She laid the baby on the bed across from me. "Esther, I'm going to help you sit up so you can feed your baby." Udeen struggled by herself to get me propped up against the wall. Then she laid the baby in my lap. She opened the button on my housecoat and put the baby to my breast. I didn't touch the baby. Udeen held her there and repositioned her, trying to get her to eat. I was ashamed; I kept my eyes closed.

"Esther, if you would put your arms around the baby, and pull her close to you, she will be able to hold on and feed." Udeen said.

I knew how to hold her so she could feed. I had seen hundreds of women breastfeeding their babies. The problem was that I didn't want to accept that I was a mother now. Udeen was so patient and loving to me. I don't know what I would have done without her. My whole family showed the baby and me unconditional love. They gathered around me and prayed that God would give me back strength in my legs so I could walk and take care of my baby.

I noticed that the baby seemed to have a hard time keeping her eyes open. "What's wrong with her, Mama?" I asked. "Why doesn't she open her eyes wider?"

"She's just a baby. She will in a couple days," Mama said.

The next morning, when daylight came I noticed her eyes were closed tight. She was awake, but her eyes were not open. I tried to open her eyes, but she closed them right away. I screamed for Udeen.

Udeen, Mama, Daddy, and everyone came running. "The baby's eyes won't open," I said between sobs.

My mom and dad tried to calm me saying, "It's okay, Esther. She's only two days old."

But I could see something was wrong with her eyes. On the third morning her eyes were swollen. She didn't even try to open them. When I tried to pull them open, she cried and cried, and I cried and cried.

This cannot be, I cried, praying to God. *I can't move my legs to get out of bed, and now I have a blind baby. If I'm going to be crippled and my baby blind, please let us both die.*

My mother started massaging my legs twice a day. I was still having pain, similar to light labor pains, and bleeding heavily. I could see my mother was very concerned. She didn't say anything to me, but she sent Daddy for my grandmother. When Grandma arrived, she told my mother to continue massaging my legs and to put heat on my stomach and legs.

"Child," Grandma said. "You need to help yourself. You have a child that you are responsible for now. You cannot be an invalid on this island and take care of a baby. Let's walk her," she said to my mother.

It took four of them to get me on my feet. They tried walking me, but I had no feeling from my waist down. Grandma then told them to start heating water. She had them bring the big washtub in and fill it half full with hot water. Then they picked me up and sat me in the tub. After they took me out of the tub, Grandma massaged my belly. Poor old soul, she worked so hard on me. It was as if God gave her special strength. I believe she saved my life that day. As Grandma massaged my belly, I could feel blood pouring out.

"Something else is coming out of me," I told Grandma. It was huge clots of blood.

"Praise God," Grandma said. "This is what needed to come out." My stomach started to feel better that day. She told the family to continue putting heat on my belly and legs and to get me out of bed and make me walk. They did it faithfully. By the seventh day, I was standing, holding onto the wall on my own. By the eleventh day, I was walking on my own.

My baby's eyes were getting worse. When Grandma looked at the baby's eyes, she said, "I think you had an infection of some kind, Esther. When the baby came though the birth channel, it got in her eyes."

I began crying. "Will my baby be blind?" I asked Grandma.

"I don't know. It depends on what kind of infection it was. Do you have an infection?"

"I don't know, Grandma. I don't feel anything."

"If you have the money, you and the baby need to see a doctor."

My daddy believed there was a natural cure for every ailment in the body. He kept us all healthy when we were growing up by boiling bushes and bark from the trees to make tea for us to drink. In fact, people came from all over the island for his cures. The moment Daddy heard my grandma say I might have an infection he was off gathering his bush medicine. By the next day, Daddy had three bottles of his bush medicine ready.

"Esther," he said, "I want you to start taking this medicine right away."

"I don't have an infection, Daddy," I told him. "I don't want to take that nasty stuff."

"This is not going to hurt you. If you have an infection, it will help you. If you don't, it will help your body to heal quicker from having the baby."

I knew my daddy loved me with all his heart, and wanted more than anything for me to be well, so I drank the concoction.

I don't know if I had an infection, but if I did, the medicine cured it. Daddy didn't know what to do for the baby's eyes because he could not give her any of his medicine. By now I was strong enough to walk around. I did not have time to dwell on myself anymore. I needed to think of how I could get my baby to a doctor. I didn't know what to do or who to turn to, so I prayed and prayed, asking God for direction.

Four days after the baby was born, everyone in the family helped me to decide on a name for the newest member of the family, and we settled on Debbie Ann. My sister Carolyn was going to the cay, so I asked her to register my baby's name with the courthouse. I wrote her name on a piece of paper for Carolyn.

When she returned home, she handed me a paper, and walked out of the bedroom before I could say anything to her. I opened the paper and read the name printed on it. Debbie Donna McLaughlin. I immediately called for someone to get Carolyn for me. She came right away. She began talking as soon as she entered the bedroom.

"Esther, don't be mad at me for changing the name Ann to Donna."

"But why would you do that, Carolyn?" I asked.

"I know two ladies with varicose veins in their legs. One of them is named Miss Ann, and people look at her legs. I don't like that name anyway."

Maybe if I had been feeling better, I would have been upset. I was depressed, and I didn't want to think about a name or fight with her. But in the end, it turned out I liked the name Donna better than Debbie, so I called her Donna.

Chapter 11

On the thirteenth day after my baby was born, I told my family the baby and I were leaving. On the morning of the fourteenth day after her birth, I got up early and packed everything in a cardboard box.

"I'm going back to the cay where I worked for Mrs. Camille. I'm going to ask her to help me take the baby to a doctor."

This was one of the most difficult things I had ever had to do. Yet I knew deep in my heart there was goodness inside of Mrs. Camille. She just had a hard time showing love to me. It didn't matter now how she treated me. I needed to be humble and ask her to please help me get my baby to a doctor. Daddy gave me five *lempiras*, and every brother and sister gave me their nickels and dimes. They cried as I left, telling me how much they loved the baby and me.

"God is going to help the baby see," my mom and dad assured me. I believed He would, too. I thanked my family for all of their love and support, and then I left.

Once on the cay I went to see the lady I used to babysit for. She was a good person. I asked her if she would let me stay at her home for a day or so. She told me I could stay as long as I needed. That afternoon I took my baby and went to see Mrs. Camille. She was shocked when she saw me. She had heard about my baby. I was embarrassed because when I was working for her, she had always told me, "If you run the streets, you'll end up in trouble."

She didn't say anything to make me feel bad. In fact, she seemed happy to see me. I told her about my baby's eyes.

"I'm sorry about your baby's eyes," she said after examining them. "You need to get some Boric acid stuff like your grandmother told you, and you need to take that baby to the doctor."

I gathered my courage and asked, "Would you please loan me one hundred *lempiras* to take her to the doctor? I'll work to pay it back."

Mrs. Camille gave me the money right away. She was happy to do it, and was pleased I was coming back to work for her. She knew she could depend on me to do a good job.

"After the doctor in La Ceiba looks at my baby's eyes, I'll come back and start working for you," I promised.

My sister Corine was working on the cay, so I went to visit her. She gave me every *lempira* she had saved, which was around forty *lempiras*. Out of that, I paid sixteen *lempiras* for a round trip ticket on a small freight boat that ran weekly from Guanaja to La Ceiba. Three nights at a hotel would cost me thirty *lempiras* more.

I was scared. I prayed the doctor would say there was nothing seriously wrong with her eyes. When the boat landed, I caught a cab. I asked the cab driver to please take me to an eye doctor. He drove me to an eye clinic.

I was thankful I had been raised speaking both English and Spanish, as only Spanish was spoken at this clinic. The doctor examined my baby's eyes, pulling her eyelids open.

"This was caused by an infection," he said in Spanish. "It happened when she came through the birth canal."

I began to cry. The doctor was quiet for a moment, and then he spoke to the nurse. I couldn't understand what he said at first, but I caught the word *ciega*, which meant blind in English. I didn't wait to hear anything more. I screamed out to God in Spanish, "Oh, please, God, don't let my baby be blind."

The nurse put her arms around me. "The doctor did not say your baby is blind or that she is going to be blind," she assured me.

"Your baby does have an infection," the doctor spoke softly. "But it's not bad. I'm going to give you some medicine for her eyes."

Not completely assured, I asked, "Why are her eyes closed all the time, Doctor?"

"Her eyes are weak."

"How … how long will she be like this?" I dared to ask.

"It will take about a year before her eyes will be strong enough for her to be out in the sunlight," the doctor explained.

Frantic thoughts crowded in on me. How will I take care of a baby that cannot see for a whole year? How will I be able to work? I knew if my sister Francine could see the thoughts in my mind, she would have said, "You should have thought about this before you did what you did."

In the outer office the nurse gave me a prescription for a salve and some drops to put in the baby's eyes. "The doctor wants you to bring the baby back in three weeks," she said.

"No," I cried. "I do not have money to travel or to keep paying the doctor. I need to talk to him again."

"He is busy," the nurse said. "I will let him know." Minutes later the doctor came out to talk with me.

"Doctor," I said, "please tell me the truth. Is my baby going to be blind?"

"I am not God," the doctor said. "If you put the medicine in her eyes as I have instructed, her eyes will get well in time."

I left the doctor's office with hope in my heart. I felt so much better walking out than when I had walked in. I caught a cab, went to the drug store, bought the medicine, and began putting it in her eyes. A few days later I caught the boat back to Guanaja. With the few *lempiras* I had left, I was able to rent a room. It didn't have a kitchen, only a toilet and sink. To take a bath, you had to fill a tub with water. Still, I was thankful to have a room. It cost six *lempiras* and fifty cents a month. I paid two months rent up front.

The next day I caught a dory to Savannah Bight to tell my family the good news. "The baby's eyes are going to be okay," I told them when I reached the house. "Will you let Nelly come to live with me and help take care of my baby while I work?" Nelly was twelve years old. She had graduated from the sixth grade, which was the highest grade that one could attend for free. Nelly was so happy when she heard me ask Mama if she could come live with me.

"I'll allow Nelly to go with you on one condition," Mama said. "You must promise to change the lifestyle you had before the baby was born, Esther. Otherwise, I cannot allow Nelly to live with you." Mama was very serious when she spoke.

I promised I wouldn't be a bad example. The next morning Nelly and I left for the cay. I purchased an old iron bed for three *lempiras*. The lady I was staying with gave me a sheet and a pillow. Nelly brought her own sheet and pillow with her. The bed was just big enough that Nelly, the baby, and I were able to sleep together with a sheet covering all three of us.

I will be grateful to Nelly for the rest of my life for how she helped me with the baby. The doctor had told me to keep the baby out of the sunlight as much as possible. He explained the glare would hurt her eyes. The room I rented had seams in the walls. Whenever the sun came up in the morning, the glare would come through the seams. Nelly took cloth and plugged every seam in that room so the sun could not shine through. Nelly sat in that bedroom all day taking care of my baby while I worked. I shared my food and took part of it to Nelly three times a day. Mrs. Camille always gave me enough food to share with Nelly.

One day Carolyn came to tell me that some American doctors were going to open a temporary clinic on the cay in a couple days. "You need to take the baby there so they can look at her eyes," she said.

Donna was about three months old, and still was not trying to open her eyes. The swelling in her eyes was gone, but whenever a little glare hit her eyes, she would close them even tighter and cry. I felt so sorry for poor Nelly who stayed inside that one bedroom month after month taking care of my baby. I had lots of time to think, and see how my mistake was causing the whole family to suffer.

When Carolyn told me about the American doctors, I wanted to go and find them right away. Many of us on the island used to think Americans could perform miracles. Early the next morning at work I told Mrs. Camille I was leaving when my morning work was done. I wasn't afraid of her anymore. I explained about wanting the American doctors to look at Donna's eyes. Carolyn had said she would go with me. She had the baby ready when I got home.

Donna was such a beautiful baby. This was the first time she had been taken out of the room since I moved there. Nelly made a little blindfold cloth to put over her eyes, and Carolyn covered her face with a little blanket. I told Carolyn and Nelly to go ahead, and I'd catch up with them. I didn't want anyone to see me with the baby. I didn't want anyone asking me questions. I already had heard people say I was ashamed of my own baby and that I would not bring her out of the house for that reason.

When we arrived at the place where the doctors were staying, we met two of them. Carolyn told them about the baby and asked if they could please look at her eyes. Donna screamed when the doctors examined her eyes.

"Her eyes look okay," one of the doctors said. "They are just very weak."

"You need to start introducing her to some sunlight," they said. "You've kept her in a dark room, so she is accustomed to darkness. She's comfortable with her eyes closed. She needs to learn she can open her eyes."

"It will take time," one of the doctors said. "Start taking her outside in the sunlight every day for a few minutes." The doctors didn't charge me for the drops they gave me to put in her eyes.

When Nelly and Carolyn got back to the room, they took off the net I had over the bed. Then they pulled out all of the plugs in the seams in the room so light could shine through. It made the room brighter. For days it seemed as though she closed her eyes even tighter. Donna was a happy baby. She would laugh, and try to feel things, acting like a blind child. It frightened me to see her behave as if she would always be that way.

I prayed and made bargains with God that if He would let my baby see I would be a good person and give my life to Him. About three weeks later when I came home to drop breakfast off for Nelly, she was excited. "Esther," she said, "Donna tried to open her eyes just after you left for work."

I did not want to go back to work. I wanted to stay home with Donna. This was the first sign of her trying to open her eyes on her own. I often wondered if she opened them at night when it was dark.

Praise God, my daughter began opening her eyes in the evening after the sun went down. I think she was so used to keeping her eyes closed that she didn't want to open them. I was able to take her out in the sunlight when she was about seven months old. It took almost a year and a half before her eyes were strong enough to tolerate the full glare of the sun.

Chapter 12

In spite of the promises I made to God that I would be good if He would help Donna to see, I didn't keep my end of the bargain, and I fell back into my old lifestyle. I continued to work hard to support my daughter, but I partied heavily every chance I could.

Donna was growing into a beautiful little girl. Every time I looked at her I knew I wanted something better for us. But I just couldn't seem to resist the temptations the devil threw my way. Udeen and her husband were living on the cay at this time, and they offered to have Nelly, Donna, and me move in with them.

Unfortunately, this gave me more freedom. I was able to work days as a domestic maid and nights at the bar. Nelly and I were both happy to live with Udeen. I had left Mrs. Camille and was working for another family who was paying me twenty *lempiras* a month, and the bar was paying me thirty-five *lempiras* a month. This was the most money I had ever earned. I was able to take care of my daughter and my sister. I also gave my mother a few *lempiras* each month.

The family where I was doing domestic work was very kind to me. They had seen me grow up on the cay, so I was not a stranger to them. Miss Hazel had two daughters and a son. Her oldest daughter had married and moved to America. She wrote often, and her mother read the letters aloud at the dinner table. Although I was always invited to eat with them at the dinner table, I never felt worthy. I would clean up the kitchen while everyone ate, but I loved listening to the letters. I think I looked forward to the letters more than the family did. She made America sound like heaven. In one of her letters, she said that she was starting a new job making tubes for color television and was earning twelve dollars a day.

Twelve dollars a day? It was hard for me to believe a woman could make that much money. On the cay I was not even making one *lempira* a day washing on the washboard, cooking, scrubbing floors, ironing, and running errands. Until I heard this, I thought twenty *lempiras* a month was great.

That day I said, "I don't know how I'm going to get to America, but one of these days I will." I began daydreaming and fantasizing about going to America. I read everything I could find on America. I asked every American tourist who came to the bar where I worked about America.

Finally, one day my dream of going to America appeared to be within my grasp. Miss Hazel's son was chauffeuring ten men around on his boat to good deep sea diving locations. While they were staying on the cay, Miss Hazel and I cooked three meals a day for the men. I also washed their clothes for an extra ten *lempiras* a week.

The men were surprised when they came to the bar and discovered I worked there, too. They joked that I was their cook, washwoman, and bartender. They invited me to go scuba diving with them, but I had to work.

One day three other men arrived at the cay in a small yacht and met up with the ten Americans Miss Hazel's son had been hosting. One of the men looked to be about fifty or sixty, which seemed very old to me at twenty-three. His name was Ted, and he owned the yacht.

"How long did it take you to get to the island from the United States?" I asked.

"We didn't come from America. We are Tahitians."

I was surprised. Ted and his friends looked like Americans to me. I thought if you had blond hair and blue eyes and landed on the island with American dollars, you were an American.

"I love the island," Ted told me. "I've decided to purchase some land and build a vacation home here."

"You want to live here, and I want to leave."

"No, don't leave this beautiful island," Ted said. Then he added, "How would you like to go back to Tahiti with me? We can travel back and forth on the yacht. I know you would love Tahiti."

I was dumbfounded. I wanted to ask him if he was in love with me, or if he wanted me to come and work for him, but I didn't know how to ask.

"How come your family didn't come with you?"

"I'm a widow and only have one son. He's married and has a family of his own."

I couldn't wait to get home that night to tell my sisters.

Udeen response was, "I thought you wanted to go to the States."

"Of course that's where I want to go, but if I can't go to the States, I will go anywhere just to get off this island."

"Don't be so anxious to run off to some place with some stranger you don't even know," Udeen said. "Where is this Tahiti place, anyway? You hadn't even heard about it before this man came here putting foolishness in your head."

Udeen knew how strong-willed and hardheaded I was. She knew I would take the chance and go.

"Did you tell this man you have a daughter?" Udeen asked. "Is he willing to take her, too?"

"Esther, please don't go with that man," Nelly broke in. "You said you were going to the

States, and I want you to send for me when you get there."

"You both need to go to bed and forget about Tahiti and the United States," Udeen said.

I couldn't wait to tell Miss Hazel the next morning. When I told her, the first thing she said was, "I thought you wanted to go to the States."

"Yes," I admitted. "But who in the world is going to help me get there?"

When the men came for dinner that evening, Miss Hazel spoke to Mr. Norman, the oldest man in the group. He always took time to talk with her. She told him about Ted asking me to go to Tahiti with him.

Miss Hazel asked Mr. Norman, "What do you know about Ted?"

"He's a good man. We've been friends for many years." Then he looked at me and said, "You will love Tahiti. It's a beautiful place. But are you sure you want to leave this little paradise?"

"You might think this is paradise, but sometimes it feels like a prison to me and I'm sentenced here for life," I replied.

"Esther really wants to go to the States," Miss Hazel told Mr. Norman. Then she turned to me and said, "Esther, I don't think you should go to Tahiti."

Miss Hazel liked me, and was giving me good advice.

Then Mr. Norman spoke words that brought joy to my heart. "Maybe I can help you get to America."

When I heard that, I wanted to grab him and hug him. I wanted to hug and kiss Miss Hazel for questioning Mr. Norman about Ted and telling him how I wanted to go to the States. Maybe my dream really would come true.

I was anxious to get home to tell my sisters the news. As I walked in the door, Donna came running to me. I grabbed her in my arms and twirled her around the room.

"Why are you so happy, Esther?" Nelly asked. "Are you still thinking about going to Tahiti?"

"No! I'm going to the States!"

"Which is it? Tahiti or the States?" Udeen asked.

"This time it's for real. Mr. Norman, one of the older men I'm helping Miss Hazel cook for, told me today that he is going to help me get to the States."

"Esther, I don't want you to think that I don't want to see something good happen to you," Udeen said. "But you are so anxious to leave this island and go to some unknown place that you could be jumping out of the frying pan right into the fire."

I didn't want to hear her advice. Nothing she or anyone else could say to me was going to discourage me. I knew if my mom were there, she would tell me the same things Udeen did. As I was getting ready for work that evening, Nelly came to me and whispered, "Esther, if that man is willing to take you to the States with him, if I were you, I would go. Don't listen to Udeen. She's not your mother. Just go, and send for me when you get there."

I stopped what I was doing, and Nelly and I laughed and laughed. "Nelly," I said, "I will send for you when I get there. That's a promise."

Nelly felt the same about leaving the island as I did, but she was much younger and hadn't been exposed to the world like I had been. I had stopped going to church and kind of lost faith in God. Now, all at once, it seemed like my prayers were being answered.

I did not get to talk to Mr. Norman for two days because he didn't come to the bar, and I didn't see him at mealtimes either. But if the truth were told, I was afraid to say anything to him for fear that he hadn't meant what he'd said.

"Are you thinking about going to Tahiti with me?" Ted asked that night when he came into the bar.

"My sister said I can't."

"Can I talk to your sister? I will take good care of you."

"I have a three-year-old daughter," I confessed.

"That's okay," he said. "I will take care of your daughter, too."

"My sister said it is too far away."

"Tell her you will be coming back and forth."

"I did, but she still said I should not go," I told him.

Ted seemed serious. If Mr. Norman didn't mention America again, I decided I would take Ted up on his offer, regardless of what my sister said.

On the third night, Mr. Norman came to the bar. I gathered my courage and asked him if he meant what he said about helping me.

"Sure, I did."

What a relief.

"First, I need to talk to my wife to see if she would like to have you come work for her. She is always complaining that it's hard to find a good worker."

When he said that, I thought of Mrs. Camille and hoped Mr. Norman's wife wasn't a slave driver because that wouldn't be good. I didn't dare say that to him. I knew I needed to tell him I had a daughter, and I knew I had to tell him before he left that night. If he talked to his wife, she would need to know I would be bringing a child with me. I don't know how I got the nerve to tell him, but as I passed him something to drink I looked right into his face and said, "Mr. Norman, I have a three-year-old girl who I would need to bring with me."

"You do?" A serious look came over his face.

"Yes, sir."

"Is there someone here you could leave her with?"

"No, sir. I could never leave my baby."

"That could be a problem. Let me talk to my wife and see what she says."

I started praying at the moment, asking God to please intervene in the heart of this woman. I knew only God could do this for me. I had never heard of anyone who was able to bring a child with them to do domestic work.

I went to Savannah Bight to tell my mom and dad what was happening and especially to ask my mother to pray that God's will would be done for Donna and me. My mother loved Jesus so much, and I knew when she prayed He answered her prayers. I had seen it happen so many times. Things we thought were impossible were made possible because of her faith in God. My mom and dad wanted the best for me, but they were afraid for me to go to America.

"It's too far away. We will never see you again," Daddy said.

"I'll find a way to come back and see you," I promised.

Thirty-eight years ago, life was so different. To us, America seemed as if it was on another planet. My parents had been isolated on that island all their lives. The furthest they had ever been was to the mainland to see a doctor, and that was so seldom you could count the times on one hand and have a couple fingers left over.

The days turned into weeks, and the weeks turned into months as I tried to patiently wait for Mr. Norman to let me know what his wife said. There were no telephones on the island, so there was no way for Mr. Norman to directly talk to his wife. In order to communicate with anyone in the United States, you had to go to the mainland. Mr. Norman made several trips to the mainland, and I was worried he wasn't going to take me with him. But finally, after two months, he returned and told me, "I have good news for you. My wife said it was okay for you to come."

"What about my baby?"

"You can bring her, too."

Words could not express the gratitude I felt to God for answering my prayers or my thankfulness to Mr. Norman for the trouble he had to go through to help me. By the next day, the whole island seemed to know I was going to America. I don't think any of my friends believed me at first. Some of them said, "I'll have to see it happen first before I believe it."

That night when Ted came to the bar, I told him I was going to America with Mr. Norman. "I'm happy for you. If it doesn't work out, my offer is still good," he said.

I walked around on cloud nine for the next couple of weeks. I think that was the happiest I had ever been. I thought about all the opportunities my daughter would have that I didn't have. The one thing I was the most happy about was that Donna would be able to go to school and get an education. I didn't have an education, nor did any member of my family. When people lived as we did on the island, education was not their first priority. Education was for the children of rich people. We struggled just to have something to eat and a dry place to sleep at night.

I obtained a copy of my birth papers and my passport. I was so anxious, I could scarcely sleep at night.

One morning Mr. Norman came to breakfast and said, "Are you ready, Esther? We'll be leaving for the US in two weeks."

I looked at him in shock. I had never heard of anyone getting the papers needed to bring a domestic person to the States that quickly. It usually took between six months to a year. I made the trip to Savannah Bight to tell my parents and the rest of my family goodbye. It was a very sad goodbye, but deep inside I was so happy. I could not express that to them.

The day finally came for us to leave. After all the goodbyes to my sisters and friends, we boarded the airplane to La Ceiba, and then to San Pedro Sula. From the airport, we went directly to the American Consul Office. I was scared because I had heard that sometimes people were turned away. We didn't have to wait long before the next officer asked for our papers. Mr. Norman explained he was bringing me to America to work for him. He gave them my passport and birth papers.

"Where are the rest of her papers?" the man asked.

"What other papers does she need?" Mr. Norman said.

"She needs an affidavit to enter the United States to work. Without that, she cannot work."

As I stood there listening to the man, I burst out crying. I couldn't hold back the tears. I couldn't believe this was happening. It was like a nightmare. Mr. Norman was shocked. He could not understand the need for more papers.

"How come I can come to this country with just a passport, and this young lady is not allowed to come to America with the same documents?"

I don't recall the man's answer, but after a little more conversing the man finally said he would issue me a temporary visa to visit the State. I don't know if he felt sorry for me or what, but he told Mr. Norman that he would be responsible for my child and me.

Mr. Norman was excited and assured the officer that that wouldn't be a problem. As I listened to them talk, my mind whirled with a mix of emotions and thoughts.

"What do you think?" Mr. Norman turned to me. "Would you like to come and visit for a couple months? You might not even want to stay in America once you get there."

I looked at Mr. Norma and the man. "If I cannot go to America and be a legal resident, how can I work to better my daughter and myself? I will go back to the island and try to make the best of life there for my daughter."

Mr. Norman had tears in his eyes.

The immigration man said, "Why not go for a visit?"

"So that I can go and not want to come back? I'd have to live my life in America as an illegal alien on the run for the rest of my life. No, thank you. I will go back home."

Before we left the office, Mr. Norman gathered all of the information he needed in order to take me to America legally.

"When I get back to the States, I will do whatever it takes to help you," he promised me.

I wanted to believe him, but I thought to myself, *He's not going to take the time to do that when he gets back to America. He will probably forget I even existed.*

I knew he knew how horrible I felt. He took my daughter and me to a beautiful restaurant. I didn't know such a nice place existed. I had never been in a place like that before, but being so sad and depressed, I could not enjoy it. I could only think about going back to the island and facing everyone after bragging about going to America. Mr. Norman tried to console me.

"I'll make arrangements for you and Donna to fly back to the island tomorrow," Mr. Norman said.

I was frightened. I had never been that far away from home alone. Here I was, afraid in my own country, and still longing to go to America.

While we were eating, Mr. Norman said, "We fly out tomorrow morning. I've made a reservation in a hotel for us."

Did he get one room or two? I wondered.

When we walked outside, he hailed a taxi. At the hotel, I was shocked. *Only rich people can come to places like this*, I thought. Mr. Norman walked up to the counter, and the lady greeted him like she knew him. She passed him two keys, and a sigh of relief went through me. A boy came and carried our luggage to what looked like a metal wall. He stood in front of a set of double doors without handles and pushed a button on the wall. The doors slid open, and the boy carried our luggage inside. Mr. Norman stepped into a little room, and holding the door, motioned for me to step in. When I got in, the doors slid shut. The boy pushed a button on the wall. It had a number "two" printed on it. The room shook, and I stumbled against Mr. Norman. Almost before I could blink my eyes, the doors to the little room opened again. I was amazed. I wanted to ask, *What in the world was that? How did that boy get us up here so quickly?*

I turned to look. I wanted to get a good look at the little room. The word "elevator" was on the wall beside the doors. I did not ask any questions. The boy walked a little way down the hall and opened the door to a room. I walked in. It was the most beautiful bedroom I had ever seen. It was icy cold inside the room. Mr. Norman stepped inside and said, "Oh, it feels great in here. If it's too cold for you, you can turn the temperature up."

"The what?" I asked.

"The air conditioner. You can turn the temperature up higher if it's too cold in here for you."

I had no idea what he was talking about. I stood in the middle of the room and looked over against the wall. There was a television, and on the nightstand beside the bed was a telephone. To top it off, there was carpet on the floor. I had read about places like this, and I had dreamed of seeing it one day, but I thought they had places like this only in America. I learned that day there were places like that for people with money in my country, too. I think my little daughter was in just as much shock as I was.

When Mr. Norman and the porter boy left, Donna and I sat on the edge of the bed and bounced up and down. She wanted to explore the room and touch everything.

"No, baby," I said. "Don't touch anything in the room. It does not belong to us, and mommy does not want to get in trouble if something gets broken."

I was curious myself. I picked up the telephone receiver and put it to my ear. Donna wanted me to put it to her ear, too. I told her it was only making a buzzing sound. She wanted to hear it, so I put it to her ear and then told her it was not a toy. I thought I would hear someone talking when I picked it up, so I was disappointed to only hear the hum.

I decided to turn on the television. I hesitated before pushing the "on" button. The screen lit up, and a bunch of lines went running across it. It made an awful sound. I quickly pushed the button and turned the television off. I wasn't about to mess with either one of those things again.

"No bath tonight," I told my daughter. "It's too cold." I couldn't wait for morning so we could leave. This was the first opportunity I had to spend the night in a beautiful bedroom, and it was the worst night I could remember. I thought we would freeze to death. Knowing what I do now about the temperature, it was probably about seventy degrees in the bedroom. I had never been in a place that cold before. I prayed all night for morning to come even though I dreaded going back to the island and facing everyone the next day.

Mr. Norman knocked on our door early the next morning, letting me know that both our flights were leaving in a couple hours—his flight back to the United States, and mine back to the island.

"If you get dressed quickly, and come downstairs, we might have time to eat some breakfast before we leave," he said.

I was so miserable and sad; the last thing I wanted was to eat. But I also did not want him to know how I was feeling. He had tried so hard to help me, and I did not want him to think I was ungrateful, because I wasn't. Donna and I were dressed in no time. Actually we did not have much to put on, as we did not take many of our clothes off because it was so cold in the room. I was thankful when I walked out of that room and started down the hallway. A couple ahead of us walked right up to those same metal doors and Donna and I followed them. A man was holding open one side of the doors; he looked at me and asked, "Are you going down?"

I didn't know how to answer because I did not know if I should get on that thing or not. Instead, I said, "I'm going to catch a plane."

"Then you are going down," he said.

I stepped into the little room, and in no time we were on the first floor. Mr. Norman was sitting in a chair waiting for me. He hurried us into a beautiful dining room and ordered breakfast. I couldn't eat. I was so sad; I had a hard time keeping from crying. I wanted to go to the United States. I felt this was my one and only chance, and I had missed it. Mr. Norman seemed to know how I was feeling. He reached across the table and caught my hand.

"Esther," he said, "I know you are discouraged, but I'm a man of my word. I promise you I will get you to America. My next trip, you and your baby will be coming along with me." The way he spoke gave me hope. We hurriedly finished breakfast. It seemed only a matter of minutes before Mr. Norman was in one cab and my baby and I were in another heading for the airport.

I dreaded going back to the island, but there was no other choice. When the airplane landed on the airstrip, I took my time getting off the plane. I hated to face everyone since I had failed to get to America. But I couldn't hide.

When my friends found out the whole story, some of them said, "Girl, you are crazy! You should have gone when you had the chance. You didn't have to come back. You could have stayed as a wetback."

"Not me," I told them. "I would rather never go if I can't get there the right way."

I was fortunate to get my jobs back. I had only been gone two days, so I fell back into my old routine quite quickly. I hoped Mr. Norman would be back, and that he would keep his promise, but only time would tell.

Back on the island, I threw myself into work, but I also began partying again with my friends. After I got off work at night, we used to steal chickens right out of people's chicken coops. We all liked fried chicken, and there was a thrill for us in stealing them.

Although I didn't think about it at the time, I had to face the consequences for my choices. How much heartache I could have avoided if I had followed what my parents had taught me from the Bible!

Chapter 13

Five months passed before Mr. Norman returned to the Island. My heart jumped when I saw him. I wanted to run to meet him and ask, "Did you bring my papers?" but I held myself in check. I was standing by Miss Hazel's steps when Mr. Norman came by and told us how happy he was to be back on the island.

"I'm tired from the long trip," he said. "I'll see you in the morning."

I don't think I got thirty minutes sleep that night. Morning finally came, and I was up early. I remember praying and asking God to give me strength if Mr. Norman hadn't been able to secure the necessary paperwork. I tried to comfort myself by saying that God knew what was best for me. My parents had told me that if I didn't get to go to the United States God had a reason.

When I arrived at Miss Hazel's home that morning, she was anxious to know if Mr. Norman had kept his word. He came downstairs around ten o'clock as Miss Hazel and I were cleaning. I looked up and saw a brown envelope in his hand. He didn't say a word; he just held out the envelope. I reached out and took it from him.

"Open it, Esther," Miss Hazel said.

I was so nervous I could hardly open the envelope. I didn't know if I wanted to see what was inside.

"Mr. Norman, am I going to the States?"

He smiled. "Read it and see what it says."

"How about my baby? Is she coming with me?" I didn't even want to read the papers if her name wasn't on it too.

"Read it and see what it says," Mr. Norman repeated.

I started reading. I saw my name and my baby's name. There are no words to express the joy I felt. "Oh, Mr. Norman! You are an angel whom God sent to this island to rescue me!" It was a miracle from God.

"I have to go tell Donna that we are going to the States," I said to Miss Hazel and Mr. Norman. "I'll come back." I felt like I had wings when I took off with that envelope in my hand.

"Guess what? I'm going to the States!" I shouted to every person I passed on the bridge. Most of them just shook their head, probably thinking, "There she goes again."

My sisters were so happy for me, especially Nelly. Now she had hope that one day I would be able to send for her. It's hard to put into words what I was feeling. I felt I was getting ready to enter the Promised Land once I touched American soil. I had always lived in such poor conditions, but I believed that was about to change.

My desires for more money and material possessions in America stood in stark contrast to my mother's simply faith that God would provide for our every meal. When we didn't have food, she would say, "The Lord will provide something for us before the day is out." And He did. There was not a day that something didn't come. Sometimes it would be late at night, but I don't remember ever going to bed without something—even if it was just a piece of coconut or a mango. Sometimes, out of the blue, a knock would come and someone would be standing at the door with some green bananas or plantains and some coconut oil. My mom would thank them, just as if she knew they were coming. My dad would take the lantern and say, "Kids, let's see if we can find a little bit of firewood so mom can fry us some plantains to eat."

God had always provided, but I wanted more from life, and I was determined to achieve my dreams. I prayed to God for guidance and that His will would be done, but in the same breath I plowed ahead, seeking my own wishes.

With the precious papers in my hand, I felt like Cinderella preparing for the ball. When I returned to Miss Hazel's house, she told me Mr. Norman said he would be back to talk with me. I thought the reason he wanted to talk with me was to tell me when we would be leaving. That night while I was working at the bar, Mr. Norman came in and sat on a stool in front of me.

"Esther," he said, "I have some bad news to tell you."

The expression on his face told me it wasn't good. My heart sank.

"My wife is divorcing me," he said.

"Why would she want to divorce a good man like you?"

"I asked her to come here with me to see if she liked this place. She said she would never give up her home to live in some God-forsaken place. I told her I wasn't giving up our home either, that we'd travel back and forth."

As he was talking, I was thinking, *I don't blame her. I wouldn't leave America to come here either. She sounds like she has good sense.* I also thought, *How in the world will I be able to work for Mr. Norman in the States, if he comes here to live?*

"What does this mean for me?" I finally had the courage to ask.

"I don't know, Esther."

As I was busy running from table to table serving people, I formulated a plan. *If Mr. Norman wants to be stupid and spend his life here, that's okay, but I don't. I have these papers in my possession. I'll leave this place, and he won't even know it.* I was scared to think this way, but I was not about to let anything stand in my way of going to America.

He could see I was disappointed. "Don't get discouraged. We will work something out."

"It's okay, Mr. Norman," I said. "I can go on my own."

"No, you can't. I'm responsible to see that you will be taken care of when you arrive in the United States. I can be in a lot of trouble with immigration if I don't fulfill my responsibilities."

"Sir, if you would please trust me, and let me go to the States on my own, I promise I will get a job and take care of Donna and myself. You will not get in any trouble."

"Esther, I really want to see you go to America. I know that's your dream. You're such a hard working girl; I believe you could make it on your own, but what about your daughter? You can't go to the United States without knowing where you are going."

Mr. Norman sat quietly for some time before he spoke again. "Do you know anyone in the United States?"

"I know a lot of people who have gone over there."

"Maybe you could contact someone and ask if you could go to them," Mr. Norman suggested.

He never would have understood, so I didn't try to explain how the people I knew in the States viewed me. They had not allowed me inside their homes when they lived here. I knew it wouldn't be any different in America. But I didn't want to change Mr. Norman's heart about how he saw me. I believed he saw me through the eyes of God. He only saw my dreams of an opportunity for a better life for my daughter and me. That night he told me I could take the papers and go to America.

I was now twenty-four years old with my whole life ahead of me. I had spent the last seventeen years feeling like a slave, and now I had the chance to start a new life without people looking at me in light of the mistakes I had made.

Chapter 14

I had the paperwork and permission from Mr. Norman to go to America, but how was I going to get there? That was the next hurdle I had to jump over. Then one day God answered my prayer and sent a small ship to the island that I knew was headed back to the States. I couldn't wait to see the captain of that ship to ask him for passage on his boat. I sat on the dock for hours waiting for the captain to come ashore. I had already learned that his name was Captain Royal. When he stepped ashore, I followed behind him and called out his name. He looked around.

"Captain Royal," I said, "would you please take me to America on your ship?"

"Lady, my ship does not take passengers. It's a freight ship."

By this time, I was walking beside him. "Sir, I need to get to America. I will work on the ship for you if you will please take me."

"Do you have papers to go to the States?"

"Yes, sir."

"Come back tomorrow, and bring your papers," he said. "I need to see if they are legal."

He didn't mention money, and I silently prayed that he wouldn't ask me if I had any money or tell me it would cost a lot for me to travel on the ship.

I arrived at the dock bright and early the next day. This time I was brave enough to board the ship. All the men started whistling at me. I asked to see the captain. I was shown to his cabin, and fortunately, he remembered me.

"Good morning, Captain Royal," I said as I handed him my papers.

He opened the envelope and studied the papers. He looked up at me and said, "You didn't tell me you had a child."

I tried to hide my panic. "Yes, sir. She is four years old. She's my baby, and I have to take her with me."

In a deep voice he said, "Okay, I'm leaving here in three days. If you want to go on my ship, be here on time."

Words cannot describe my joy. I was one step closer to setting foot in America. I sent word to my family that I would be leaving for the States in three days. In all the excitement, I forgot to ask the captain where in the States we would land, but that wasn't important to me. I thought it would be the same in the States as it is on the islands—whenever a boat landed everyone ran to the docks to see who had arrived. I knew a number of people who had gone to the States. I figured I would recognize someone who came to the ship and they could tell me where I could get a job. Looking back, it is hard for me to believe how naïve I was.

I had saved a few dollars, but I badly needed to buy a few things for the trip. God was watching out for me, His lost child, and He caused one of my employers to pay me extra, one hundred and twenty-five American dollars!

My friends threw a going-away party for me, and my whole family came from Savannah Bight and spent the day with me. The last day was sad; everyone was crying. My mom and dad gave me advice and reminded me that if I made good choices God would take care of me. Everyone pleaded with me up until the last day to leave Donna and send for her once I knew where I was going. But my answer was always the same. "No!"

The day of our departure finally arrived. As I walked toward the ship with my family and friends, there was joy and sadness, laughter and tears. I felt so much love from my family and friends that I was able to get on board that ship without any fear of facing the unknown. As the ship pulled away from the dock, I waved my last goodbye and watched the crowd fade into the distance. Suddenly, I felt all alone. All around me were sailors—Donna and I were the only females on the ship.

Captain Royal was a nice man. There was a set of large bunk beds in his cabin. He explained that since there were so many men on the ship and no accommodations for a woman he wanted my daughter and me to sleep on the bottom bunk in his cabin. He reminded me a lot of my dad.

"There are too many men on my ship," he said. "I feel I have a responsibility to get you and your daughter safely to the States."

My mom and dad told me they asked God to send angels to keep us safe, and He did. The weather was beautiful; the ocean was as calm as a lake. The dolphins following the ship put on a show for Donna and me, causing the only stir in the water. We stood on the deck for hours watching them.

I was amazed to see how vast the ocean was. It went on as far as the eye could see. I wondered how the captain knew which way to go. We sailed for six long days. On the seventh day, I awoke to hear the men shouting. The captain was at the wheel.

When he saw me, he said, "We made it! You are in America."

I looked around, but I could only see what looked like smoke. The captain told his men to drop anchor. "When the fog clears, you will be able to see the dock," he said.

I had never seen anything like fog before. I had heard about fog, but it never occurred to me to ask what it was. This was the first of many new things I would discover in my new world.

Around ten o'clock I heard the captain tell the crew to pull up the anchor. I was standing beside the door looking out when the captain opened it. Cold air hit me. I thought I was going to freeze before I got away from the door. I grabbed the blanket from the bed to cover us.

"I'm cold, Mama," Donna said.

A lady had given Donna a little red sweater when we left the island and were boarding the ship. I didn't want to take it, but she said, "You might need it when you get there."

I had never worn a sweater in my entire life. I had heard and read that sometimes it was cold in the States, but I hadn't paid much attention. I quickly opened my suitcase for the sweater and put it on Donna. After the fog, the cold was the second new thing I was experiencing, and I was still on the ship.

I was anxious to see what America looked like. I felt the ship moving and could hear when it reached the dock. I got out of bed and opened the door. I walked out on the deck and looked down at the dock. All I could see was a bunch of rugged looking men pulling on ropes. I walked toward the front of the ship and looked down. I was shocked. The water was black and dirty. Our water was clear as a crystal—our ocean was a beautiful blue.

I searched the dock for the people who came to see who had arrived on the ship. All I could see were the men working on the dock. There was not one woman on that dock. That's when I panicked. What was I going to do if no one I recognized came to the dock? I went back inside the cabin. Donna was still covered up in bed. I knew she wouldn't understand what I was saying, but I began to talk to her.

"Donna, we are in trouble." For the first time, I was really, really scared.

It seemed like an hour before Captain Royal came back to the cabin. I had taken out my money as he stepped inside.

"Captain Royal," I said, "how much do I owe you for bringing us here?" I only had ninety dollars, but that was a lot of money to me.

He hesitated, than said, "Oh, give me fifty dollars. That will do."

I couldn't imagine being able to come all the way to America for fifty dollars. That amount included three meals a day for Donna and me. I was thankful he didn't say one hundred dollars, as I didn't have that much. Praise God, I still had forty dollars left.

"Get your passport, and all of your papers ready," he said. "In a few minutes, immigration will be coming on board to check the ship and make sure everything is legal. Then they will give us the okay to get off the ship." He smiled at me. "I enjoyed having you and your daughter on the trip. I hope everything works out well for you both here in America."

I think he could see how scared I was, although I didn't say a word about it to him. He was getting his things together when the immigration men knocked on the door. I saw their badges, and I knew I couldn't let them suspect I was scared. I pretended to get Donna ready. The two men checked the captain first before asking for my passport and papers. While one checked my papers, the other checked our luggage. It was a relief when the inspection was finished.

"Are you going on to Louisiana?" one of the men asked.

"Yes, sir." I nodded my head. I was so afraid they were going to ask me more questions, but praise God they didn't.

"Are you ready to get off this ship?" Captain Royal asked. He picked up one of my suitcases and started out the door.

I took the other one, caught Donna's hand, and followed him off the ship. As we walked along the dock, I looked around. A sign said, "Port of Tampa."

"This is Tampa?"

"Yes," Captain Royal said. "Where did you think it was? Isn't this where you are supposed to meet your party?"

We were off the dock by this time, and there were taxicabs nearby. Captain Royal walked toward one of them. I reached out and grabbed him and then burst out crying.

He turned around. "What's wrong, child?"

"Sir, I don't know what to do. I don't know where to go."

Captain Royal stood and looked at me in disbelief. "You're telling me someone isn't meeting you here?"

I managed the words, "No, sir."

"What about the family your papers say you are going to work for?"

"Sir, it didn't work out—"

"So you decided to come on your own?" he interrupted.

"Yes, sir."

"I'll be doggone! You made me bring you all the way from the island on my ship, and you didn't even know you were coming to Tampa." He shook his head. "Where did you think you were going?"

"To the States, sir."

"You are in a state right now. It's a big one, at that." I think he was really upset with me.

"Tell me, what do you want me to do for you?"

"I don't know, sir," I said.

He repeated my words after me, "I don't know, sir."

I was scared and ashamed that I was putting this poor man through this, but I wasn't sorry that I came, not for one second.

"Do you know anyone who lives here?" Captain Royal asked in a stern voice.

Again, we both repeated the words, "No, sir." He was slowly realizing that I didn't know anything, not where I was or what to do. He motioned the cabdriver away, walked to a small building, and set my luggage on the sidewalk.

He took a deep breath. "How much money do you have?"

"Forty dollars."

"Forty dollars," he repeated. "How much money do you think that is? Don't say it—I don't know, sir." Then Captain Royal said, "All right, little girl, I want you to tell me everything, and I want the truth. You can get me in a lot of trouble for bringing you here."

I guessed he was thinking, *She looks like an adult, but she has the intelligence of a little girl.* I wanted to defend myself, but then I thought, *You can call me anything right now; just please don't leave me here.*

But before I could speak, he asked, "Did you take those papers from those people?"

"No, Captain Royal, I didn't steal the papers. He gave them to me."

"What kind of man is he to give you papers and send you to a foreign place alone with a child?"

"He's a good man. He was only trying to help me," I said.

"Do you have their phone number?"

"No, I don't."

"How about his family?"

"No, sir."

"So, you are telling me you don't have anyone's phone number."

I shook my head. I was tired of saying, "No, sir."

He looked at me and said, "I don't know what to do with you. My wife is in New York."

I said, "That's where I want to go."

"Hush, child, you think you have problems now, what in the world would you do in New York? I can't take you to my house, my wife would kick us both out when she returned and found a young girl in her home." He put his hand in his pocket and pulled out some coins and walked to the other side of the little building. There was a box on the wall with the word "telephone" on it. I watched as he put the money in a little hole, then his fingers went to work on it. He put the phone to his ear and started talking.

I pulled Donna's hand and said, "Look at the captain. He's talking on the telephone." I was fascinated to think you could put money in a box and talk to someone. He talked for a while. I knew he was talking about me. I prayed, *Dear God, please don't let him call immigration on me. They will send me back home.*

The captain hung up the phone, put more money in, and began talking again. This time he didn't talk as long. When he hung up the phone, he came over and picked up the two suitcases and started walking. Donna and I followed behind him like two lost puppies. He stopped walking where the cab was when we first arrived. We stood there for what seemed a long time. Finally a cab came.

"Let's go," he said.

With a little hesitation, I got in the cab. I wondered where he was taking me, and after a few minutes I finally asked him.

"Why?" he asked. "Are you scared?"

I just looked at him.

"You should be," he said. "It's about time." Then he asked, "Do you know a lady by the name of Adela? She's from your hometown."

"No, sir."

"Then, maybe you know her family, her mother's name is Miss Maybell."

"I know her."

"Okay. I talked to Adela. She's married to my son. She said I could bring you by. Maybe you can stay with her until you can figure out what you are going to do with yourself."

"Thank you, Captain Royal. I'm sorry for putting you through this."

Now that I realized he wasn't taking me to immigration, I was able to relax. It was a short ride to Adela's house

I was nervous, wondering how Miss Adela was going to feel about my little girl and me coming to her home without being invited.

Chapter 15

God was so faithful to me; He planned my whole trip. Captain Royal and Miss Adela were such a blessing when I arrived in Florida. Miss Adela opened her home, and her heart, to Donna and me. She was sad, and she had reason to be as her husband was very sick. She had seven beautiful, well-mannered children—three boys and four girls.

Miss Adela's husband had a brain tumor and was nearing the end of his life. I arrived at her house on March 8, and her husband died on March 25. I never got to meet him, but I know he was a lucky man to have had a father like Captain Royal, a beautiful wife, and seven precious children. I needed Miss Adela, and she needed me. God placed us together to help each other. As Miss Adela dealt with the loss of her husband, I was able to be help out with the children

I had fantasized about America and all the new and exciting things I would see and do. I believed all my wounds would be healed and all my problems solved. But I spent the first three months in shock. It was not at all what I expected from the books I'd read and the movies I'd watched. Nonetheless, there were many things I marveled in.

I loved the television. I could sit and watch it all day. The telephone also fascinated me. But I was embarrassed to let anyone hear me talking on it, and it was difficult to dial. My finger would pop out of the holes as I dialed, and I often missed one or two numbers. I watched the children pick up the phone and talk to their friends. It was easy for them.

The washing machine was the most amazing thing to me. I could not get over it when I saw Miss Adela put a huge load of clothes in the washing machine. In no time she was taking them out, and they were all clean. It was unbelievable to me. I could only think of the hours I stood washing on that washboard at home, and this machine did the job in minutes. I learned a lot from Miss Adela and the children. She didn't drive, so that limited the places she went. I stayed and helped her in the home until she was able to cope with the loss of her husband.

Miss Adela talked to a lady living next door who was a preschool teacher. She offered to help me get my daughter in school. I was very thankful. She even offered to take Donna to school and bring her home until Miss Adela could help me figure out transportation for her.

My first job in America was an experience I will never forget. I never dreamed there would be such a gross job in America. Miss Adela told me when she was feeling better she would help me find a job. It was hard for her with the seven little ones, and no transportation. But I couldn't just stay at her home and not work. One day we caught a bus and went looking for a job. I was amazed at the things I saw that day. We went to downtown Tampa. I saw huge, tall buildings, department stores, restaurants, traffic lights, and many cars. Amazingly, everything was painted. I looked through big plate glass windows at beautiful clothes and shoes. Miss Adela took me into Grants. We had lunch in the restaurant of the department store. Everything was so beautiful to me.

"Maybe you could try to get a job in one of these stores," Miss Adela said.

I panicked. "No, No, I can't work in these stores. I wouldn't know what to do."

"They will teach you."

I didn't want to even try to get a job there. Everyone was moving too fast for me.

"If you can get a job downtown, you can easily catch the city bus to go back and forth," Miss Adela said.

I didn't want a job downtown. I was not ready to catch a bus and get lost. Everything seemed too complicated to me. I was beginning to think I had made a mistake. Maybe I should have never come to the United States.

For the next few days, Miss Adela helped me look for a job. She took me to a canning factory, a fruit factory, a packing factory, and finally to a chicken factory. The people at the chicken factory told me to come back the next morning. I had a job. I had been in the States for two months when I finally found work.

Miss Adela took me back to the chicken factory the next morning. After helping me fill out the application, she left, saying, "I'll have someone pick you up after work."

A lady took me to the area where I was to work. The place was gross. If someone had told me people worked in those conditions in America, I would never have believed them. The lady showed me around and told me what I would be doing and what was expected of me. Then she took me to a room and gave me a pair of high boots and a long, yellow apron. After I put on the boots and apron, she took me into the work area. Lots of men and women stood beside what looked like big long freezers full of water, with ice floating in them. When I looked inside, I saw hundreds of chickens floating there. The lady showed me where I was to stand each day. The place was freezing. I was scared and miserable. I knew I needed to work, so I was thankful to have a job even if it was gross.

Miss Adela showed me how to catch the city bus, but I soon discovered that the factory was only about a thirty-minute walk from her house. I decided to walk, as I didn't have the money to ride the bus every day. Walking was no problem for me; it had been my main form of transportation all my life. If I wasn't walking, I was in a boat or a dory. After a few days, I became acquainted with Sarah who worked beside me. She offered me transportation, explaining she drove by the house where I lived. I gave her five dollars a week for taking me back and forth to work.

I don't know what I would have done without the support and friendship of Miss Adela. By staying with her, I was able to send a few dollars to my parents and save enough money to rent a place for Donna and me. I was thankful and happy to have a place of my own.

I worked at that nasty chicken factory for several months. The city finally closed the factory down because of sanitation problems. My friend, Sarah, and I went job hunting. I felt more confident now, but I was disappointed that life in the States wasn't turning out as I had expected. Sarah and I were hired at a fruit-packing factory, but the job only lasted a few weeks. They could only hire us for fifteen or twenty hours per week. We both needed to make more money than that.

One day Mr. Tringally called. He had taken a fleet of shrimp boats to Honduras and had been at the dock when I left. Although I had never met him, my friends and family had. There were no strangers on our island; we made friends with everyone who came there, which I discovered was completely opposite to life in America. Nelly had given him my address and phone number and asked him to call. I was so happy to hear him say he had talked to Nelly.

"Is Nelly okay?"

"Yes, everyone back home is fine. But your sister is very worried about you. Your family needs to hear from you more often." Then, he asked, "When can you come to pick up your letter?"

"I don't know where your place is, and I don't have a way to get there. Could you please bring the letter to me?" Thinking back, I realize it was bold of me to ask a rich man like Mr. Tringally to bring me the letter. But, if the situation were reversed, I would have taken the letter to him.

Mr. Tringally came that evening. It was good to see someone who had just come from my island and could give me news of my family.

"Are you doing okay?" he asked.

I broke down and told him I wasn't doing well. I explained about the job situation. I felt comfortable talking to him even though I didn't know him, but I knew he had been in Honduras long enough to understand our culture.

When I finished explaining about my situation, he said, "I can get you a job at the shrimp factory."

"I don't care where the job is as long as I can make enough money to take care of my daughter and me."

"The manager at the shrimp factory is a personal friend of mine. I take shrimp to that factory." He reached in his pocket, pulled out his wallet, and gave me one hundred dollars. "Buy something for your daughter and yourself."

I was stunned. I didn't know what to say except for thank you.

"I'll call you tomorrow and let you know when you can start work." The next day he called and said, "My son will be over tomorrow to take you to see the manager."

The next morning a car pulled up in front of the house. A handsome young man knocked on the door and introduced himself, saying, "My dad sent me to take a girl named Esther to the shrimp factory."

I got in the car with the young man. It was a long ride to the factory. He took me to the office where the manager gave me an application and said I could start work right away.

"I can't start for a couple days," I told him.

"Take the application along, and bring it back when you can start."

The young man took me back home. He told Miss Adela where the job was. At first she was shocked. "How are you going to get back and forth? That place is in Dover?"

Then Miss Adela remembered that she knew a lady who worked there. She called her and told her about me. Then she asked if she would give me a ride back and forth if I helped out with the gas. Thankfully, the lady agreed. Two days later I was on my way to the shrimp factory. I took my application in and was assigned a spot, just like at the chicken factory. It was another stinky, nasty place, but it was a job and I needed work.

The ladies I worked beside were very unfriendly. One of them was especially mean to me. Every morning each worker was required to pack a certain amount of boxes in a certain amount of time. I was a fast worker and had no problem completing my assignment. The mean lady would slip one or two of her boxes into my pile every chance she got. I complained to the manager that walked the floor, but she ignored me. One day I caught the lady putting three of her boxes in my pile. I called the manager over and told her what happened. She just said, "You are just trying to get out of doing your boxes, Esther, and you want someone else to do them for you." I wished every day that I didn't have to go to that shrimp factory. I didn't mind the work; it was the mean cold-hearted women I worked beside that I minded.

Around four-thirty one Friday evening at the shrimp factory, just before the end of my shift, a voice came over the loudspeaker. "We are in the middle of the shrimp season. We have lots of shrimp coming in, and need everyone here tomorrow. Please be here."

My heart started to beat fast. I knew I couldn't come to work Saturday. It was the Sabbath. I had heard that you were fired if you missed work. I couldn't afford to get fired. But I thought back to my growing up years and the importance of the Sabbath.

When I lived at home, my mother and father took us to Sunday School every Sunday, and any other time the church doors were open. When I was sent to Mrs. Camille's home, my mother asked Mrs. Camille to please send me to church.

"We need to have all the work done by four-thirty today," Mrs. Camille told me on Friday morning of the first weekend I was at her home. "You have to go to church on Friday nights."

"I don't go to church on Fridays," I said.

"If you are going to live in my home, you will have to go on the days I tell you to go. Every Friday night and every Saturday, you will go to church."

That evening two little girls stopped by Mrs. Camille's house to pick me up. She had arranged this with their mother. I liked that the church had a children's program. When it was over, the children said, "Everyone is welcome to come back to Sabbath School tomorrow."

I couldn't wait for Saturday morning. In my church back home, we had to sit with the big people and be quiet. This church had church just for children. I used to wish our Sunday School back in Savannah Bight was like this so my brothers and sisters could have fun in church, too. My mother had taught us to repeat the Ten Commandments. She said everyone should know them because they taught you right from wrong. We would repeat them twice a day, so by the time I was seven, I knew all the "Thou Shall Not's," as we called them. At Mrs. Camille's church when they asked the kids what the Ten Commandments were, I held up my hand and said, " I can say them." The teacher hugged me and told me she was proud of me. When the Sabbath School teacher began talking about the fourth commandment, I was the only one who didn't know why we were in church on Saturday instead of Sunday. I asked the teacher to explain it, and she did, but I still didn't understand. However, it didn't matter to me; I liked the church because they did lots of fun things. I told my mom when she came to see me that Mrs. Camille made me go to church on Saturday. It didn't seem to bother my mom.

"Does Mrs. Camille go with you?"

"No, Mama, but I know where the church is, so I can go by myself."

Mrs. Camille saw to it that I went to church every Saturday, even though she and her husband never went. I am so thankful today that she made me go. I became a Sabbathkeeper because of Mrs. Camille. Eventually my whole family became Sabbathkeepers. Mrs. Camille instilled in me the need to keep the Sabbath day holy. All the other days she worked me like a little slave, but come sunset Friday evening I could rest until sundown Saturday evening.

In spite of all the hard times and bad choices I had made growing up, I had never worked on Saturday from the time I had learned it was God's holy day. I wish I had stood firm on all of the other principles as I did on the Sabbath day, but I was determined to keep the Sabbath.

I decided to go see the manager and explain why I couldn't come to work on Saturday. By the time I found him, I was scared and shaking.

"What can I do for you?" he asked when he saw me.

"Sir, I wanted to let you know I cannot come to work tomorrow."

"Why can't you?" he asked, looking in my eyes.

"Sir, it's my Sabbath."

"You're what?"

"My Sabbath. It's the day I go to church," I explained.

"I respect you for your religion, but you need to be here tomorrow."

I didn't say anything. I just turned and walked away. I knew it wasn't an option for me.

"You don't need to pick me up Saturday morning," I told the lady I rode with.

"Aren't you afraid of being fired?"

"I don't want to get fired, but I do not work on Saturdays."

The lady was sure I would be fired if I didn't go to work. "I know you are new to this country, and you need your job, but you need to realize this kind of factory hires and fires people every day."

By the time she dropped me off, she had convinced me I would be fired. So I told her not to pick me up Monday morning. I believed her because of the manager's attitude when I told him why I couldn't work on Saturday. I didn't know what I was going to do, but I knew I had to stand firm in what I believed. I had lived a double standard for the better part of my life, knowing right from wrong but always making excuses. Still, there were certain things I refused to compromise, and the Sabbath was one of them.

I was worried. I had no one to turn to. I knew when I told Miss Adela she was going to say, "Child, you know that you need to work. I don't know what you are going to do now."

By Tuesday I was sick with worry. I picked up the phone and called Mr. Tringally. When his secretary answered, I asked to speak to him. When he answered the phone, before I could say anything, he asked, "How's the job going?"

"That's the reason I'm calling you," I said. Then I explained what had happened. He listened, and then said the same thing three other people had said.

"Esther, you need to work."

If anyone knew that, I did. I didn't need to be reminded. When I called him, I was thinking, *Maybe Mr. Tringally has a shrimp boat going back to Honduras, and maybe he would allow me to go back home on it.*

"You need to go back to work, Esther," he said before I could ask.

"I'm not going back to that place so that man can fire me."

"You won't get fired. I'll call my friend and talk to him. I want you to go back to work in the morning." Mr. Tringally said.

Thinking back, I can't believe how very naïve I was. There is a scripture in the Bible where God says He winks at our ignorance. He must have gotten tired of winking at me because of the bundle of trouble I got myself into.

I called my coworker and asked her if she could please pick me up on Wednesday morning.

"Did they call you and say you could come back?"

"No."

"When you get there, they will tell you that you are fired, and I cannot bring you back home. You will have to sit outside all day, and they might not even want you on their premises."

"They are not going to fire me," I told her.

Early Wednesday morning she picked me up. When we arrived I walked behind her to the clock. My card was still in the slot. I took it out and clocked in and went right to my spot and stood there. The lady who passed out the boxes came by and stocked my little overhead area. I started working just as if I had never missed a day. I was never questioned as to why I did not come to work for the three days. That had to be another time God winked for me.

Things were starting to go a little better for me. I was beginning to feel that maybe everything would work out. Of course, that would have been too good to be true. That nasty old devil couldn't stand to see good things happening to me.

I was beginning to feel more comfortable in my surroundings. Donna and I even started catching the city buses and going downtown. Sometimes I would even venture into Grants or Crest and order a coke and French fries, which both of us loved. As we walked along the street, Donna would tug on my hand and say, "Mommy, look at that doll," or whatever she saw in the store windows.

"One of these days Mommy will take you into one of these stores and buy you dolls and pretty clothes."

After working for about two more months at the shrimp factory, I began praying every day that God would help me find a different job. I believe God has His way of working things out for those who believe and trust in Him.

One Friday evening, just before quitting time, the voice over the loudspeaker said, "We are working the next three Saturdays. We want everyone here." This time the voice added, "We will not be making any exceptions."

I stopped working for a minute and just stood there. I asked under my breath, "Lord, what am I supposed to do now? You know how much I need to work. Why are you letting this happen?"

I knew I could not come to work, so I didn't even bother to go talk to the manager. I knew he didn't want to hear anything I had to say. When I clocked out that Friday, I knew I would never return to the shrimp factory.

When I got in the car, the lady I rode with said, "Miss Esta (that was the way she pronounced my name), what are you going to do? You have to work on Saturday. He said three Saturdays this time. I bet a lot of people are going to be fired this time. He didn't ask if people could work. That's not right. It's unfair."

"You don't need to come pick me up ever again. I will never go back to that place," I told her. I thanked her for taking me back and forth to work, paid her the five dollars for the week, and said goodbye.

This time I didn't call Miss Adela or Mr. Tringally. I was going to make it on my own or ask to be shipped back to my country. By Monday morning, however, I was panicking. My paycheck was seventy-nine dollars, and I had managed to save sixty dollars. I was more scared that day than the day I arrived in the States. I came with hopes and dreams, but that Monday I felt hopeless. During the short time I lived in the neighborhood, I didn't really get to know anyone. I had always left for work at five-thirty in the morning and returned home around six-thirty in the evening. The lady who drove me dropped me off at the babysitter's house in the evening, and Donna and I would walk home. I only saw daylight at my house on weekends.

Chapter 16

Three weeks went by and I still didn't have a job. I did plenty of looking, but nothing was working out. One morning that third week of no work there was a knock on my door. When I opened it, a woman was standing there. I didn't recognize her.

"I'm one of your neighbors," she said. "No one has seen you for a while, and we were wondering if you had moved. I don't mean to be nosy, we just wanted to know if you were okay."

"Yes, ma'am, I'm okay. I don't have a job, and I don't know what I am going to do now."

"What kind of work can you do?"

"I was working at the shrimp factory," I said. Then I went on to tell her about my Sabbath.

The woman stood there listening to me. Then she said, "It might be hard to find a job where you don't have to work on Saturdays. But I will talk to my husband when he gets home this evening. Maybe he can help you."

I thanked her, and she left. There is a scripture in the Bible where Jesus says, "I will never leave you, nor forsake you." Sometimes I forget that promise, get discouraged, and lose my faith, which I was doing then. I tried to hold onto my dad's words, "Esther, God will always be right on time for you."

At eight o'clock that night, there was a knock on the door.

"Who is it?" I asked.

"Your neighbor's husband," the voice said.

I opened the door and invited him in. He introduced himself and told me he was a pastor. I told him my story, and I believe he understood when I explained why I couldn't work on my Sabbath.

He stood there a moment. "Young lady," he said, "I don't know what I can do for you. I can't promise anything, but I will try to help you find a job. Be ready at eight o'clock in the morning. I'll pick you up, and we'll see what I can do for you."

The pastor was at my door at eight o'clock the next morning. I was a nervous wreck. I had prayed all night that he wouldn't take me to another factory. The people I had met at the factories seemed angry and used foul language. I felt uncomfortable around them. I spoke English well, but I couldn't understand American accents when people spoke fast to me.

It was nice to see a different part of Tampa as I rode with the pastor. He stopped in front of a big white building. It looked like a factory to me, and my heart sank. But when we went inside, it wasn't stinky or nasty like the other factories. The pastor spoke to a lady, she called someone on the telephone, and in just a few minutes a man came. The pastor went over and talked with him. I couldn't hear what they were saying, but felt they knew one another. The man from the factory came toward me saying, "Follow me."

I did, and the pastor followed, too. I was scared. I didn't know what kind of a place this was, or what they did here. Perhaps the man thought the pastor had told me what they did. It looked like the man was going to hire me. I began to worry. What if I didn't know how to do whatever the job required? Perhaps it was something I needed an education to do. The man led me into a small room. There were a couple of tables and chairs.

"Sit down. I'll be right with you."

Through a glass window I could see the pastor sitting in a room across the way. The man returned, reached under a counter and pulled out a sheet of paper and a pencil. He placed the paper and pencil in front of me. Then he put something that looked like a clock in front of me. I wanted to ask about it, but didn't want him to know how dumb I was. If he knew how naïve I was about certain things, he probably would have had second thoughts about hiring me.

"I'm going to set this timer. You have fifteen minutes to complete this test."

He did something to the clocklike gadget, and the timer started. I suddenly felt like I was going to freeze to death. My legs started to shake. I picked up the pencil and stared at the ticking thing in front of me. I had no clue how to take the test. When the timer went off at the end of the fifteen minutes, I almost jumped out of my skin it frightened me so. The man entered the room and stood in front of me. I looked at him, and he looked at me.

"What happened? You didn't do the test."

I was so embarrassed. I hung my head, and said, "Sir, I didn't know what to do." Even now, I can't believe what the man did next. He reached down for the test sheet, balled it up in his hand, and threw it in the trashcan.

"I'm going to pretend you did that test," he said.

I just sat there. He went back to the counter and pulled out a long sheet of paper and placed it in front of me. I knew what that was; I had filled several of those out before. I was so nervous after the ordeal with the test, there was no way I was going to be able to fill out an application. The man left the room. I looked through the window. The pastor was still sitting in the same spot watching me. I went to the window and beckoned for him to come to the room. He came right away.

"Would you please help me fill out this application?"

He was happy to help. We filled out most of it until we came to the part that asked if I was an American citizen.

"I wonder if this is going to be a problem," he said.

"I'm here legally," I told him. We completed the application, but I still didn't know where I was, or what kind of factory this was. The man came back and took the application. When he saw that I was not a U.S. citizen, he looked surprised.

"You're not a citizen?"

"No, sir, I'm not." That's when I discovered where I was.

The man said, "Here at Honeywell we are making some parts for the Vietnam War, and we cannot hire anyone who is not a U.S. citizen." He was really sorry—I could hear it in his voice. He apologized many times that he couldn't hire me. We thanked him and left. I was sad as we left the factory. But then I realized that was not the job God had prepared for me. That was the reason it didn't work out. God had another job planned for me. I remembered that He knows the beginning and the end. If I had gotten the job at Honeywell, I might have had the same problem over working on the Sabbath that I did at the shrimp factory. Later, I learned that the Honeywell factory closed down three years after. I believe that was another reason I didn't get the Honeywell job. God was watching over me. He was preparing me for something better the whole time.

The pastor was still willing to go out of his way to help me even though I was ready to give up. I felt the pastor was an angel in disguise. When we left the Honeywell factory, the pastor drove me to another place. This building looked quite different, and when we entered, the atmosphere was also different. I saw children going in and out of the doors.

There was a lady sitting behind a desk in a big office as we walked in. The pastor went up to the window and asked the secretary if he could speak to the principal. I didn't have any idea what a principal was, as I had never heard of anyone with that title. I could tell this was a school, although I had never seen a school like this. We sat in the lobby for about fifteen minutes before a little, short lady came out of her office and introduced herself to the pastor.

"I have a young lady here who needs a job," he told her. "I was wondering if you could help her out." Then he turned to me and said, "This is the principal of the school."

"I'm Mrs. Biser. What kind of job are you looking for?"

I shrugged my shoulders and said, "Work."

Thank God for the pastor. He spoke up right away. "She just came from another country and needs help."

"I don't have anything available at the moment," she said

The pastor didn't even let her finish speaking. "Mrs. Biser, I know there is something around this school you can use her for. She really needs your help."

I thought she was going to say, "Sir, leave my office," because he was so bold. But he had spoken very kindly, and I believe God softened her heart that very moment.

"Let me think about it," Mrs. Biser said. "Could she check back with me in the morning?"

"Yes," the pastor said, and then he shook the principal's hand and said, "Thank you."

When we got into the car, the pastor said, "I believe you have a job."

"I hope so." The pastor had no idea how scared I was. The only school I had been in was on the island, and it had been made up of benches, a black board, and a teacher. I couldn't think past the school on the island. I had wanted to tell the principal and the pastor about the minimal education I had received while on the island, but I had been speechless.

The pastor took me back home. He didn't offer to take me any place else. "Be ready for work in the morning at eight o'clock."

I hadn't heard Mrs. Biser say she was going to hire me. But the pastor was confident that I had a job. At eight o'clock the next morning I was ready and waiting on my porch waiting when the pastor arrived. He was right on time. When I got in the car he said, "Are you ready to go to work this morning?"

"I don't know."

"You are going to do okay," he assured me.

Sure enough, when we arrived Mrs. Biser hired me even though she didn't have a specific job for me. After the pastor left, she pointed to a chair and asked me to sit and wait until she could get back to me. While I waited, people came in and out of the office. Some were dressed nicely and looked professional, while others were plainly dressed. I wondered what all of these people did at the school.

After what seemed like forever, Mrs. Biser came out of her office and asked me to follow her. I was afraid, alone, and lost all at the same time. I walked beside the principal to a building with double doors. She opened one of them, and we went in.

"This is our lunch room," she said. There were little children sitting around tables eating. I had never seen so many little ones at one time.

"These are the kindergarten children. They have an early lunch."

I wondered if their parents brought food here for their children. On the island the children walked home every day to see if there was anything to eat. Most of the time, there wasn't.

Mrs. Biser showed me the kitchen area. There were about ten women cooking and serving the children. Plates of food sat in rows on the counter. The children came through and picked up a tray. I had never seen anything like this before. There was so much food I could hardly believe it.

The principal introduced me to the lady working the cash register, and then said, "I am going to start you out working in the lunch room. Your job will be to assist the children if they need help. You will also keep the tables clean, and clean the tables after each class. I'll talk to the lunch room manager and have her give you your meals every day for keeping the tables clean."

I was so happy. One of the reasons I had wanted to come to America when I was a little girl was so that I could have lots of food to eat. Now I was going to be working in a lunchroom, and I was going to get paid for working and also get my food. Only in America could this happen.

The principal took me to another part of the school. As we walked along, she said, "This part of the school is where the handicapped children are taught."

I had no idea what she was talking about. I had never heard the word "handicapped" before. On the island there was no place for handicapped people. If you were unable to take care of yourself, it was better if you had never been born. The few people who had something wrong with them were made fun of, harassed, and called "retarded." When I was a child, I heard of a family who had a crippled boy. No one ever saw him. The other kids said the retarded boy couldn't walk or use his hands and that he drooled. He was kept locked up in the house until he died.

Mrs. Biser showed me the classrooms. I saw all the little handicapped children as I walked through the building. Many were not able to use their hands or feet. I felt like crying as my thoughts went back to that poor little boy who stayed locked up in that house all his life just because he was handicapped. Here there were beautiful classrooms for all the handicapped children. The children were treated like real people. I was ashamed of how I had been raised to view handicapped people.

Then the principal took me to a big room with all kinds of equipment. There were a couple women there with some of the children on tables and tricycles and by walking bars. "This is the physical therapy room," she said.

I had never heard those words before either, but by now I was smiling and pretending I knew what she was talking about. I don't know if she planned for me to work in that room or not, but one of the ladies asked, "Did you bring us some help?"

"Yes, Esther can work with you when she isn't cleaning tables." Then she said, "I have to get back to my office now." She left me in the physical therapy room, saying, "Report to the therapist when you arrive in the morning, then go along to the lunch room."

That's how it happened. Whenever I wasn't in the lunchroom, I worked in the therapy room. I never would have dreamed that I would work in a place like this. I didn't do much that first day. I helped children on and off the exercise tables and back and forth to their classrooms. It was hard for me that first day, seeing so many children with so many deformities. I was afraid to touch some of the children. I had never experienced anything like this before, and no one explained anything to me. Everyone seemed to take it for granted that since I got the job, I must know what was required.

There was one physical therapist and two occupational therapists working in the room. The children scheduled for treatment came in all throughout the school day. It was fascinating to see the way the therapists worked with the children. It was difficult for me to watch the children try so hard to make their little bodies move and function. It was heartbreaking. It was beautiful to see how the therapists touched and handled the children. They hugged them and held them in their arms. They treated them like normal children. The children responded just as my little daughter did when I gave her love and affection.

During that first day, I watched the physical therapist as she worked with each child. She made each one feel special, and the children worked so hard to get their bodies to do the things she asked of them. I liked her and felt drawn to her. She didn't say much to me, but she seemed to know how new and unusual this school was to me. She took time to introduce the children to me and explain their disabilities.

By the time I made it home I felt I had seen and learned more in that one day than I had in the eight months I had been living in America. I wanted to tell someone about my new job, and since there was only my five-year-old daughter available, I told her. That night I got down on my knees and told God how thankful I was for the job, and for my healthy little girl.

A whole new world opened up to me. Every day was a new experience. I couldn't wait to go to work each morning. As I began to get to know my coworkers and fall into a daily routine, I began to feel more comfortable. I thought, *This is the America I wanted to come to, and this is the place God knew I needed to be at. If I had a little bit of education, I might make it.*

I was running into problems in the classroom when the children needed help. I had never taken English and was unable to help the students when they asked me about a verb, adjective, noun, or pronoun. In order to not let the children know I didn't know the answer, I would look at it and say, "Didn't you listen when the teacher explained it to you? You need to ask your teacher for help."

Sometimes I would walk out of those classrooms feeling so dumb. That's why I decided I needed to go to school and get book sense to go with my common sense. That's how my Mama would have put it. The nearest adult education classes were held at Young Elementary School. That evening on my way home from work, I got off the bus near the school and registered for a class four nights a week, Monday through Thursday. I filled out the registration card indicating I would like to start in the seventh grade. If questioned, I could tell them the school on the island only went up to the sixth grade. That way I wouldn't have to tell them I had never gone to grade school.

"I'm going to school at night," I told Donna.

She giggled. "Mommies don't go to school."

"I need to go to school so I can help you with your homework."

Donna still thought it was funny, but asked, "Where am I going to stay while you are in school?"

"You'll have to go with me."

"No, Mommy, I won't get to watch TV."

I wasn't thinking of my daughter when I made the decision to go to night school. "Donna, I really want to go to school, and you'll have to be a good girl so the teacher will let me bring you with me."

I hadn't checked on the bus schedule. There wasn't a bus going from my house to the school. I had to catch a bus from my house to Ybor City, then another bus to school. This meant I had to leave home an hour earlier to get to school on time. I took a small cushion, a blanket, and a few toys for Donna to play with. The first evening I found the teacher, Mrs. Hill, to be a very understanding lady.

"I don't have anyone to take care of my little girl, and I really need to come to school."

"It's okay as long as your daughter doesn't disturb the other students," Mrs. Hill said.

I had to walk about four blocks to catch the bus in the evening. The class ended at ten o'clock, so with the long bus ride and walking, I didn't make it home until eleven thirty. The hardest part was that most of the time Donna was asleep, and I had to carry her over my shoulder for the four blocks. It wasn't easy, but I was used to carrying loads from the time I was a little girl. All that hard work carrying loads on my back paid off. I did this for several months, then one night the teacher was in her car and saw me.

She stopped and asked, "Where do you live?" When I told her, she asked, "What time do you and your daughter get home?"

In response to my reply, she said, "It's too dangerous for you to be out here catching the bus with your daughter every night. You need to be very careful." She drove away.

The next evening at school, Mrs. Hill called me to her desk. "Would it be okay for me to ask one of the students I know very well if he could drop you off on his way home from class?" The student's name was James. He was a family man trying to earn a diploma, and was already transporting two other students.

"I'll be happy to take her," James said. "It's not far out of my way."

Mrs. Hill assured me James and his other passengers were all good people, and she knew them personally. I was so thankful to be able to get home an hour earlier.

School was not easy for me since I had never learned the basics. It was hard to grasp the new, advanced material, and I struggled to keep up. But Mrs. Hill was a good teacher, and she took time to explain when the class didn't understand. American history was my favorite subject. I couldn't get enough of reading it. I was in America and grateful for the privilege to attend school and learn its history.

Chapter 17

I had promised myself if I ever came to America I would be true, honest, and work hard to become an American citizen. I wanted freedom for my daughter and me. I asked what I needed to do to become a citizen, and I was able to learn the history needed for the test. When the day finally came for me to take the test to become a citizen, I was a nervous wreck.

I was so proud of myself the morning I walked out of the building after taking my citizenship test. I knew others had similar experiences as I did, and some worse, but that day was my day. A letter arrived with an appointment date for me to be sworn in as an American Citizen. I was so anxious for that day to come. I wrote my family and told them I would soon be a citizen of America. I missed my family so much. I wanted to share with them all the things that were happening in my life.

I rode the city bus to work each day. One day, a friend, Mona Lee, and her husband, Alejandro, came to visit me. He asked if I drove a car.

"I haven't learned how to use a washing machine, much less drive a car," I said.

"I have a car I will sell you for three hundred dollars."

"What kind of a car is it?" I asked. "Is it a big old monster like the one you are driving?" Alejandro was driving a big station wagon.

"No, it's a 1961 Chevrolet. Don't be like Mona Lee. She hasn't learned to use the washing machine either, and she won't try to learn to drive a car."

"It's not easy to learn how to do all these new things," I said.

"I feel sorry for you. Here you are in America and you are still washing your clothes in a washtub. Get your clothes together, and I'll take you to the laundromat and show you how to use the machine."

I had always wanted to learn, but I was afraid I would mess something up. We went to the laundromat, and Alejandro showed us both how to do the laundry. Even as I followed his instructions, I doubted I would dare use the machines on my own.

After my friends left that day, all I could think of was the car he wanted me to buy. I began imagining myself driving a car. I had saved almost four hundred dollars, so I had more than enough to pay for it.

The next day, I told my coworker Jan Renyard about the car.

"It would be nice to have a car," Jan said.

"Do you think I should buy it?"

"That's up to you, Esther. If you think you can trust your friend that it is a good car, and you want to drive, then you should get it."

I called Alejandro that evening and told him I wanted the car. The next morning Jan gave me a book to study in order to qualify for my driver's license. I paid for the car and my neighbor drove the car home for me. I felt I was making progress. I had a good job and owned a car, but I didn't have a license, tags, or insurance, and I didn't know how to drive. I was so proud of that car. I started it up every evening and washed it every Sunday for two months until I saved enough money for tags and insurance. But who was going to teach me to drive?

Jan suggested I contact a driving school, but first I needed a restricted license. Poor Jan stayed after work so many times to help me study for that license. Finally, I felt ready to take the test. Jan was doubtful, but she took me to the Motor Vehicle Department for the test. I prayed, and she nervously waited.

I don't know who was happier when I walked out of that place with the restricted license, Jan or me. No one could ask for a better friend.

Jan was not the only coworker who looked out for me. Dorothy Kotz, Patricia Moll, and Kitty Getz were all so kind. Another friend Mrs. Reeves offered to have her dentist husband treat Donna for free. And I couldn't forget the kindness of Mrs. Biser for hiring me at the school and the pastor for helping me find the job. When I think back on all of these people and the love they showed, I know it was because a loving God was watching over Donna and me.

Jan called the driving school and arranged for them to give me lessons. I could only afford to pay for three lessons. I had paddled lots of dories, and even steered a motor dory, but driving a car was going to be totally different. Now I was getting ready to get in a car with a stranger. I did what I knew how to do best—I prayed.

At the end of the first lesson, the instructor said, "You did a good job for your first time on the road." He praised me again at the end of the second lesson.

When he came for my third lesson, I asked, "Sir, could you take me today to get my license?"

"I don't think you are ready. You only had two lessons on the road, ma'am."

I didn't argue. I knew he was right, but he didn't understand I didn't have money for more lessons.

"What do you want me to do?" the instructor asked.

"Take me to get my license."

He directed me to the Motor Vehicle Department, telling me when to turn as I drove. I prayed all the way. When we arrived, I went inside and told the man behind the counter I wanted to take my driving test. I then waited for my turn. A short man carrying a clipboard in his hand came out a side door. He paused a moment, then called my name. I was shaking as I followed him outside to the car. I don't remember what I did, but as the car moved ahead first one orange cone, then another disappeared under the car.

"Sir," I cried out, "what do I do now?"

"Stop the car," he said. He slid out of the seat and walked back to set those cones back up. Then he got in. "You may try it again," he said.

My guardian angel must have taken over for me then because the next thing I remember was following the man back into the building. He went straight behind the counter. I didn't know whether he was going to keep my restricted license and tell me to catch the bus home or tell me to learn how to drive and try for the license another time.

To my surprise, and the surprise of my driving instructor, the man handed me my license. When I looked at it, I didn't see the word "restricted" on it. I had a real driver's license!

The man must have seen the shocked look on my face because he said, "Please don't take that car on the road by yourself for a while. Get someone to drive with you."

I was so proud of myself as I walked out of the building. My driving instructor didn't say a word. I think he was too shocked that they had given me my license. How I wished my family and friends back home could see me. I didn't have any biological family here to share my joy with, but I knew my friends at work would be very happy for me, especially Jan, who had faith I could do it.

I knew what the man from the Motor Vehicle Department had said was right. I should have an experienced driver in the car with me, but I didn't have anyone who could ride with me. That is, no one others could see, but I knew my guardian angel was with me.

I could hardly wait to get home that day. I wanted to show Miss Adela my license and let her see me driving. I called my friend Mona Lee to tell her the good news.

"I'm studying for my license now, too," she said.

That evening I told Donna we were going for a ride.

"Mommy, are we going to still have to bring our groceries home on the bus?"

"No, sweetheart, you and Mommy will go shopping in the car now."

By now I had become so involved with the children at the school I didn't see them as helpless handicapped children anymore. They were beautiful. Some of the boys and girls were so smart. It was amazing to see the things they were able to accomplish. I fell in love with them and enjoyed every moment I spent working with them and some of the families I met.

The dreams of acquiring material things was not as important now that I had developed relationships with so many good, honest people. God knew I was a stranger in a new land. He prepared a special group of people to show me His love for honoring Him by refusing to work on His holy Sabbath day. I know He did this for me as I never again had to explain to an employer why I couldn't work on Saturday because it was the day Jesus wanted me to keep holy.

My dream when I came to America was to work, earn lots of money, and have fun without anyone watching me and telling me how to live my life. But once I got settled, I realized that I had to be accountable to Donna. Furthermore, as I became friends with my wonderful coworkers, I felt accountable to them. Praise God, between my coworkers and Donna, maybe I made only half the mistakes I would have made if I had been free to go anywhere and do anything.

My job became my life. I reveled in the love and affection from the children. Each day I felt driven to help them. I loved my job, and the people I worked with, especially the children.

Now that I could drive things began to change in my personal life. I was so thankful I didn't have to ride the bus to work anymore or carry the groceries home on the bus.

One Sunday I said to Donna, "I'm tired of washing on this washboard. Let's drive to the laundromat. If I can learn to drive a car, I can learn to use a washing machine." I had been so scared to use a washing machine that I had purchased a washboard and was doing laundry the only way I knew how—by hand.

"Let's go, Mama," Donna said. "I will show you how to use the washing machine."

"What do you know about a washing machine?"

"You just put your clothes in with some soap, and it will wash your clothes."

"Donna, hush, and let's go."

I was a little nervous thinking about trying something new. Donna had said she was going to show me, and she meant it. There were so many other things she helped me figure out. When we arrived at the laundromat, some people were there folding clothes. I took my time getting our clothes out of the car, hoping the people would leave. I didn't want them to see me if I messed up. I had only brought one load of colored clothes for this first attempt. I chose a front loader. Donna helped me put the clothes in, and I let her close the door. She wanted to put the money in the machine, but I told her to wait until I put in the soap. I poured in about three cups of soap, and once the soap was in, Donna put in the money. The clothes started to spin.

"See, Mama," Donna smiled. "I told you that was all you had to do."

That was pretty easy, I thought. But a few seconds later, I couldn't see the clothes, only suds. Suds started coming out of the top of the machine. When I turned around, I saw one of Donna's shirts that had fallen on the floor. I picked it up and thought, *If I put the soap in through this little hole, I should be able to put the shirt in through the same hole instead of opening the door to the washer.*

I forced the little shirt through the little soap hole. I heard a funny noise, but I worried the suds would pour out if I opened the door. I prayed no one would come until I could get finished and out of there.

"Mommy, Mommy," Donna cried. "The machine isn't going around anymore."

The machine had stopped. I panicked. I didn't want Donna to know I had broken the machine, so I said, "What in the world happened?"

"I don't know, but it stopped, Mommy. What are we going to do?"

"We are going to take our clothes out and go home." I opened the door of the front loader machine. Water, suds, and clothes came tumbling out on me. Water splashed all over the floor. I pulled my washtub in front of the machine and started wringing the water from my clothes. Donna and I were both standing in water and suds.

Some people started to came in to wash their clothes. When they saw the water on the floor, they left. I got my clothes out of the machine and swore I would never try this again. My washboard was a much safer option.

I was getting better with my driving, but I began to get tickets. I made wrong turns, held up traffic several times, and drove down a one-way street. After receiving three tickets in two months,and attending two defensive driving schools, I realized driving was costing me too much money. Plus, I was earning too many points on my license. Until I started driving a car, I didn't realize how great it was to have my own transportation. The car enabled me to go wherever I wanted. This car was the first thing I owned here in America. In Honduras I only owned a small kerosene stove and that old iron bed I bought for three *lempiras*.

But now that I owned something that I could call my very own it was costing me a lot of money. I had to make a decision about the car.

Chapter 18

To earn a little extra money, I got a part-time job on the school bus. I got the handicapped children on and off the bus, made sure they were buckled in, and watched them carefully for any medical problems that might develop during our ride. The extra money enabled me to send some to my parents.

By now I was feeling confident that everything was going to work out for me in America. The friend who sold me the car visited us often. Other friends learned I was in America and visited, so I didn't feel as homesick. One day one of my friends said, "Why don't you go out sometimes and have a little fun? You might meet a good man and get married."

I had been thinking along that line for a while, but I was scared, and I worried about who would care for Donna if I went out. When I first moved, I didn't know anyone I could trust to take care of her. Now I did have a neighbor whom I had met with a little girl about Donna's age. As we got to know each other, we discovered we were both Seventh-day Adventists. Mrs. Niome invited me to go to church with them. I hadn't been going to church. I was still keeping the Sabbath, but since I didn't have to report to anyone, I had decided to take a break from church. In my heart I felt I was a good person and had gone to church enough in my lifetime. I loved Jesus with all my heart. I prayed every day, and I knew God was blessing me, so I figured I didn't need church.

One Sunday my friends told me about a nightclub they enjoyed going to. The devil was listening, and he saw this as an opportunity to trap me once again in old habits. It was just a week later that Mrs. Niome asked if she could take Donna to church with her and her daughter. I agreed, happy for my little girl to go to church. I wanted her to learn about Jesus. After church that Sabbath, Donna's little friend asked if she could spend the night with her. I had never left her alone with anyone at night since I had been in America. Both girls began asking me at the same time, and that's when the thought hit me—*If she spent the night, I could go to the nightclub*. I agreed, and that Saturday night around eight o'clock, I got all dressed up.

By the time I got into my car, I was a nervous wreck. I had not ventured out at night by myself before. I really wanted to go dancing and see what a nightclub was like in America. I missed dancing and having fun.

When I was a child and was about to do something wrong, my heart would beat faster. That little voice, which I believe is my conscience, never failed to warn me. Most of the time I would ignore it, just like I was doing that night. I had been doing okay avoiding the temptations of the world until my friend urged me to go out and have fun. That's the way the devil works, especially with young people, making them feel as if they are missing out on something.

My mom always told me, "Let your conscience be your guide."

"You don't want me to have any fun, Mama, that's why you say that," I'd respond. I had a conscience, and it was always reminding me what my mama said.

Right then, I was not listening to my conscience. I was getting older, and I wanted to meet a man and get married. That's one of the other reasons I came to the States. The warning signs of cold chills and a fast heartbeat signaled that I was about to make a mistake. But like so many times before, I wasn't about to let that stop me. I was on a mission, my mom would say, to see what kind of trouble I could get myself into this time.

Following the directions my friend gave me, I had no problem finding the place. I pulled into the parking lot, parked my car, and sat there. A few people went in and out. It was very quiet. It was a lot different from our bars back on the island. Those doors were always wide open, and you could hear the jukebox playing before you got inside. I got out of my car, walked up to the door, and pulled it open. I was shocked. It was dark inside. There were only a few people sitting around some tables, and a couple men sitting at the bar. A band was playing. I made my way over to a table and sat down. I felt out of place. I wanted to get up and leave, but the urge to stay was stronger. A girl came to the table and asked what I was drinking. I ordered a Coke. When she brought it back, it looked like an alcohol drink with a straw. She had a glass filled with ice, and half the coke had been poured in.

"That's a dollar," she said.

I only had five dollars with me. I thought a dollar was a lot to pay for a Coke. When I left the island, Cokes were a dime, and we didn't serve it in a fancy glass with ice. Here they made the drink look fancy. The smoke was strong. Everyone was smoking cigarettes. I hated sitting there inhaling the smoke. People smoked in the bars back home, but the bars were built over the ocean, and the doors and windows stayed open. There was always a sea breeze blowing through the buildings.

I decided I'd better not drink too fast. At a dollar a Coke, the five dollars wouldn't go far. There was a man sitting alone at another table. Every time I looked over, he was gazing at me. I was a little nervous, but I had come hoping to attract someone. The man finally came over and asked me to dance. I wanted to, but I didn't know how to dance to the music that was playing. I said no. When I emptied my glass, the man returned to my table and asked if he could buy me a drink. I said. "No, thank you."

"Would you mind if I sat with you?" he asked. "Or are you expecting someone?"

"No, I'm okay sitting alone." I just had the feeling that I shouldn't let this man sit with me. The bar was getting crowded. I didn't feel comfortable at all. I wasn't excited like I thought I was going to be. Maybe it was because I had been away from this lifestyle for so long. I sat there feeling very lonesome while the band played and people danced. A strong urge to leave came over me, but song after song, I kept telling myself, *After this song is finished, then I'll go.*

I was on my third Coke, and I made myself a promise to leave when the glass was empty. The devil had other plans for me. His trap was set, and I was about to walk into it. If only I had listened when I felt that urge to leave, but no, I had to stay and listen to one more song. At that moment a man came straight up to my table and asked, "What are you drinking?"

I should have said, "None of your business, thank you," and left. But he didn't give me a chance to answer. He simply motioned the waiter over. "Give her what she wants," he said.

Instead of refusing, or leaving, I said, "Another Coke, please."

The man walked away. I didn't even look to see which way he went as he disappeared in the crowd. I didn't want another Coke, but I continued to sit there and sip on it. The urge to leave got stronger, but I ignored it. I glanced up and saw the man walking toward my table again.

"Would you like to dance?"

I refused because I didn't know the song.

"Is it okay if I sit with you?"

"I don't care," I said.

He pulled out a chair and sat down. "Why don't you want to dance?"

"The music is too fast for me," I confessed.

"If they play a slow song will you dance with me?"

I smiled, "yes."

"My name is Phillip Brewster."

I can't explain how I felt just then. I thought I would be happy to meet someone, but I wasn't. I just wanted to leave.

Phillip pulled out a cigar and lit it. He smoked as he talked. "I don't go to bars a lot, but maybe the reason I'm here tonight is to meet you."

The band began to play a slow country love song. I used to love to dance to those old heartbreaking country songs back home on the island. It made me a little lonesome sitting there listening to the music. I recalled the fun I used to have with my friends. We'd put our dimes in the jukebox and waltz across the floor. If there weren't enough boys there, the girls would dance together.

"Will you dance with me now?" Phillip asked. The song was half finished before we made it to the dance area. He put his arms around me. I could smell his cigar. I hated the smell, and pulled away from him. I was thankful when the song finished, and we walked back to the table.

"I have to leave now," I told him.

He talked me into staying longer. I sat and listened to him for a while. He told me a few things about himself, the kind of work he did, and that he was divorced with three children, two boys and one girl. He was ten years older than I was. Several times he asked for my telephone number.

"I have a little girl," I told him. "And I really do have to leave and get home to her."

"Will you give me your phone number before you go?"

I hesitated, but then I gave him the number. He seemed like a gentleman, and in no way did he show me any disrespect.

"Can I walk you to your car?"

We left the bar together. I said goodbye when we reached my car, and he left. I don't know why I wasn't even a little excited. I felt more sad than happy.

When I went to work Monday morning, I told my friends I had gone dancing. Everyone wanted to know if I had met anyone. I told them about Phillip, but I wasn't excited like most girls when they meet a guy.

"Was he good looking?"

"Did you give him your phone number?"

"Did he say he'd call you?"

I thought about the questions. Phillip wasn't bad looking. He was tall and thin at six feet four inches, with dirty blond hair and blue eyes. He worked as a drywall finisher. I didn't know what a drywall finisher was until Jan told me.

A week went by, and Phillip didn't call. I thought about him a couple times and wondered what he looked like in the daytime. It didn't bother me that he didn't call. Still, it was embarrassing since I'd told my friends he was going to call.

It was at the end of the second week that he called. I pretended I didn't remember who he was.

"I bought you a Coke, and we slow danced, but you had to leave shortly after. I was hoping I'd see you at the club again," he said.

"I probably won't go back there," I told him. We talked for about an hour, and by the time we hung up, he had talked me into letting him come by on Saturday night to see me. I wasn't sure I wanted him to come. I was feeling lonesome, but I didn't feel one stir of emotion for him. I decided it wasn't going to hurt anything to see him one more time.

Secretly I missed my sister telling me, "You shouldn't let a strange man come to your house!"

Phillip came bearing roses and a box of chocolates. It was the first time a man had given me flowers. He looked older than I remembered, but I had always been attracted to older men.

I didn't invite him inside, but I sat on the front porch with him. I didn't want him to get the impression that because I was living alone I allowed strangers in my house. He started to light a cigar, and I asked him not to do so on my porch. I was afraid I had insulted him, because he didn't stay much longer.

"Can I call and come back to see you again?" he asked as he was leaving.

I didn't think he would come again because of the cigar, but I was wrong. He called the very next night.

"Would you like to go to the movies next Saturday?"

I had only gone to a movie once since I'd been in America, so I was happy to go. Phillip started coming over frequently, taking my daughter and me places and showing us around. I couldn't decide if I wanted Phillip to be my boyfriend or not, but he was determined to prove he had fallen in love with me. He was a gentleman, but I hated his cigars, although Phillip didn't smoke around me.

Phillip came to my job, and my friends met him. No one had anything negative to say about him. I decided to give him a chance. I had never dated a man for a long period of time, but Phillip was serious. He continued doing everything possible to assure me he was for real.

I had to admit I liked Phil more and more the longer we were together. I began to feel pulled between work and school and spending time with him. He did not have an education, so I received no encouragement from him to continue pursuing my high school diploma—I had made it to the ninth grade and was determined to graduate. Fortunately, my friends at work kept telling me how proud they were of me for going to night school. It was their encouragement that gave me the incentive to go on.

I wrote to my family about Phil. He was driving me back and forth to school now. I tried in vain to convince him to attend school with me and get his diploma. He wasn't pleased that I was going there four nights a week. Phil was very possessive of me, and I mistook that for love. After we had dated a while, he brought his children, two boys and a little girl, to meet me.

After dating for nine months, Phil asked me to marry him, and I said yes. Deep down in my heart, I didn't feel as happy as I should have about marrying him. Subconsciously, I was worried about getting older, and not being married, so I plowed ahead in spite of the red flags that should have halted me in my tracks—Phil's possessiveness, his divorce, and his three children.

In addition to the big news about the wedding, I also had other important news to share with my family. I was an American citizen. Donna and I attended the citizenship ceremony with a crowd of other people who were being sworn in as citizens. Tears streamed down my face, as they did on the face of many of those waiting there. I placed my hand on my heart and repeated the Pledge of Allegiance with joy in my heart. I said the words loud and clear as I had practiced. I felt a moment of betrayal to my country of Honduras, but I had no regrets for my decision. I walked out of that building that day praising God for the opportunity to become an American citizen. When I returned to work that day, everyone hugged and congratulated me. When I wrote to my family, I promised to show them my passport as proof when I came to visit. I could now travel anywhere just like other Americans did.

I'd had so many dreams when I came to the States, and marriage was one of them. I told Phil about my dreams, and the things I wanted, and in turn he told me all the things I wanted to hear. He promised we would fulfill those dreams together. I knew my dreams could become a reality. I was accomplishing so many things on my own by having faith and believing my prayers would be answered. I saw no reason why I couldn't fulfill my dreams with Phil. He said he wanted the same things I did.

I completed the tenth grade, and then decided to quit for a while to prepare for my wedding. It was 1971, and I promised myself I would return to school after I was married. No matter how small a wedding is it takes a lot of work to put it together. My friends at work decided they were going to give me "a real wedding." I didn't have any family in the area, and all of Phil's family lived in Ohio. I had planned for us to be married by a justice of the peace, and then invite a few friends to celebrate with us, but my friends wouldn't hear of it. My loyal friends from work decided they would each pay for part of the wedding expenses—my cake, dress, shoes, photographer, and invitations. Phil and I had a beautiful outdoor wedding with about thirty people at the home of my friend Patricia.

Phil and I rented a house, and I began my new life as a married woman. I soon realized that living with someone is totally different from dating him. I began to get to know Phil, and he began to get to know me. It was difficult for me to adjust to being married. I was surprised to find I didn't like married life as much as I thought I would. I lost much of my freedom. I couldn't make decisions on my own anymore. That was hard for me since I had been making my own decisions practically all my life.

I quickly discovered that Phil was a very jealous man. I was blinded to this before, believing his jealousy to be concern for my welfare. I tried to convince him there was no reason to be jealous, but he would respond, "I'm afraid of losing you to a younger man."

I figured maybe a new setting would be good for our blossoming marriage, so I suggested that we visit Honduras so he could meet my family. Phil was excited about the trip. He had never been out of the country, and once we arrived he was fascinated seeing the way I used to live. Then, less than a week and a half into the visit, Phil threw a jealous tantrum in front of my family. This was his first and biggest mistake. He was jealous of them. He accused me of not giving him enough attention. I was scheduled to stay for a few more days, and I was angry and ashamed at his behavior.

"I'm not going to play your games," I told him. "You can pack up and leave. I wanted you to meet my family, and you're acting like a fool. That's the first and last time you'll ever come with me to visit my family."

In the midst of the ups and downs of our early days of marriage, I soon discovered I was pregnant. I was very sick, and the doctor didn't know what was causing me to be so ill. By the time I was three months pregnant, my feet and hands were swollen. I had cramps in my stomach and was hemorrhaging. I went to work every day, but I was so sick I could scarcely do my job. My coworkers watched out for me, and I was able to continue working. The doctor never advised bed rest, and he continued to be puzzled why I was in constant pain and bleeding so much.

When I was four and a half months pregnant, I was in so much pain that my friends at work urged me to go to the hospital. I hesitated as the day before the doctor had told me "everything looked normal." I tried calling Phil's workplace to see if he would come and take me back to the doctor. I couldn't reach him, and my friends were growing more and more concerned about my condition.

"If you don't want to go to the hospital," my friend Dorothy said, "then you need to be home."

One of my friends drove me home in my car, and another followed. Phil called while I was on my way, and they told him what was happening. He got home as my friends were getting ready to leave. When Phil saw the pain I was in, he picked me up and rushed me to the hospital.

Poor little Donna was frightened, but I was in so much pain I couldn't comfort her. Phil was able to have me admitted to the hospital right away. He left Donna in the hospital lobby and followed me to the room. I was worried about my baby being left alone in the waiting room. Phil didn't want to leave me, but I begged him to take my daughter home and put her to bed. It was the first time Donna had been alone with Phil.

My doctor was out of town, so the hospital arranged for another doctor to see me. I was crying as the pain was so bad, but no one seemed to care. "Blood is pouring out of me!" I cried to the nurse. I was passing big clots of blood. She put on a pair of gloves and checked to see if it was the fetus.

"It's just blood," she said. She removed the soiled pads, and placed clean ones under me.

"When is the doctor coming?"

"He'll be in to see you soon," the nurse said. She closed the door behind her as she left. I was more afraid there in that hospital than I had been on the island with my sister helping me deliver Donna. I thought I was going to die that night. I prayed that God would not let me die alone in a hospital room.

I pressed the call button repeatedly and waited for someone to come, but no one came. Suddenly, I felt as if I was going to take my last breath. I tried to raise my back to push myself higher on the pillow, and as I did, felt the baby come out. I remember trying to scream, but I don't know if any sound came out. I remember seeing the baby, and the last thing I remember is placing it in the bedpan. I don't remember anything else after that.

The next thing I remember was people all around me asking me why I didn't push the call button. Someone said, "The baby is dead. It's a little boy."

I don't know what else happened that night. I was devastated. I don't know what I said or did, and I was hardly aware of them as they cleaned me up and left me alone again. The next morning I asked about my baby.

"The baby was dead," the nurse said. "Would you like the hospital to take care of it?"

"Yes," I murmured, not knowing what else to do.

Phil came the next morning after taking Donna to school.

"I asked them about the baby," he said. "They said you told them to dispose of it."

I was shocked. I couldn't believe people in a hospital would refer to a baby that way. A nurse came in that morning and said a doctor would be in to perform a D and C. I was sad about losing my baby and shocked at the way I had been treated.

I tried to take comfort in the words of Solomon, "There is a time and a purpose for everything under the sun. There is a time to be born, and a time to die." I felt the people in the hospital had treated me poorly, but another scripture comforted me and reminded me that God knows what is best for us, and everything happens for good to those who love the Lord.

My mom and dad had instilled in me the knowledge that God loves me regardless of how I feel about myself or how many mistakes I've made. I knew that Jesus would never leave or forsake me. I cried to Him that night in the hospital. He heard my cries and delivered me. I will never understand why the baby died, but I have to trust that God knew what was best.

Chapter 19

In 1974 I brought my sister Nelly to America to visit me on a three-month visa. Her dream of coming to America was finally coming true. What a blessing it was to have my sister with me. Nelly was a very reserved person, very different from me. She had grown into a very responsible, godly young woman. She reminded me so much of my mother with her daily worship and praising God for everything. When the visa expired, immigration refused to extend Nelly's time, and she had to return home. It was a sad day when she had to leave. I promised her I would do whatever it took to bring her back. Out of my seven sisters, Nelly was the only one, at that time, who had the courage or desire to come to America.

I was finally able to arrange for a two-year school visa for Nelly to attend a local community college. I didn't know how I was going to be able to afford to pay for her schooling, but I knew somehow God would find a way. School was the only way she could stay in America. I registered Nelly at Hillsborough Community College without knowing how we would pay for it, and then we both prayed. I'm so glad God understood me and my hasty decisions that I would then pray about after the fact. Nelly spent quiet time with the Lord each day. I would see her on her knees and hear her singing the same beautiful hymns our mother used to sing when I was a little girl. I was too busy, and wasn't interested in spending my spare time worshiping.

"You are not setting a good example for your daughter," Nelly told me. "You should be taking her to church and teaching her about God."

Nelly started taking Donna into her bedroom and reading Bible stories to her. Nelly thought I was a heathen because I wasn't going to church. Every once in a while when I woke up on time on Sunday morning, I would get Donna ready and let her ride the bus that came through our neighborhood picking children up and taking them to Sunday School.

When Nelly found out what I was doing, she gave me a piece of her mind. "I don't want you to think I'm telling you how to raise your daughter, but I'm surprised you can put Donna on a bus with strangers and send her to a church where you don't know what they are teaching her." I did feel guilty after Nelly put it that way. I knew my neighbors were Sabbathkeepers, like I was supposed to be. I hadn't wanted them to know, however, as I didn't want them to start inviting me to church. Nelly wanted me to take her to church. That's when I decided to ask my neighbors if they would mind taking Nelly and Donna to church with them on Sabbath morning. They were more than happy to, and they invited me to come along. "Maybe one day," I told them.

I had borrowed money from the credit union and made a down payment on a house. It needed a lot of work, but Phil knew how to do repairs. Saturdays and Sundays were the only two days we had time to work on the house. Phil was so jealous he didn't want me to go anywhere without him. It had gotten so bad that he followed me to work every morning. I had to be to work at five thirty to ride the school bus to pick up the children. Phil swore I was meeting another man before I got to the school bus. At first, it didn't bother me as I thought he really loved me—I didn't realize jealousy was a disease that Phil harbored in his heart.

Phil became harder to live with every day; he constantly accused me of being unfaithful. To make matters worse, he was antisocial. None of my friends were welcome in our home.

"I'm your husband," Phil informed me. "If you need someone to talk to, you can talk to me."

He was so possessive that he made Donna tell him everything she and I did together. She tried her best to keep him happy. I was embarrassed that Nelly was seeing the life I was living with Phil, but I couldn't hide it. I became so tired of him constantly accusing me that I began to resent him.

I knew husbands and wives could have problems, but I had never heard or seen anyone like Phil. He tried to suppress his jealousy at times, but he had no control when it exploded. The Bible said jealousy originated in heaven, and it was so evil and vicious that one third of the angels were affected by it. Phil became so consumed with jealousy that he began hiding my underwear, my toothbrush, and even the soap so I couldn't take a bath.

I asked Phil to see a counselor, but he swore there was nothing wrong with him. I had no complaint about Phil working and doing jobs around the house. There were days when one would never know there was a flaw in our marriage. But all too often jealousy raised its ugly head and our home became a living nightmare.

My sister's two years in America were going to expire soon. We received a letter informing her she would have to leave on a certain date. I wanted and needed Nelly to stay. Phil and I had joked many times that Nelly needed to find a boyfriend and get married so she could continue living in America. Phil offered to introduce her to a couple of fellows he worked with, but Nelly wasn't interested. Without Nelly knowing, I asked Phil if he thought any of the fellows he worked with were decent enough. I suggested he set up a blind date. I knew Nelly would never go along with the idea if she knew what we were planning. Between us, we invited a guy over to go to the wrestling matches with us. Nelly didn't pay any attention to him. When Phil came home from work the next day, he told me Eddy was interested in getting to know Nelly. I told Nelly what he said.

Nelly said, "Esther, I don't know. I will never get involved with any man who is not a Christian."

I didn't want Nelly to have to return to Honduras.

"Please give Eddy a try."

Nelly said, "I would rather be shipped back home without any hope of ever returning to America, Esther, than to stay here and go through what you are going through with Phil."

But, nevertheless, she agreed to go on one date. Years later, I asked Nelly what she said to Eddy on her first date. She said, "Esther, I told him I would never marry a man who wasn't willing to allow God to be a part of his life." She was open and honest with him, and Eddy decided Nelly was worth it. He began studying the Bible, and within two years Eddy was baptized and he and Nelly were married. Now, twenty-eight years later, Nelly and Eddy are still married. When I look at them, it reminds me that God is in the business of transforming lives.

Nelly and I had grown very close to one another. When she decided to marry Eddy, I was happy for her, but sad for me as Donna and I wouldn't see her as often.

After Nelly moved out, Phil and I decided we would put our house up for sale and buy a nicer home. I was concerned about doing this, but I wanted a nicer home, and I thought that once we had a nicer home Phil would realize I loved him and would stop being so jealous. Deep inside, I knew I was fooling myself again, but we moved forward anyways. Of course, things didn't get better; in fact, they grew worse. We had been in the new house for only eight months when I knew I couldn't live with Phil any longer. His jealousy was escalating to the point that he was taking parts off my car so I couldn't use it.

I had started going to church and was feeling good about that, but that was another source of controversy. Phil did not like the idea of me going. He accused me of only going to church to see the men. He still had Donna reporting to him my every move. One day I heard her tell him a man was looking at me; another time she told him a man honked his horn at me as we walked along the street.

Phil wanted to rule my every move. He complained I was doing too much for Donna and not giving him enough attention. One day when I arrived home after taking Donna to swimming lessons, I found the house completely locked down. He had sticks in the windows so they could not be opened, and he had pushed the couch against the door. It was his way of punishing me for taking my daughter to the pool. I called the police to report that my husband wouldn't let me back into my house. "That's a domestic problem," the officer said. "There is nothing we can do about it."

One Sabbath I tried to start my car to go to church and discovered he had taken the distributor cap out. That was my breaking point. I decided I would not take any more abuse from him. I was devastated. I didn't want to get a divorce. I worried about what people would think of me. I felt like a failure, but I couldn't take his controlling ways any longer.

The Bible tells of people clothed in sheepskin who are really wolves underneath. Marriage can sometimes bring out the worse in a couple. Love can turn to hate. I had lost all respect for Phil, and I wanted out of the marriage. I was ashamed to tell my friends at work of my problems with Phil. They were like family to me and had put so much into the wedding. Now I had to tell them my marriage was over after only six years—for me it had been six years of misery.

I knew asking Phil for a divorce wasn't going to be pleasant. Sometimes I thought Phil didn't realize what he was doing. There were times when we got into fights, and we would both say ugly things to one another. Then, ten minutes later, Phil would not remember anything about it—or he pretended he didn't. He would accuse me of doing something that wasn't true, then minutes later he would put his arms around me and tell me how much he loved me.

"Get away from me," I'd say. "You are lying. If you loved me, you wouldn't treat me this way."

Phil would act surprised and say, "What way? What way am I treating you?"

When I reminded him of what happened, he would say, "You're lying. I would never say anything like that to you!"

Sometimes, as ashamed as I was, I was thankful Nelly had seen what had happened when she lived with us before she was married. Nelly knew what I was going through, and she confirmed that I wasn't crazy. She saw firsthand how Phil acted and what he said.

"Esther, I feel sorry for you," Nelly often told me. "How can you tolerate living with him?"

Phil was so unpredictable, I was afraid to tell him I wanted a divorce. A few times when he accused me of wrongdoing, I would say, "One of these days, I am going to leave you, Phil."

"You will never do that to me," Phil would always respond.

I was worried what he would try to do if I left. I would have to leave the house, because I knew he would never leave it. I needed money to leave, and I had no extra money after the bills were paid. I felt trapped.

During my lunch hour, I looked for a place to live near the school where I worked. It was the only time I could go anywhere alone without having to account for my time. I found an apartment about a mile from work and was able to borrow enough money from the bank to pay the first and last month's rent. The situation was getting more desperate every day. I knew the Bible didn't approve of divorce, but I also believed that God didn't want me to live in such an abusive situation.

Phil worked for different construction companies as a drywall finisher. He had never been asked to go out of town on a job. But the day after I secured the apartment, Phil came home and told me his boss had asked him to go to Sarasota, Florida. The boss needed him to help on a job that had to be finished in three days. The company would pay for his motel and other expenses.

As I listened, I knew beyond a doubt that God had heard and answered my prayers. I had paid the rent on the apartment without knowing how I was going to approach Phil to tell him I was leaving and wanted to take my belongings. This was my opportunity. This was the answer to my prayers. I had already talked with someone about moving me, so I called them and made arrangements for the next day.

Phil didn't want to leave me alone for three nights, so he decided to stay the night and leave at three o'clock in the morning. I had planned to stay up and pack so I would be ready for the movers, but I modified my plans. The moment Phil left at three o'clock in the morning, I got out of bed and began packing. I called work to let them know I wouldn't be coming in. I was able to get most of my things packed. Nelly and Eddy came over with the movers. We took two truckloads over to the apartment. I left my living room and bedroom furniture for the following day. It was only a half hour after I returned to the house when I heard the key turn in the front door. Phil walked in. I wasn't surprised to see him; I was just thankful I had made it back home before he got there. I still don't know if he suspected I was going to do something while he was gone or if it was his jealousy that brought him back home that night. He seemed satisfied to find me home and in my nightgown. Everything was still in its place in the living room, bedroom, and bathroom. He went to the kitchen and opened the cabinet where his coffee cup was kept. I had left glasses and cups for him, so he didn't notice anything was missing. He finished his coffee and went straight to the bathroom to get ready for bed.

"Why did you come home tonight if you have to leave at three in the morning again?" I asked.

"I missed you and didn't want you to be alone."

When Phil left at three, I got up and began packing again. By six o'clock that evening, I had everything out of the house that I was taking. It was such a relief. I went back to the house that evening to be sure everything was clean and to leave a note letting Phil know I was sorry our marriage had to end this way. When I stood in the doorway and saw the empty living room with just a couch and a chair, I began to cry. My marriage was over, and my life felt as empty as the living room looked. As I went through the house making sure everything was clean, I thought about the six years of my life I had spent with Phil. I thought how precious life is, and how we take it for granted. I didn't know how this was going to affect Donna and my life. This was not the example I wanted for her. I felt so helpless. I had wanted my marriage to work, but I couldn't make it happen. It takes two to make a marriage. I hadn't waited for the right partner God had intended for me, and I was suffering the consequences of my choices.

I left a note on the counter, *"Phil, our life together is over. This is my choice. I don't expect anything from you. I'm sorry it has to end this way. Esther."* I walked out of the house and closed that chapter of my life.

Phil showed up at my job early the next morning. He made all kinds of promises, begging for another chance. It was sad to see him this way. I had told him many times that some day if he continued to treat me the way he did I would leave and not come back. He pleaded with me to tell him where I was living. I knew it would take him a while to discover where I lived because I was still riding the school bus, and he didn't know where I parked my car. I hoped he wouldn't learn where I was. When I had closed the house door behind me, I knew I wasn't ever going back. That evening I prayed I would be able to erase the six years of pain from my heart so there would be no memory of it. It was years later before I discovered that Phil had not only hurt me, but he had also hurt my daughter. Donna will carry the scar he left with her for the rest of her life.

I decided I was going to pick up the pieces of my life and put the past behind me. The road I had traveled those six years was one of those roads my dad had warned me about. I felt a little disoriented, but I hadn't allowed Phil to control my emotions or my self-esteem. I was fortunate to have the support of friends and my beautiful sister, Nelly, who stuck by me and gave me encouragement. Most of all, I learned to lean on Jesus. I asked Him daily to place His loving arms around me and to continue to lead me on a path closer to Him.

It was hard to start all over again. I lost all I had worked for and was in debt to my bank. I knew I couldn't sit around feeling sorry for myself. I had gotten myself into this mess, now I needed to figure a way out. A night job? Yes, that would be the answer. It would enable me to pay off the bank. I was so fortunate to have my sister with me. She worried about me as I was still making hasty decisions and wanting everything done yesterday.

I applied for a position at a nursing home, and was hired right away. Those days you didn't need a diploma to take someone to the bathroom, change a diaper, or put food in someone's mouth. Nelly was willing to keep Donna at night for me, so I was able to start work right away.

Chapter 20

Toward the end of my marriage with Phil, I had started attending church. I realized how I had deprived Donna by not teaching her about the most important person in life—Jesus—the way my mom had taught me. She made Him real to us, and we all fell in love with Him as little children. I have never fallen out of love with Him. I had just strayed away.

Without a doubt, the most important gift a parent can give to their children is to instill in them the love of God. He loves us so much that He sent His only Son to die for us. As I considered the number of years of spiritual teaching I had failed to provide for my daughter, I decided it would be best to send her to a Seventh-day Adventist school. I knew that if she attended church school she would receive a good spiritual foundation.

At church I met Dr. Abbott and his wife. Their children attended the local Adventist school, and they offered to take Donna back and forth for me. The extra job helped me pay for Donna's schooling.

Because I was holding down three jobs, I seldom saw my daughter. I left home at five-thirty every morning and rode the school bus to pick up the children for school. Then I worked all day in the classroom before riding the bus again to take the children back home. At four o'clock I would jump off the bus and run into a McDonald's rest room to change into my uniform and hurry to the nursing home to clock in. I was tired all the time, but I enjoyed every moment I spent working with the elderly people. All my life I had been comfortable around older people. I leaned on Jesus more and more to get me through each day. All the jobs were rewarding. I felt I was doing something worthwhile. I was able to take my Bible and songbook to the nursing home. After my rounds in the evening, I would go from room to room and read and sing to some of those precious old people who never had anyone visit them.

Three weeks after I left Phil, he discovered where I was living. One evening he knocked on the door. Nelly opened it and found Phil standing there.

"Did Esther leave me for another man?" he asked.

Nelly assured him that I didn't. Phil began stalking my apartment. Every night when I returned home from work, his car would be parked in back of my apartment. I guess he was checking to be sure I didn't bring a man home. I was concerned at first, and I thought about calling the police, but Phil never got out of his car to bother me. I felt sorry for Phil, but not sorry enough to take him back. Phil sat in his car outside my apartment in the evening for a couple weeks and then stopped. He never bothered me again.

The job at the nursing home helped me pay off some bills, and after nine months, I was able to stop working the night job. Donna and I were doing okay. She was a happier little girl and could now bring friends home to play. She wasn't scared or embarrassed that her friends would see or hear her mom and stepfather arguing or fighting.

I decided to return to school for my diploma. I was determined not to quit until I had it. It was a lot harder for me to attend school this second time around. There were so many things on my mind, and I felt as if I had flushed six years of my life down the drain. Now I needed to piece it back together. Going to school and earning a diploma was one of the things I had promised myself I would do if I ever got to America. Donna was getting older, and I wanted to set a good example for her.

I was single again and free to do as I pleased. I knew I had to be strong and not get out of control. I was thankful I had started going back to church. Instead of going dancing, I went to church socials, prayer meetings, and church outings. My whole outlook on life changed when I decided I wanted to follow Jesus all the way. It was the best decision I had ever made.

I began to get to know my church family, so when I found out that a mother of three had been killed in a car accident, I pitched in with the rest of the church to support the family. Her death left a nine-year-old girl, Stella, two younger boys, and their father alone. The children attended the same Seventh-day Adventist school as Donna, and Donna and Stella were friends. Mrs. Abbott, the lady who drove Donna to school, also drove these three children.

A couple weeks after the funeral, the pastor encouraged the congregation to continuing lending a hand to the family. After church I told the children's father, "If there is anything I can do to help, please let me know."

Right away, Stella asked, "Can I come home with Donna?"

Stella often came to visit; the boys only came a few times. Stella took on a lot of responsibility after she lost her mother as she tried to be a mother to her two brothers. As I got to know her, I realized Stella was a very intelligent girl.

One day Stella told me that her dad was not her real dad. She and her oldest brother were stepchildren, and just her youngest brother belonged to her stepfather. She wasn't happy at home and preferred to stay at our home. I often kept all three children overnight. The children seemed to enjoy being with Donna and me.

Randy was the oldest boy, and Steven the youngest. Their father, Matt, had a girlfriend by then, and he spent a lot of time with her. Matt didn't have a steady job and was gone a lot. I kept the children so they would not be left alone. The children became more and more attached to me.

Matt found a night job and began attending some kind of mechanic school through a government program. He only made a small salary, but he offered to pay me to keep the children at night since he worked until eleven-thirty, five nights a week. Matt and his girlfriend, Claire, were having trouble, mostly because of the children. Claire was younger than Matt and had a hard time dealing with the children. Randy was a difficult child, and Matt had no idea how to care for him. Stella missed her mother. Matt wanted the children to accept Claire, but Stella refused. The boys didn't care one way or the other; they just wanted someone to take care of them. Claire wasn't ready to take on the responsibility of a ready-made family, and she finally moved to Massachusetts.

During this entire time, Matt continued coming to church. I admired him for bringing the children to church every Sabbath. He even preached sometimes when the pastor was away. Meanwhile, I was praying for God to send me a godly man. During the two years since I had left Phil, I had made a promise not to marry unless the man was a Christian and shared my same faith. I thought if a man loved God, he would treat me the way my dad treated my mom—with love and respect.

Matt came every night after work to pick up the children. He didn't arrive until twelve o'clock, which meant waking the children for the ride home. They hated it and fussed every night. Finally, Matt asked if the children could stay overnight, and he would come early in the morning to take them to school. I was relieved, as I worried about waking the children each night. Matt continued to stop each night after work, even though the children were spending the night. I began to look forward to Matt coming even though it was so late and he could only stay for about thirty minutes.

I told God I was getting old and wanted to get married again before I was too old. I was used to telling God what I wanted and then working hard to make it happen. Then I convinced myself that God had answered my prayer. I also told God I would never go searching for a man—I asked Him to send one to my door as I sign that I should marry again.

During this time I continued working on my education, and with God's help I earned my high school diploma. My graduation date finally arrived. I was so proud as I walked across that stage to receive my diploma. I can't explain the joy I felt knowing I had accomplished one of my dreams. How I wished my entire family could have been there to see me. Many of my friends came to celebrate the happy event with me.

Matt and I began spending more time together, and the children seemed to be happy that we were doing things together, especially Stella. I began dreaming what it would be like to be married to a man who loved Jesus.

"God," I said, "I will be the best wife, just like my mom was to my dad."

Matt and I grew closer, and I wanted to believe it was God's doing. My prayer had been that God would send the man He wanted me to love to my door. Was Matt the answer to my prayer? Once again, I should have seen the red flags. Matt was still in love with Claire and having a hard time accepting that she had moved away. He traveled to Massachusetts many times to see her, but because of the children, things couldn't work out for them. Matt needed someone to help him care for the children. He showed me just enough affection and said just the right words to make me feel that I was that person. Matt was having a hard time dealing with Randy. There were problems at school and at home. He was ten and still having a difficult time dealing with his mother's death. Randy's problems were deeper than Matt could handle alone. I had never dealt with a child like Randy, and could only think he was acting this way because he needed a mother to care for him. More and more, I felt that these children needed me.

One day Mrs. Abbott called and asked me to come to her home. When I arrived, she began telling me how she had tried to help Matt with the children after they lost their mother. The Abbott family was kind and beautiful. I had come to know them well, and I knew they wanted what was best for Matt's children.

"Esther, this is really not my business, but I know you and Matt are courting. I know you care for the children," Mrs. Abbott said. "I believe you would be a good mother to the children, and they really need you, but," she hesitated, "I have been trying to find the right words, and I still don't know how to say this. As a friend to both you and Matt, I don't think you should continue the relationship."

I was shocked when Mrs. Abbot began talking, but I was speechless for a few moments when she stopped. I took a deep breath and released it, trying to make sense of what this dear friend had just said.

"Why do you feel this way? Do you think I'm not good enough for him?"

"Oh, no," she said. "I would never think that about you. On the contrary, I know you are a hard-working woman, and I believe you have big dreams for your future. I don't think you realize the big responsibility you would be taking on."

I didn't understand what she was trying to tell me. All I could think at that moment was, *Lady, you have no right to tell me what to do with my life.* I had come to her house expecting her to congratulate me and give me encouragement; instead she was warning me not to continue my relationship with Matt. I left Mrs. Abbott's home that day tormented with different thoughts. *Mrs. Abbott doesn't like me. She thinks I am not good enough for Matt and his children. But maybe since she is such a godly woman, God is using her to tell me this.*

I couldn't wait to get home to call my sister.

"Nelly," I said, "you won't guess where I just came from."

"Where?"

"Mrs. Abbot's house."

"What were you doing way over there?"

"She invited me to come so she could tell me what to do with my life. Nelly, I didn't even know she had a basement in her house. That's where she took me to talk to me."

"What was so important she couldn't tell you over the phone?" Nelly asked.

"She said I should stop my relationship with Matt because she doesn't think I know what I am getting into."

There was silence on the end of the line.

"Nelly? Are you still there?"

"I'm here, and I heard what you said. Esther, I know you are upset with Mrs. Abbott for trying to give you good advice."

"What do you mean 'good advice'?"

"Esther, what Mrs. Abbott said to you today is what I have been wanting to tell you from the day you first told me about you and Matt."

I was angry, and I gave Nelly a piece of my mind. Nelly listened to me until I was through talking, then she said, "I'm sorry, Esther. You know I love you and want to see you happy, but I saw what you went through with Phil. You are still not over that tragedy. You need healing before you get into another relationship."

"I don't know what you are talking about. There is nothing wrong with me. I don't need you or Mrs. Abbott to tell me what to do with my life."

When Matt came to see me that night, I told him everything Mrs. Abbott had said. Matt listened while I told him how I felt about her trying to interfere with us.

He didn't say much at first. Then he murmured, "She's good about telling people what to do."

God was sending me warning messages because I was about to make another mistake. But I was hardheaded and so caught up in pleasing myself that I did not stop and think. I was too stubborn to listen to those who cared about me.

One Wednesday evening when Matt stopped by my apartment, he acted nervous.

"What's wrong?"

He hesitated, and then said. "Oh, someone set up a blind date for me. I got a call from this lady last night. Someone told her about me, and she's coming all the way from up north to meet me this weekend."

I couldn't believe what he said. I managed to ask, "And you want to meet her?"

"Well, she is coming from so far away, I thought I would."

The whole time he was talking, I was thinking, *What about us? You met me already.* I didn't say it out loud as I didn't want him to know I was jealous. I was hurt and angry. I don't know why I didn't explode and let him know how I felt, but I kept quiet.

Matt acted as if he didn't see anything wrong in seeing this other woman. All this time I had thought Matt was a God-fearing man, a man I could trust.

"She's flying in on Thursday evening," Matt explained. "I told her she could stay at my house while she's here."

I've heard it all! I thought. "You mean she is going to stay at your house? You and her alone?"

"Esther, she doesn't have money to go to a motel. I offered to let her stay at the house. I don't see any harm in it. She will be in one bedroom, and I will be in the other one."

All I could think was *I hope no one I know ever finds out about this. They will think I am a fool to accept this kind of behavior from a man I am seeing every night.* But what he said next made it even worse.

"Do you think the children could stay here with you and Donna for the next couple days? That way I can spend some time with this woman without being disturbed by the children."

Even now, I can't believe I agreed to let him take advantage of me like this. The woman came, just as Matt said she would. Matt picked up the children for school Thursday and Friday morning and dropped them back off after school. I was so upset and embarrassed..

I took the children to church Saturday morning only to discover that Matt was already there with this other woman, sitting near the front of the church. I sat in back with the children. They did not even notice their father during the church service. I tried to get the children out just as the pastor said "Amen." On my way out, members of the church asked me what was going on between Matt and me. Everyone wondered when he walked in with another woman.

"Ask him" was all I said. The children and I left the church without speaking to Matt. Monday morning he came to pick up the children before taking the woman to the airport. She was in the car, so the children got to meet her.

I did not see Matt until Monday night when he knocked on my door. I opened it, amazed at myself for being happy to see him. Matt was treating me like a fool, and I was allowing him to do it. He pretended nothing was wrong. I had all kinds of questions to ask him, but he swore nothing happened between him and the woman.

"That's hard for me to believe," I said.

Matt didn't seem to care whether I believed him or not. He intended to please himself. I was determined to make him tell me how he felt about the woman.

"I felt obliged to give this woman a chance," Matt said.

"What about you and me? What about our relationship?"

"Esther, I love you. I know I will not find anyone to help me with the children like you do."

I wanted to tell Matt to get out of my house and never come back. But like the fool I was, I could only think of the children needing me.

Matt said, "The woman tried to attract me with her eyes. Every time she looked at me, she would flirt and roll her eyes. It bothered me the whole weekend. It really turned me off."

Our relationship continued as if the episode with the woman had never happened. Shortly after that, Matt asked me to marry him. That was what I had been praying for when our relationship began, but now I wasn't sure. Matt had disappointed me many times by staying in contact with Claire. He had a close relationship with her family and didn't want to break away from them. He had a new job with a car dealership and would stop and visit with Claire's family every day as he passed their home on his way to work. He didn't seem to think his children needed him at home.

In hindsight, Matt really didn't have any room in his heart for me, but he knew I was capable of taking care of him and the children, and he needed my help. I don't think Matt was capable of distinguishing the difference between needing me and loving me. I realize now that I was trying to fill his need in hopes he would love me. I think I knew he didn't love me like I wanted him to, but I convinced myself that once we were married it would solve any differences between us. I was sure it would work out if we both committed our lives to God and to each other with our marriage vows. We would love and respect one another.

Many times my friends cautioned me, saying, "Do you realize what you are getting yourself into?" I didn't want to hear it. All I could think of was three children needing a mother to help guide and teach them.

Matt and I talked to a pastor about marrying us. We set the date, and good friends of ours offered to let us get married in their home. Two weeks after the date for our marriage was set, Matt's ex-girlfriend Claire came to visit her family. Matt spent many evenings visiting the family while she was there. I told Matt it was wrong and that I didn't think it was very fair to me. He ignored me and did what he wanted to do.

One evening Matt came to pick up the kids. I was upstairs in my bedroom. I had parked my car in back of the apartment, so he didn't know I was home. The phone rang. We both picked up the phone at the same moment—Matt downstairs and me upstairs in the bedroom. He grabbed it the moment it rang; it was clear he was expecting the call and didn't want Donna or the other kids to pick up the phone. The moment I put the phone to my ear I recognized Claire's voice. I couldn't believe he would have Claire call my home. I didn't say anything; I just listened to the conversation.

"I need your help," she said.

"I'm here for you," Matt responded. "What can I do?"

"You know I am planning to leave tomorrow, but my car broke down. I need you to look at it for me. I don't have the money to take it to a garage."

Matt is a mechanic, so he quickly assured her. "I'll get that car going for you. Remember, I'm here for you."

"What about Esther? She will get mad if she knows you are fixing my car."

"Don't worry about Esther. You need your car fixed. I'll leave the children here with her when she gets home, and I'll come over."

"Matt, I don't want to cause any problems between you and Esther. I know you are planning to be married. She cares a lot about the children, and I know they need a mother."

"I would like you to be their mother," Matt said. "I can take care of our marriage plans if you would give it a try."

"I think Esther will make a better mother for the children. I don't want to cause any trouble between you."

"I'll be there as soon as she gets home," Matt promised Claire as he hung up the phone.

I hung up my phone and went downstairs a few minutes later. I was angry and wanted to tell him to get out of my apartment and never return. In retrospect, I wish I had had the courage to speak those words to him that day. I was a fool for allowing Matt to treat me that way. He had no idea I had overheard the conversation. The second he started to give me the excuse as to why he had to leave the children with me, I said, "Matt, you are such a liar, and a cheat! I know where you are going. I heard you and Claire talking. I heard everything you said to her. Why don't you leave and not come back?"

"Oh, Esther," Matt said. "You know I love you. I would have never asked you to marry me if I didn't love you."

"You are a liar, Matt. The only reason you are marrying me is to have a mother for your children."

"That's not true," Matt said, putting his arms around me. You heard me promise Claire I'd fix her car. She's waiting for me, and I want to do it for her."

Matt left, and I didn't see or hear from him until the next afternoon. The episode was soon forgotten. Matt had his way of doing things, like bringing me flowers or taking me shopping for a new dress. I convinced myself that he cared for me and things would change once we were married.

Matt's stepdaughter Stella tried to warn me many times. She had good insight into the relationship between Matt and me. At first, whenever she would say something, I thought it was because she was afraid I was taking her stepfather away from her. I wish I had listened to her warnings.

Time passed, and soon the day for the wedding was at hand. We had a nice ceremony, but we didn't have money for a honeymoon, and with four children, we couldn't go anywhere anyway. Donna and I moved into Matt's house with him and his three children. Now I was the mother of four children, two girls and two boys.

Everyone was right. I had no idea what I was taking on. Our marriage was in trouble before it even began. I can see how unrealistic I was thinking marriage would change Matt. In reality, I was the one who needed to change. When I think back on everything that happened before we were married, it is hard for me to believe I willingly married him. It was a one-sided relationship from the beginning. I loved and wanted to care for Matt's children. Matt had told me he was tired of taking care of them alone and needed help. In some ways, I needed more help than Matt did. It was important to me to be needed.

Chapter 21

I am not ashamed to admit that both my marriages failed because I rushed ahead without waiting on God. I wanted to do things my way. I didn't want to wait. Rushing ahead to fulfill my desires brought pain and heartache. It is sad because I meant for my choices to be for good, but time after time they backfired on me. I hadn't learned what it meant to completely wait on the Lord to show me His plan for my life.

This time four innocent children were unfairly caught up in this unhealthy family situation. In my heart I wanted what was best for the children, and I think Matt did, too. However, Matt made no commitment to the children or me. I tried many times to get Matt to understand that I did not marry him to be his slave; I wanted to be his wife. I didn't feel it was too much to ask him to carry half the responsibility of the family. I wanted him to take the role of a father in the home. He refused. Even though he read the Bible every day and could quote it from Genesis to Revelation, he apparently didn't think it applied to him.

The conflict in our home began to have its effect on the children. The children were constantly exposed to ugly comments we said to one another. There wasn't much laughter or happy times in our home. As parents we didn't set a good example for the children. Randy, the oldest boy, rebelled; Matt had no control over him. Stella was twelve years old and had witnessed many problems between Matt and her mother. She had her own problems with him—Matt often accused Stella of things the child didn't do. Stella disapproved of the way he treated me. For these and other reasons, she and I bonded from the time I became her stepmother. .

I have asked God's forgiveness for my part in our marriage and the example I set for the children. I have peace in my heart with God now, knowing I did try to make our marriage work.

Things continued to go from bad to worse. Matt liked to flirt and have women pay him compliments. I discovered that Matt often visited two other women on his way home from work. Many times he didn't return home until nine or ten o'clock at night. This caused arguments and fights. Of course, I put on a front for my friends and coworkers. They all thought I had a good marriage. Some of them would say, "You are lucky to have a husband who loves the Lord and is good to you." I thought to myself, *I would rather have a husband who did not profess to know God than the fake I have.*

I was unhappy and scared. My second marriage was failing, and I didn't know how to save it. I asked Matt several times to go to our pastor for help. He refused, saying, "You probably went to the pastor already and told him bad things about me. You need help, not me."

Every once in a while, things would appear to go smoothly between us. Rays of hope would enter my heart. *Maybe we could work things out*, I would think. Sometimes I felt strongly that he wanted our marriage to work, but still he refused to commit himself to the family. It seemed that every time we were getting along, the devil would throw something into our path.

Claire was a continual problem, but so were her sisters. Claire had two sisters who lived nearby, and they did their best to make my life miserable. Every Sabbath when we went to church, Matt sat with Claire's family instead of with the children and me. It was so embarrassing. Matt was a deacon, and we were both well known in the church. I would pray and ask God to give me strength to bear this disgrace.

One Sabbath I overheard one of the sisters tell Matt that Claire was coming home. The next Sabbath Claire was in church with the rest of her family. You would have never known Matt was married based on how he acted around Claire. After church one Sabbath, I asked the children to wait for me in the foyer, and I went looking for Matt. I walked around to the back of the church and saw Matt and Claire leaning against the wall talking. I went to the pastor's office and asked him to please come and talk to Matt and Claire.

"We were talking about spiritual things," they responded when Pastor John said it didn't look good for Matt to neglect his family and spend time with Claire.

"That's what I am here for," Pastor John said.

I was hurt and decided I couldn't take the situation anymore. I wanted to leave Matt that very day, but I had no place to go. I started making plans. Things became worse and worse. I couldn't get over Matt being so bold and disrespectful right there in church. I was desperate to leave him, but I had already borrowed money from my bank to remodel our home.

At work on Monday, I broke down and told my best friend, Dorothy Kotz, what had happened and what I had been going through. I told her I wanted to leave. She knew I was desperate, crying out for help, and she offered to loan me money for an apartment. I started looking for a place. Matt began arguing with me every day. One day he was so angry he threatened to hit me.

"Don't you touch her," Stella cried.

Matt came toward me, and Stella jumped on his back to keep him from hitting me. He grabbed her, threw her down the hallway and rushed back toward me. He started hitting me. I tried to fight back. Stella tried to keep him from hurting me, but we were no match for him.

Donna grabbed the phone and called Nelly and Eddy and asked them to come over. They lived about forty minutes from our house, and we were still fighting when they arrived. He had me on the floor. Nelly and Eddy pulled him off, but Matt continued fighting. He grabbed me and picked me up and three times tried to throw me out the front door. Eddy blocked the doorway every time. Donna called Pastor John. He came and tried in vain to settle things between us.

Unbeknownst to Matt, I found a house the next day. Two days later I went to work as usual while Eddy and another friend came and moved my belongings to the new place after Matt left for work. Stella asked to live with me, and I agreed. I went back to the house to be with the boys until Matt got home from work. He tried to talk me into changing my mind. I felt bad for the boys. They were victims of this awful situation, but I was a victim too and had been physically and mentally abused. I didn't stay to talk with Matt, as I found I was beginning to feel sorry for him. Leaving wasn't easy for me. I didn't want to leave, but I felt I had no other choice. Matt wanted to know where I was living, but I refused to tell him.

Donna and Stella were happy I had decided to leave. They were tired of the constant turmoil in the home. After about a week Matt discovered where I was living. I had sympathy for him and the boys, and every day after work he came over with them. Before I knew it, we were living as husband and wife again. Stella was very upset and begged me not to return to Matt. She knew him better than I did, having lived with him longer and seen how he had treated her mother.

"If you don't go back to my stepfather, I'll take care of you," Stella promised.

"You are only seventeen, Stella. You need to finish school before you can even get a job."

"I will as soon as I can. Then I'll take care of you."

Matt was able to convince Stella he would never raise his hand to me again if I would give him another chance. Two months later I agreed to return home. We both made an extra effort to get our marriage on track. We were trying hard to get our family back together. Stella was not happy that I was trying again, but she respected me and wanted to see me happy.

Unfortunately, it wasn't long before it was like it was before I left. To make matters more complicated, one month after I returned home, I discovered I was pregnant. I was shocked and frightened. This was unthinkable. With the problems Matt and I were still confronting, this was not a good time to bring another child into the world. To top it off, I was thirty-nine years old. In a panic I told myself I was too old to have a baby. The doctor assured me I wasn't too old. I was in good health and should have no problem with the pregnancy. This eased my mind somewhat.

Shortly after I discovered I was pregnant, Matt and I got into an argument, and he accused me of being pregnant with another man's baby.

I felt Matt had stabbed me in my heart with those words. He knew it wasn't true; he just wanted to say things to hurt me.

"Oh how I wish I was pregnant by another man instead of you," I cried. "You do not deserve me, or this baby." From that day onward Matt accused me of being unfaithful. I prayed and asked God to help me stay calm and not allow him to upset me. I was living with my husband knowing he had doubts whether the baby I was carrying belonged to him. That was not a good feeling.

I wasn't feeling well and was working too many long hours. I had to board the school bus every morning at six o'clock and ride all over Tampa picking up the handicapped children. After getting them to school, I worked in the classroom all day and then helped bus the children back home after school. Some days I worked from six o'clock in the morning until six in the evening. I tried to keep a good attitude and be positive, praying that God would give me a normal, healthy baby.

Having a baby at thirty-nine and wondering if you are going to have to raise this child yourself is not a pleasant thought. As the baby grew inside of me, so did the thought that this fate would become a reality. I spent many sleepless nights crying for the little baby.

Often as I rode on that school bus, it would hit a bump in the road and I would grab my stomach and hang on. I would say to myself, *Esther, I know the road is rough, but hang on. You will make it. You have traveled rougher roads than this, and God saw you through. He will get you through this, too. But, Lord,* I would cry silently, *speak to my husband's heart so he will take the responsibility of a godly man for his family.*

God answers our prayers in many ways. I felt the special presence of God throughout my whole pregnancy. I asked Him for it, and He showed His presence to me through many beautiful people. It is hard to explain how many good things happened to me. My health was great. I was able to work until six days before my baby was born.

Chapter 22

I gave birth to a beautiful little baby girl on April 22, 1983—two days before I turned forty. Donna was twenty years old at the time, attending a community college and dating a young man named Rick. He decided to join the army and was preparing to leave for training. I thought, *This is great. They were getting too serious about one another. This will give them time apart to think about their relationship.*

I was happy, but not for long. Shortly after Rick told us he intended to join the army, he was over for supper one evening.

"Mom and Matt," Donna said, "Rick and I have something to talk to you about."

"I'd like permission to become engaged to Donna before I leave for training," Rick managed to say. He had the engagement ring in his pocket. I think they had decided to get engaged whether we consented or not. In a way it didn't surprise me. Shortly after their engagement, Rick left for training.

I expected the girls to want to leave home as soon as they had the opportunity. Stella graduated from high school one month after baby Heather was born. I knew she wanted to leave when she finished school. She had been so disappointed when Matt and I had gotten back together. She couldn't understand why I had returned to the abuse.

Stella found a nice, safe place to live. I was sad to see her leave, but I knew she was miserable living in the house with her stepfather. The house was very empty with Stella gone. When she was home, she did little things for me, letting me know how much she appreciated me. I missed her very much. Stella is the most beautiful, loving stepdaughter any mother could ask for, and I love her very much. I knew Donna wanted to leave home for the same reasons Stella did, but Donna kept everything inside and became cold and distant. I never knew how she was feeling. She didn't show her emotions. I was sad and disappointed in myself.

So much happened at one time—Stella graduated, Donna got engaged, and I had a baby. Everyone accepted Heather, and she was loved by her two brothers. They were happy to have a little sister, and Matt was a happy father, too. In fact, having a baby in the house seemed to bring some level of peace and happiness to our home. Heather was a blessing for me, but I was filled with joy and sadness at the same time.

Three months after Donna and Rick's engagement in 1981, the army scheduled Rick to transfer to another state. They wanted to get married so Donna could go with him. I was disappointed. I had been looking forward to Donna spending time with Heather and me. Matt and I, along with Rick's family, planned a wedding, and two months later Donna was married and gone. A year later Donna and Rick had a beautiful baby girl, and I became a grandmother. I felt a little strange becoming a grandmother while Heather was so young, but Donna thought it was neat that the girls would grow up together. The joy Heather brought gave me peace and helped me deal with Donna and Stella leaving home.

As he grew older, Randy continued to give us problems. He was impossible to handle. He refused to obey, and Matt had absolutely no control of him. Matt felt it was easier to let Randy have his own way rather than try to deal with him. My younger stepson, Steven, was a good boy, but I knew scars would surface eventually because of the tension in our home.

Matt had become pretty good about pretending everything was okay. I knew it wasn't, but I was pretending for the children's sake, especially since we had brought another child into this marriage. Matt decided we should move to the country. We took out a second mortgage on our home so we could afford to purchase the country home. It was not my dream home, but it was what we could afford. There were five acres of land with the house, a barn, and a stable for horses. The garage, separate from the house, had been made into a one-bedroom apartment. Matt loved the place.

The boys were not happy. They didn't like leaving their friends in the city. My husband had good intensions thinking if the boys were in the country, maybe they wouldn't be exposed to some of the bad things in the city. It was years too late for Randy, and his bad examples were beginning to rub off on Steven. I found it difficult adjusting to country living at first, but for the boys it was even harder. They had to change schools and make new friends. The move was not good for them. Randy's behavior became even worse. He refused to go to school, and Steven followed his example.

I had to leave home an hour earlier to take Heather to a babysitter, and then be on the school bus picking up kids. When I left home in the morning, Matt and the boys were still asleep. I asked Matt many times to at least get out of bed and walk outside with me and the baby as it was dark. I didn't think it was asking too much. I was hurt because of his lack of interest in his daughter and me. I even suggested if he would get out of bed when I was leaving, he could get the boys up and make sure they got on the school bus before he left for work. But that never happened.

The boys constantly made excuses for not attending school. They would always say that they missed the bus. Of course, there was absolutely no reason for missing the bus. It stopped right in front of our driveway. If the boys missed the bus, it meant their father had overslept and couldn't take them to school as he was already late for his job. He would get them out of bed and tell them to get to school whatever way they could. It was too far and too dangerous to walk, and they had no interest in school anyway. They would hide inside the garage or barn until their father rushed out of the house trying to make it to work. After Matt left for work, the boys would break into the house—they broke many windows and door locks getting into the house. Then they spent the rest of the day doing exactly what they wanted to do.

I tried to emphasize to them how important school and work was, but no one paid any attention to me. I was frustrated with my husband for allowing the boys to get away with not going to school. Randy began getting into trouble in our neighborhood. I had no control over what went on in my home. There were days when I walked in my front door and my sons and their friends would run out the back door. The whole house would stink like marijuana. They all smoked pot and chewed tobacco.

The boys would leave whenever I got home so they wouldn't have to listen to me. Some days I just sat and cried. I didn't know what to do. I prayed for the boys, but prayers can only be answered when a person is willing to let the Holy Spirit into their heart.

With Donna and Stella living away, and the boys out of control, Matt and I resorted to screaming at one another. I was so tired of fighting and arguing that sometimes I felt it was better not to talk to Matt at all. It didn't bother Matt, as he wasn't home much anyway. I would get so upset when I didn't know how to handle the latest problem with the boys or needed Matt's input on a decision that should be made together. I didn't realize he stayed away from home to avoid the children and me. I was torn. Heather needed a father, but every fiber in my body kept telling me that she did not deserve to grow up in a home where there was no love or respect between her parents and siblings. Matt pretended to love our daughter. It is not easy for me to use the word "pretend" as anyone who saw him with Heather when she was little would have believed he was a great father, but he fooled everyone, including me.

Chapter 23

I hired a babysitter, Miss Gray, to come to our home to care for Heather. Every day when I got home from work she would complain that our oldest boy was smoking pot in the house with his friends. Matt refused to listen when Miss Gray and I tried to tell him what Randy and his friends were doing in the house while we were away. One day when I arrived home from work, Miss Gray was very upset.

"You are not doing anything about Randy. I cannot babysit in this house for you anymore. I'm sorry."

I was sorry, too. It wasn't easy to find someone willing to come to our home to care for our daughter. I understood, but I was angry. I was losing my babysitter because of Randy. Miss Gray was still there when Matt came home. I wanted Matt to hear about the problem with Randy from her. I was holding Heather in my arms as I tried to explain to him about Randy, but he became very angry.

"I'm tired of listening to you every day!" he shouted as he walked toward me. "You're always complaining about Randy. Why don't you do something about him?"

"He's seventeen, Matt. He won't listen to me, and now I'm losing my babysitter because he is doing drugs in the house while she is here with the baby. They are exposed to it."

I knew my husband was frustrated with Randy himself. He didn't know what to do, but he wasn't given me any support or respect in front of the boys. Matt was out of control; he came at me as if he was going to hit me. He put his hand in my face and shouted, "Shut up! I'm tired of your mouth!"

I was still holding Heather, so I slapped his hand away. That made him even angrier. He pushed me, pinning me against the wall. Miss Gray was screaming at both of us to stop fighting. She tried to pull Heather from my arms, but I couldn't release her because of the way Matt had me pinned against the wall. Miss Gray was finally able to get Heather away from me and ran outside with her.

What happened next was a nightmare. I was no match for my husband. When he was angry, he became a wild man. He followed me out of the kitchen, down the hallway, and into the bedroom. I fought back the whole time. He threw me across the bed, and I ended up with half of my body hanging off the bed. My head was jammed between the bed and the wall. He struck me again and again on my left arm in the same spot, right below my shoulder. It was as if he was trying to break my arm. When I was finally able to turn over on my side, my left arm was hurting so badly I couldn't use it. I was frightened to think my husband would try to hurt me this way knowing I was nursing our baby. When I was able to stand up, I was crying and holding my arm.

"What are you crying for? Look at my neck where you scratched me," Matt snarled. "What am I going to tell my coworkers tomorrow?"

At that moment, I didn't care what I had done to him. I was worried about the baby and Miss Gray. We lived way out in the country, it was dark outside, and there was no place for Miss Gray to go. I managed to get outside and found Miss Gray standing behind the car crying. Mosquitoes were biting Heather and her. I was so ashamed Miss Gray had witnessed what had just happened. I apologized, telling her how sorry I was.

Miss Gray tried to comfort me in return. "I'm sorry you had to go through an ordeal like that," she said. She was a kind woman. I understood why she couldn't continue babysitting for me.

That night I wished I had never met Matt. I wanted him out of my life. I didn't have the strength or the courage to leave, and I didn't want to accept the fact that my second marriage was now hanging by a thread. I couldn't see how it could last much longer. I discovered something about Matt then that I was puzzled about. After a big fight Matt could calm himself down and act as if the fight had not happened. There was no remorse for what he had done. His personality changed from night to day. I wondered if he was a good actor or bipolar.

I had done my best for the boys, and they still had lost all respect for me as a mother. I was just another person living in the house cleaning up after everyone and working every day to make sure we had a roof over our heads. I was tired of carrying the entire responsibility for our family. I was the one who worried if we had enough money to pay the mortgage or the electric company. When we didn't have enough, I had to find a way to make up the difference. I was in debt to my sister, my daughter, and my bank.

I will never forget when our lights were going to be turned off for the third time that year. Whenever I told Matt we needed money for the electric bill, he ignored me. That was his way of dealing with anything he didn't know how to handle, or didn't want to handle. These were the times I would become so upset with him.

Two days before the lights were going to be turned off, I placed the bill on the kitchen counter. "Look at the date; it's due on the seventeenth," I told Matt. "In two days we will be in the dark if we do not pay the bill."

He didn't say anything. He knew he didn't have to worry about it. He felt it was my problem, not his. Later, I realized I was wrong assuming I had to be responsible for everything. Yet,

I am one of those people who need to know that things are going to be done on time. I panic and scramble to rescue the situation. My husband knew this and took advantage of me. The day before the deadline, I stopped by Nelly's house on my way home from work.

"Nelly, my lights are going to be turned off again if the bill is not paid by tomorrow. Would you please loan me two hundred and seventeen dollars until I get paid on Friday?"

For the first time, my sister said, "No." She had always loaned me money when I asked. I was shocked.

"Why, Nelly? Why don't you want to loan it to me? I do not owe you any money. I always pay you back."

"Esther, it's not about you paying me back. It's about you not letting your husband take responsibility sometimes. Make him be a man this time and figure out how to pay the electric bill."

"He won't pay it. Heather and I will be left without electricity. The boys will go to their friends, and Matt doesn't even get home until late. I don't want to be out in the country alone without lights." I tried to convince Nelly.

"You don't have to stay out there without lights. Tomorrow, if he doesn't pay the bill, pack some clothes and you and Heather come and spend the night with me."

I didn't like the idea, so I called Donna and told her the problem. "Your Aunt Nelly refused to loan me the money. Can you loan it to me?"

"Mom, I think Aunt Nelly is right. I feel bad for Heather and you. I will loan you the money, but I wish you would take Aunt Nelly's advice and make him take the responsibility this one time. Pack some stuff for Heather and yourself and come spend the night with me, or go to Aunt Nelly's."

It was embarrassing to have my sister and daughter give me the same advice. I was not happy with them. I was also thinking about my neighbor living across from us. I knew she would be over the next day wanting to know why the lights were off again. She would ask if I needed her to bring candles over.

When I got home that evening and looked at the meter box, there was no tag or lock hanging from it. There was nothing on my front door, and this was the day they were supposed to turn off the lights. I opened the door and turned on the light switch, and the lights came on. I was so happy; I walked straight to the kitchen and called Nelly to tell her.

"He must have paid it, but the bill is still on the counter where I left it."

"He didn't need the piece of paper to pay the bill. Just be thankful he paid it." Nelly said. "I told you to stop running ahead. When he realizes you are not going to pay the bills, he will."

"Nelly, this is like a miracle."

When Matt came home that night I didn't mention anything about the bill to him, and he didn't say anything to me. I was thankful Matt was acting responsibly at last and the problem with the electric bill was solved. Only it wasn't. The power company just gave us another day.

Instead of turning the lights off on the seventeenth, they waited until the eighteenth. I didn't pay any attention to the meter box when I passed it, but when I reached the front door, I saw the tag hanging from the doorknob.

At that moment, I was so angry with my husband I began crying. Every day he proved he didn't care for us. The lights were just another problem he knew I would fix if he ignored it.

It was a Wednesday evening. Matt and the pastor of our church were good friends. The pastor had asked Matt to lead the prayer meeting for him that night. I knew Matt would make sure he was home in time to get ready for the seven-thirty meeting. Sure enough, Matt came walking in the door at six o'clock.

Heather met him at the door saying, "Daddy, daddy, make the TV work."

"Baby, it's not working?"

"No, Daddy. Fix it."

I looked at him and said, "Why don't you tell her what's wrong with the television?"

He pretended he didn't hear me. Heather followed him into the kitchen insisting he fix the TV.

He turned around and said, "Honey, we must have had some bad lightning come through here and mess up the TV today. Daddy has to go to a prayer meeting. When I get home, I'll fix it for you."

I wanted to scream at him, *You lying dog! Why don't you tell her the truth? The lights are off because you didn't pay the bill.* I didn't say it, but I couldn't help thinking it.

An electric pump controlled water from our well. Therefore, when the power went off, we didn't have any water. Matt was dirty and greasy from his work as a mechanic. He had to be at the prayer meeting in about an hour, and he needed a bath. Matt grabbed a pail and went outside to the well. There was a faucet on the holding tank. He was able to get enough water to wash up a bit and shave. In no time he was all dressed in his suit. He took his Bible, gave Heather a kiss, told her goodbye, and went out the door.

I packed a few things and went to Donna's for the night. When I returned home the following day, the lights were back on. Someone might think, *What's the big deal? No lights for one night.* To me, it was the principle of the whole thing.

My sister was my best friend, and I could count on her for good advice. But I felt she didn't understand what I was going through. I had come to despise Matt. He professed to be a godly man and was always willing to give a Bible study or conduct a prayer meeting. He would stop and help anyone in need. His good deeds for others made him appear to be a good man. All of these kindnesses made it hard for me to understand him. How could this man be so willing to do good things for others but have no time for his family?

Our relationship was so bad it no longer bothered me that he didn't come home. However, it broke my heart knowing how much Heather loved her daddy. She couldn't understand why he wasn't home by her bedtime. Most of the time, when he did come home on time, he would bring Heather a toy or some candy.

The hardest part of our marriage was that Matt refused to take any blame for the destruction of our family, and he never said he was sorry. He just said he wouldn't hurt me again. I know I had faults, too, but I wanted our marriage to work.

When a friend told me that Matt had confessed to her that he had only married me so that I could take care of his children, I was heartbroken. Even with all the abuse, I didn't want it to be true. I wanted to believe that he loved me.

I promised I wouldn't say anything to Matt, but when he walked in the door that evening, I was sick to my stomach thinking of how he had used me all those years. It would not have hurt so badly if Matt didn't pretend that he was a good husband and father. At home he was a completely different person. It was very hard for me to even want to continue to live in the house with Matt after I learned what he said.

He knew something was wrong the minute he walked through the door. I wanted to say something to him that would hurt him so badly he would never forget it. I finally broke down and told him what was bothering me. He admitted he said those words, but then he attempted to smooth things over. "But that was when we first got married, Esther. Over the years I have learned to love you."

"You are a liar. You are a selfish man who only cares about yourself. One day you are going to have to stand before God and give an account to Him for the way you have treated the children and me. It's a shame the children had to suffer for so many years because of your selfishness."

I was blaming him for everything, but then I thought of something my parents instilled in me. When I was a little girl and my brother or sister did something to me I thought was unfair, I would go straight to my mom and dad to complain. Many times I wished I didn't because they would say, "If I ask your brother or sister will the story be the same?"

"There are two sides to this story," my dad would say to me. "Do you want your mother and me to intervene, or do you want a little more time to think about it before we call your brother or sister?"

Sometimes I would say, "Daddy, I'm telling the truth. You can call them right now." But sometimes I would have to say, "Wait, I'm coming right back." They knew that when I said that I wouldn't be back because I would have to admit the part I played in causing the problem. My parents did their best to teach us to be truthful and honest.

It was a struggle to be fair to my husband, but I needed to question myself. Was I being completely honest with Matt? It wasn't as easy as when I was a little girl. I just wanted to tell him, *It's all your fault!*

My dad's words came to me. "It takes two to make a marriage. Be honest."

My thoughts began to dwell on all his selfish acts. But then I realized that I had put the tools in his hand and gave him permission to use them. The children needed a mother, and I was vulnerable. Matt discovered it the minute he met me. I was an easy prey.

Number One: I was looking for someone to want and love me. Matt wasn't capable of loving as he was too in love with himself.

Number Two: I was still in a grieving process from an unhealthy divorce. Matt was going through rejection from the woman of his dreams. From stories he told me, he too had suffered rejection at an early age. We both were looking for acceptance and love when what we needed was healing from our past.

Women are battered and abused every day for no reason. No woman or man should ever feel they have that authority over another. God ordained marriage in the Garden of Eden between Adam and Eve. God made us to love and enjoy the companionship of one another. I believe the devil knows how important marriage and families are to God. That's why he works so hard in the hearts of men and women to bring strife and discontentment to break up families. As many beautiful things as there are on this earth, I don't think there is anything as beautiful as a bride and groom on their wedding day. Whenever I go to a wedding now, my prayers are for the couple, that they will allow God to be a part of their marriage. Without Him, nothing will last. I don't think there is anything on this earth that can start out so beautiful and end in so much hate. I believe God hates divorce because so many of His little children are hurt by it, while the devil loves it because it destroys families.

But although God hates divorce, I don't believe He intends for people to stay in abusive relationships. He wants us to be happy. God made us to be a helpmate for one another, not a doormat. God is a kind and loving God. He sees and understands what happens behind closed doors. It breaks His heart to see us abusing one another. If you are afraid to leave an abusive marriage, seek professional help and ask God for wisdom to make the right choice.

God has been my Comforter throughout my entire life. He has watched over me even though I turned my back on Him many times and went my own way. My mom and dad always told me Jesus would love me regardless of the choices I made. They told me Jesus hates sin, but He loves sinners. Sometimes I didn't want to listen to them because I didn't think I was doing anything that bad. I didn't see, or understand, what they meant. I was having fun. How could that be sin? My parents never stopped praying for me until I understood I was a sinner. From that moment on, I discovered I needed Jesus. Even though I'm still a sinner, I know Jesus loves me.

Chapter 24

I have never been able to talk about the incident that is documented in this chapter, but this is part of my story, and I need to share it. Donna and her husband and daughter had moved back to Florida and were living with us until they could find a home of their own.

Randy had left home, and we hadn't heard from him in about a month. He had run away from home and been living with an older woman. Then when he came back, he got in trouble with the law for stealing from our neighbor. I was honestly glad that he was gone, since no one could get through to him, especially not Matt, and he caused nothing but trouble in our home.

Donna was taking care of two-year-old Heather, but I still hurried home after work to spend time with my little girl and grandbaby. This day as I hurried toward home and pulled into the yard, I saw Steven standing in the driveway crying. He had a bloody nose. I jumped out of the car, anxious to know what had happened. He was so upset he could hardly talk.

"It was Randy," he managed to say. "My own brother stole my dirt bike." The bike had been gone for about a month. Apparently Randy was back in the neighborhood and when Steven confronted him about his bike, Randy had punched him in the nose.

I was so frustrated. I was at work all day, and Randy knew that. He was taking advantage of things while I was away. Matt was not happy about Randy's actions either, but he, too, was at work during the day. Randy had run out of places to live and had decided to come back home. He was only seventeen, and Randy knew we were still legally responsible for him.

Steven told me that Randy had come home angry. Randy had gotten a job not far from where we lived. He had worked there three days, and then left. A few days later Randy had returned to the job to collect his pay. The boss accused him of stealing a piece of equipment and refused to pay him until Randy returned the missing item. Randy lost his temper and got in a punching fight with his boss. He was still angry when he got home, so Randy took it out on Steven when Steven asked about the bike.

"Come in the house, Steven, so I can get you cleaned up," I said.

"No, Randy is inside. I don't want him to beat on me again. I'm going to wait out here until Daddy gets home."

I left Steven standing outside crying. When I reached the porch, I saw the front door was wide open. Randy was standing by the entrance with his hands on his hips. He was watching television. My heart sank when I saw him. I didn't want this boy back in my home, but I knew I didn't have a choice. I would have to tolerate him until he was eighteen.

When I stepped inside, I asked, "Why is the door wide open and the air conditioner on?"

Donna was sitting in the living room with the two babies. "Mom, the door has been open since Randy came in. He's just standing there watching TV. I asked him to close the door and he told me to shut up. He said I didn't have any rights here in this house. I am married and shouldn't be here. He cussed me out with every four-letter word for no reason, and he did it in front of the babies."

I didn't know what to say or do. I was standing beside an angry six-foot man who had just gotten in a fight with his boss and then beaten up his younger brother.

"Why did you come back here to cause trouble again in my house?"

Randy began to yell and scream at me. "This house belongs to my dad, too. You have no right to tell me anything!"

"I have every right to tell you that you cannot come and go and do as you please in my house."

"Shut your mouth!" he yelled, adding a bunch of four-letter words after his command.

"Get out of the house, Randy," I said.

He stepped out on the front porch and picked up a rock from beside the sidewalk. He walked back to the front door. "If you don't shut up, I'll knock your head off with this rock!"

There was a machete in the house. "Randy, if you raise that rock to hurt me, I will stop your hand with that machete."

"Don't argue with him, Mom!" Donna cried. "He's completely out of control. I'm going to call the police to get him out of here!"

I was so upset. I felt I had been pushed to my limit with Randy. Matt was never home when Randy did these things. I always had to struggle with him alone. Matt had never wanted to deal with his son's problems. Donna called the sheriff, and then things happened so quickly. The sheriff who responded to the call was the same sheriff who had taken Randy to juvenile detention on charges of stealing from our neighbors, but then released him the next day.

Randy met the sheriff in the driveway. "My stepmother threatened to kill me with a machete!" he told her.

Donna tried to explain what had happened, and that she had called because Randy was threatening to hit me with a stone, but she didn't even let Donna finish speaking.

"Step outside, Mrs. Vance," the sheriff said. "Did you threaten to kill your stepson with a machete?"

"No! I told him I would stop his hand with a machete!"

"Mrs. Vance, I have to arrest you for threatening a minor with a weapon."

My daughter tried talking to her again, but the sheriff refused to listen. She would not allow me to go into my house. My poor little baby was crying. She wanted to be nursed, but I couldn't even go to her.

Within a few minutes there was another sheriff's car in the driveway. My neighbor from across the street could see what was happening. She came over and tried to talk to the sheriff. "Arresting her is unfair. I know some of the things that boy has done to her over the years! He broke into my home and stole from me." At seventeen, Randy already had nine encounters with the law.

The sheriff insisted she had to arrest me because Randy was a minor. In the fifteen years I had lived in this country, I had never experienced prejudice until that day.

"Where are you from?" the sheriff asked, noting my accent.

"My husband will be home in a little while. Could you please wait until he gets here?" I asked. "If you talk to him, he can tell you what I've been going through with Randy."

The other sheriff was standing on the porch. He didn't have much to say. Steven was still standing in the yard with a bloody nose. He wanted his dad to see what Randy had done to him.

"Stay with her," the lady sheriff said to her partner. "I need to talk to the other boy and see what's happened to him." I think she thought I had hurt Steven.

She was surprised when Steven told her Randy had hit him. She called Randy over and asked him if he had hit his younger brother.

"Sure," Randy said. "But I was just playing around with him. It was an accident."

"It was no accident! You did it on purpose because you were mad."

"If he wants to, Randy, your brother can press charges against you for assaulting him," the sheriff told him.

I didn't know if Donna had called Matt, or just by chance he came home on time that day. When I saw his blue car coming down the road, I just knew he would talk to the sheriff and try to get her to understand what was happening in our home with Randy.

The sheriffs walked over to meet Matt as he got out of his car. Steven hurried over to his dad.

"What's wrong with you?" Matt asked Steven.

Steven began to tell him what happened. The sheriff apparently didn't want me to hear what was being said. She told them to step away under a big oak tree where I couldn't see or hear them. I was told to sit in the swing on my front porch. I sat there waiting and hoping my husband was talking to the sheriff on my behalf. I heard Matt laugh out loud. I thought, *How in the world can he be laughing when I am sitting here waiting to be arrested?*

My little daughter was inside the house crying. Donna came to the door. "Mom, what do you want me to do about Heather?"

"Try to get her to drink a little juice and some water till I can nurse her." I was so upset,

I don't think I could have held my baby and nursed her then. I had never been involved with the law before. I was so ashamed Donna had to see this, but I was also thankful she was there to take care of Heather.

After what seemed like forever, the two sheriffs came back to the porch.

"Mrs. Vance, your stepson wants to press charges against you."

"Where is my husband? How come he didn't come and talk to me?"

The lady sheriff said, "Oh, he talked with Randy, and he wants to press charges."

"What about what Randy did to Steven? What are you going to do about that?"

"That is between your husband and his sons. Mrs. Vance, I need to put handcuffs on you and take you to the car."

Right then I realized my husband wanted me to be arrested. She had waited to handcuff me to see what Matt would tell her. Matt never came to say, "Esther, I'm sorry this is happening to you." He didn't even come up on the porch where I was. I never had the chance to speak to him on my way to the sheriff's car. I saw him and the two boys standing under the oak tree talking. The sheriff put me in the back of the car and closed the door. They both walked back to where Matt and the boys were and talked and laughed with them for about another ten minutes. I couldn't even cry anymore. I sat in that sheriff's car and looked at Matt. It was as if he was a complete stranger.

Matt knew our baby was in the house and needed me, but he didn't seem to care. I try very hard not to think about that day, but it is hard not to. I know God was looking down from heaven and saw exactly what happened. I know it hurt Him when I told Randy what I did, but I also know He saw my heart and knew I would never hurt my stepson. Yes, I was very angry with him that day, but God knows I would never have used a weapon on him.

There is a chapter in the Bible that says "Everything happens for good to those who love the Lord." That was one time I could not understand what good could come out of this. I still ponder why this had to happen to me. There is another verse in the Bible that says, "Lean not on your own understanding, but in all your ways acknowledge Him and He will direct your paths." If my mother hadn't taught me these beautiful scriptures from the Bible, I don't think I could ever have made it this far. My dad used to tell us that the Bible says to love your enemies, bless those who curse you, and do good to those who hate you. Sometimes it seems as though evil prevails, but I know God is always in control, and we do not see the big picture. Jesus says He will never leave us or forsake us. It's very hard sometimes when it seems as if the people we care about are the ones who hurt us the most.

As I sat in the sheriff's car that evening watching my husband and stepson, they seemed to be gloating. They looked as if they were rejoicing over what was taking place. It was very hard for me to watch them. Why was Matt treating me this way? I was the mother of his little girl. God knows I had never done anything intentionally to harm him or the children. I only wanted what was best for us. Matt acted as though he was getting revenge.

The Bible says that the eyes of God travel to and fro upon this earth. He sees everything that each and every one of us does, and He hears every word spoken. I know He heard the conversation between the sheriff and Matt and Randy when the sheriff asked what they wanted her to do with me. Matt left it up to Randy.

"I want her to know how it feels to go to jail," Randy said.

"If that's my son's decision," Matt said, "then I have to go along with it."

The sheriff asked Steven if he wanted to press charges against Randy for punching him. Steven did not want his brother to go to jail, so he asked his dad what he should do.

"Don't do it, Steven. If Randy ever wants to go into the service, he doesn't need that on his record."

Matt made the choice that day to keep Randy from being arrested, but he sent me to jail.

We tend to blame God when things don't go our way or when something bad happens. God gets the blame every time. I don't understand why we blame God when bad things happen. All I know is that the Bible tells me that God loved me so much that He gave His only Son to die to save me. I don't know what kind of a person I would be if I didn't believe that Jesus loves me.

While I sat in the sheriff's car, I thought about Jesus. Just because He loved us, He was misunderstood and was killed. He was innocent of all evil that was brought against Him. He called on His Father and said, "Father, forgive them for they know not what they do." Whenever bad things happen, people call on God either for mercy or to curse Him. If people had the heart and mind to do to Jesus what they did, who am I to think I should go through life and not suffer hurt and pain?

It's such a wonderful experience to know Jesus personally, to know He knows you by name. He has already gone through everything you are going through, and more. But we must read God's Word if we are going to know Him. Until He became my personal friend, He didn't mean too much to me. I knew He was my mom and dad's friend, but I didn't know how they got to know Him so well. One day I discovered I needed Jesus, and I called on Him from the bottom of my heart. I realized His sweet Holy Spirit was there all the time just waiting for me to give Him permission to begin His work in me.

God gave us ten simple rules to follow—the Ten Commandments. He said, "If you love me keep my commandments." The word "if" is used many times in the Bible. To me, it is the most important two-letter word in the Bible. Most of us do not like rules, but God knew we needed some standards to follow. He said not to take away from, or add anything to the Ten Commandments. The first four commandments are to show loyalty to God, and the remaining six to each other. He asks us to write them upon our hearts and teach them to our children. My parents talked to us about them when we woke up in the morning and before we went to bed at night. We thought they were trying to make our lives miserable and boring. We didn't realize it was because they loved us so much.

In Proverbs 22 the Bible says to train a child in the way he should go so that when he is old enough to make decisions he will chose right instead of wrong. The Bible didn't say we would always make the right decision, but He gave us the right to choose. When I read the Bible, I see how compassionate Jesus was to those who were rejected and made to feel worthless. John 8 tells the story of the woman accused of adultery. The Bible doesn't mention a sister or friend being there by her side, and I'm sure she must have felt so alone. The sad part of the story is the same people accusing her were her abusers. Jesus, in His love and compassion, saved her from being stoned. Recalling this story gave me strength that day, as I knew I wasn't alone. I put my trust in God, knowing He would take care of me. He sees the end from the beginning. He knew what was happening, and He saw ahead to what was going to happen.

After what seemed an eternity sitting in the back of that sheriff's car, she came and drove me to the jail. She stopped in front of a building, opened the door, and told me to get out. Inside, she placed my pocket book in a locker. She took me to a small holding cell and locked me in there. That day the poem entitled "Footprints" became real to me. Jesus carried me in His loving arms that day. He knew I couldn't have gone through it alone. About an hour after I was placed in the cell, the sheriff came to the door.

"Mrs. Vance, as you know we do not have a jail here. We transport our inmates to the next town."

I don't know why she said "as you know" as I had no idea where the jail was located. I thought they were going to keep me in that cell. Her next words were unbelievable.

She said, "Mrs. Vance, I just got off the phone with your husband. This is the deal. I told him you are under a five thousand dollar bond. You need five hundred dollars to get out of here tonight, or you can talk to a bondman. There is a second option, and I explained both to your husband. The other one is for you to be transferred to jail tonight and see the judge in the morning. Your bond will be reduced to one thousand dollars, and you will only have to pay one hundred dollars."

What she said next was like a stab in my heart. "Your husband wants me to ask if you would spend the night in jail because he doesn't have the money to get you out tonight."

I couldn't believe what I was hearing. I had a baby at home who I was nursing, and her father was willing to let me go all night without nursing. He wanted me to spend the night in jail.

I have to keep repeating how thankful I am to have had parents like I did. The Bible has all of these beautiful promises for every situation. I don't know if there is another mother in this entire world who called on God on behalf of her children as my mother did. Whenever she gathered us for worship, she would always pray that the Holy Spirit would give us faith to believe Jesus would answer our prayers. We had to pray, and it had to be out loud. My mom and dad taught us to pray for each other, plus the whole world. They loved Jesus so much; they wanted all of us children to love Him, too. They tried to teach us to trust and depend on Him for all our needs. We were young and often would rather have been outside playing instead of inside praying. My mom would make me mad sometimes because I always asked Jesus for all kinds of stuff. She would wait until everyone was through praying and say, "Children, you don't need to name all the things you want. Jesus knows our needs. Let's ask Him to give us what is best for us." We always had to end our prayers with, "Thy will be done." My mom and dad had faith in God and always looked for something good to happen on the next day. They had that peace the Bible speaks about—"The peace that passes all understanding."

I felt that peace my parents had as I stood listening to the sheriff. Instead of getting angry, I said, "Please don't tell me anything that Matt said. I don't want to hear it. I can pay my own bond. I have five hundred dollars in my pocketbook. Please bring it to me. I need to go home to my baby as quick as I can."

The sheriff said, "I have to call your husband and let him know. He is waiting for your answer. He said that if you stay in jail overnight it would save him four hundred dollars."

"Tell him I don't need his money."

"I still need to call him and let him know you have the money. He needs to bring the papers for your house for collateral."

All I could do was whisper a prayer and ask God to touch Matt's heart so he would not refuse to bring the papers. As the sheriff walked away from the cell door, I knew everything was going to be okay.

The pieces all began to fit together. Years ago when I offered to pay Nelly back five hundred dollars I owed her, she had told me not to. I knew she meant it, but I was determined, all these years later, to pay her back, and God knew I would need the money today. He made sure Nelly wasn't home that evening when I stopped by to give the money to her. I was able to stand in that cell and give God praise. Before this, I had trouble understanding a promise in the Bible that my mom often repeated. She would say to us children, "When God is for you, no man can be against you. Even though sometimes it seems as if the whole world is against you, Jesus will never leave you."

I know I could have called Nelly, or any of my good friends, and they would have been right there to help me. But I felt so degraded. I didn't want anyone to see me in this condition. The only thing that kept me from falling apart was my relationship with God.

Matt finally came with the papers for the house. He also brought Heather and Steven with him. When I walked out of the cell and into the room where he was waiting for me, I looked into his face. He had no remorse for what had happened to me. He acted as if I had just gotten off an airplane from a vacation. Maybe at that moment I was being very ungrateful, but I thought how cruel and mean to bring my little girl and stepson to this place. There was absolutely no reason to bring them. Donna was at home and could've taken care of Heather.

After I was released, I went to the car and got in the back seat with my baby where I was able to nurse her. On the way home, we passed McDonald's. Matt had the nerve to ask me if I wanted him to stop and get me something to eat. How could he think I could stop anywhere to eat? I felt as if my whole world had caved in on me, and my husband wanted to take me to McDonald's.

Listening to Matt and Steven talk in the car on the way home opened my eyes. I learned how cold and unsympathetic my husband was toward me. I remember saying to God, *I don't want to live with this man any longer.*

I looked at Heather, and my heart broke for her. She loved her dad and got excited when she saw him. I believe in his own way he loved her, too. He was very good about entertaining her. He bought every new toy that came on the market, and when he was home, he played with her. He gave her piggyback rides and wagon rides. Whenever he was around, he spent quality time with her. I was heartbroken because I knew the decision I was about to make would leave Heather without her dad. I was so exhausted and sad; I couldn't see myself going through life living like this any longer. I felt as though I couldn't spend another day in the house with Matt. My mind was made up. The thought of leaving Matt had been lingering in my heart for a long time, but I kept praying it wouldn't become a reality, especially since I had Heather. I knew she would be the one who would suffer the most. Steven was young, too, and I knew he would suffer as well. I made up my mind on the way home that Matt would never have another opportunity to make me feel inferior or abuse me again.

I arrived home and walked inside. I felt dirty and embarrassed to think my daughter had witnessed me being arrested. Donna was thankful I didn't have to spend the night in jail. She was very upset that her stepfather had been so cold and had no remorse for what had happened to me. Donna told me that when the sheriff pulled out of the yard, Matt walked inside the house and told her he was hungry. He asked her to fix him dinner.

"Mom, I did, but I was so angry with him, I wanted to tell him to fix his own supper."

"It's okay," I told Donna.

"Mom, I didn't want him to bring Heather to that jail, but he insisted he wanted her and Steven along. I think the only reason he did not bring Randy, too, was because the neighbor from across the street came over and told him he should not have Randy here when you got home. She told him it wouldn't be fair to you."

I was very thankful to my neighbor for being so thoughtful. I don't know how I would have reacted if Randy had been home when I got there.

"God sees every injustice that is done to his children," I told Donna. "That's why we all should be very careful how we treat each other. I'll be okay, but I can't wait to get into the shower."

When I stepped into the shower, I began to cry. I cried and cried. The shower washed my tears away as the water poured down my face. After the tears, I prayed and asked God to help me not to hate. I really had to pray that prayer again and again, because I knew I was capable of hating if I allowed my feelings to control my thoughts. When I stepped out, the feelings that came over me were not anger, nor sadness, but a feeling of relief. *Yes. God willing, I will go tomorrow and file for a divorce.*

I didn't want to have any contact with Matt, verbally or physically. I knew his character. Matt seemed to be able to block out his unusual behavior. He did a good job pretending and making me believe that I was the abuser. He had a way about him that made me feel I deserved to be abused. I knew when Matt came to bed he would act as if nothing had happened. And then he would blame everything on me. Tonight was no different.

Matt got into bed and wrapped his arms around me. My back was turned toward him. I took his arms and threw them off me.

"Matt, you are a sick man. How can you think I would want you to touch me tonight after what you did."

"I did not do it, honest," Matt said. "Randy wanted to press charges against you. I had nothing to do with it."

I knew arguing with him would not solve anything. I said some ugly words to him that I should not have said, but at that moment I didn't care. I just wanted him to know how I felt.

Chapter 25

I was up and dressed early the next morning. I called my job and took the day off. I was still so devastated by what had happened that I didn't want my neighbors to see me.

As I walked out the door, my daughter said, "Mom, don't cry. You are a strong person. Don't let this man continue to do this to you. He doesn't care anything about you. Leave him and his sons."

Every word Donna said to me was true, but all I could think was, *What about Heather?* All the way to the lawyer's office my heart was breaking with sadness knowing Heather would not understand. I knew Matt would tell her he did not want a divorce. That was the truth; I was taking care of him so why should he want a divorce? I knew what he would tell her when she was older, but I knew it was the right thing to do. I had to be strong for myself that morning when I talked to the lawyer.

After I explained everything to the lawyer, she asked, "Are you sure this is the only way to solve your problems?"

I said I was sure. She said, "If you want me to take your case, it will cost you five hundred dollars. You will need to give me one hundred and fifty dollars today to begin the process."

I wrote her a check. She explained a few more things, gave me a list of information she would need, and set another appointment. I was very stressed and sad as I left her office. I felt Matt had given me no other choice. I comforted myself by saying, *Esther, this is long overdue. God sees what you have been going through.*

Many times my dad had told me, "Search your heart before you jump to conclusions. Remember, there are always two sides to a story."

Out loud, I said, "But Daddy, this is different. That was when I was a little girl and wanted to be told I was right. Now I have a little girl, and it doesn't matter if I am right or wrong; she will end up being the victim."

I prayed and prayed, asking God to show me if I was making the right decision, but it seemed as if He was silent. Then, it hit me. I had already made the decision on my own.

Matt had no idea I had gone to a lawyer. He thought everything was going along as it always did. I treated him very cold, but I had done this before whenever he treated me badly. He thought I was too much of a coward to leave him. Instead of Matt trying to keep our marriage together, he was in complete denial that we had a problem at all.

Matt used Heather for a shield whenever he was home. He bought her something just about every day. She didn't want to go to bed at night until her daddy got home because he always brought her some candy or a toy. I knew the divorce was going to be the hardest thing I would ever do to my daughter because she really loved her daddy.

The day came for my second appointment with the lawyer. She said, "You'll need to leave twelve dollars to pay for the sheriff to serve the divorce papers to Matt. Where do you want him served, at home or on his job?"

"At home. It will be less embarrassing for him."

"If you want the papers served at home, you can give them to him yourself and save twelve dollars."

During our conversations, she had asked me many times if I felt safe living in my home with my husband. I'd told her I didn't feel any danger. I never thought at any time my life was in danger. Matt wasn't a bad man. He is no different from any other person who makes bad choices, and that includes me. The Bible speaks of those who have a form of godliness but deny the power of God to change. If we are truly connected to Him, God would help us to keep from hurting one another.

I talked to my mom about my decision to leave Matt. I wish I could have talked to my dad as well, but he had passed away some time before. How I long for the day when Jesus will come in the clouds to take His children home to heaven where there will be no more pain, suffering, death, or evil. I also look forward to that day because I'll see my dad again.

I found myself calling on God more and more. The more I called on Him, the more real He became to me. I needed Him to get me through this. I felt so guilty over what the divorce would do to Heather. But I could no longer handle the abuse. I had lost every inch of respect for Matt. Every time he had raised his hand to me, or called me names, it had killed a little bit of the love and respect I had for him. He didn't physically abuse me many times, but it was awful when he did. The last time he abused me, I had told him, "Matt, if you hurt me physically again, you will regret it." I think he knew I meant it. Once Matt stopped the physical abuse, he completely denied he ever abused me in any way, and in spite of the fact that my sister, her husband, and my daughters saw him abuse me, Matt swore it didn't happen. He called me a liar and said he had never touched me. I don't know if he was able to block it out, or if he was trying to make me believe I was going crazy.

What makes a woman stay with a man and allow him to hurt her and her children? Some women even lie and cover up the abuse. My story is just one of millions. I have friends who confided in me after they learned of my situation and told me about the abuse that takes place in their homes. When I heard what their husbands were doing to them and their little children,

I might have refused to believe them if I wasn't going through similar experiences. When God put woman and man on this earth, He did not intend for them to abuse one another. We were created to serve Him and enjoy each other's company. Marriage is a lifetime commitment, and I understood that. But it takes two to make a marriage work. The Bible tells husbands to love their wives like Christ loves the church. It doesn't stop there; God wants a wife to love and respect her husband because he is responsible for the family. God holds each one of us responsible for our actions.

The day I picked up the divorce papers, I didn't know how Matt would react when I confronted him with them. I had isolated myself from him for almost a month, and he had no idea the divorce papers would be waiting for him when he came home. I was anxious. I rehearsed the words I would say to him again and again in my mind. As usual, he was late getting home. I approached Matt just as he walked in the door. I knew if I waited it would be harder for me to tell him.

I said, "Matt, I'm divorcing you."

He looked at me as if I was speaking a foreign language.

"I mean it. I have the papers for you to sign right here."

He did not say anything. I don't think he believed me. If he did, he acted like he didn't care. He went straight to the bathroom, took his bath, and returned to the kitchen. I placed his dinner on the table. He still didn't say a word to me. When he finished eating, he went to the living room and sat down to watch television. I took the divorce papers and went to the living room and placed them on the coffee table right in front of him.

"Matt, here are the divorce papers. You need to sign them so I can take them back to my lawyer. I'm going to divorce you because you don't love me. I'm the mother of your daughter, and you treat me like dirt. You have no respect for me—you never had—and it has gotten worse." I took a breath. "Matt, I really don't know who you think you are, but I know I deserve better than you have been treating me. I don't want to be married to you any longer."

Matt ignored me and continued watching television. He never said a word to me. I didn't know what he was thinking as he had never been this quiet before. He was always ready with an answer, so his silence was something new. I think he was surprised, as he never thought I would leave him.

Matt finished watching his television show. He didn't even look at the divorce papers; he got up and went to bed, still not saying a word to me. I was upset. I wanted some kind of response from him. Perhaps I wanted him to say something negative to me so I could tell him again why I was divorcing him. I guess he decided he wanted no part in an argument that night, or for the next two weeks. We hardly exchanged a word. The papers sat on the table. I looked at them every evening when I got home from work, hoping he had signed them, but he hadn't. After two weeks had passed, and it looked like Matt wasn't going to sign the papers, I broke the silence about the divorce.

"Matt, I don't know what you are thinking, but I have decided I am going through with this divorce whether you sign the papers or not. I can do it without you signing."

He heard the tone of my voice and knew I meant it.

"I don't know why you are doing this, Esther. I don't want a divorce. I want us to continue to be a family."

"Matt, we have never been a family. I've always felt like your doormat, and I'm tired of it. Please sign these papers so we both can move on with our lives."

Matt begged and pleaded with me not to divorce him, but I was determined it was for the best. I was tired of being abused. I had been warned about Matt before we were married, but I thought I could change him once we were married. We were not compatible at all. It didn't take me long after the wedding to realize I had married the wrong man.

Several days later, I told Matt I would let my lawyer know he refused to sign the papers. He grabbed a pen and signed them.

"There, take them to your lawyer and do what you have to do," Matt said. Then, in another voice, he said, "Why don't we get a legal separation. It will give us another chance to work things out."

I have to admit I wasn't thinking like a good Christian when I heard his words. In my heart I didn't want to make things right with Matt. I knew I had made those vows "till death do us part" but the hurt was much stronger now than those vows. My heart had been wounded badly. I didn't believe words or promises would be able to mend the broken pieces and hold them together for a period of separation. Then I thought of Heather being separated from her daddy. A little girl needs her dad. My own dad was my world when I was a little girl. There would be a big void in Heather's life if her dad was not a part of it. I decided to talk to my lawyer about a legal separation if Matt would agree to leave the house and give me some time for healing. There would be no limit put on the time he could spend with his daughter, but the agreement had to say he would stay away from me. I was very skeptical. In spite of my doubts, I was willing to give the separation a six-month trial. Matt became very upset when I told him he would have to leave and find a place of his own for six months.

The very next day, without Matt knowing, I made an appointment with my lawyer to discuss the legal separation. When I told her Matt wanted us to try a legal separation, she explained that there is no such law in the state of Florida called a legal separation.

"If that is something you and your husband want to try before you go through a divorce, try it. But I have to tell you that you have no legal grounds to stand on."

I was very disappointed as I left her office. I told her I would put the divorce "on hold" and pray. She wished me luck. Every fiber in my body told me to go through with the divorce. I was so disappointed to learn I would not have any legal rights that I didn't want to discuss the situation with Matt. Even though I had decided to place our divorce "on hold," I still wasn't sure what I wanted to do.

Matt continued to take Heather to work with him. One morning he left his job saying he needed to take the customer's car for a test drive on the way to the babysitter's house. He stopped at a Circle K convenience store, got out, and left Heather in the car. In the few minutes it took Matt to go into the store, Heather climbed into the front seat and put the car in reverse. It rolled under the semi parked behind them. Thank God my baby didn't get hurt, but there was a lot of damage to the customer's car.

I pleaded with Matt to get out of bed in the morning in time so he could drop Heather off at the babysitter's home before getting to work on time. He paid no attention to me. The garage where he worked was directly across from the dealership. Whenever he needed a part, he would run across the highway between cars to get it. If our daughter were with him that day, he would leave her in a car until he got back. I didn't know he was jeopardizing our daughter's safety until the day I went to his dealership. Heather was four and a half years old, and she loved her daddy. He was her idol. I couldn't understand how my husband could love Heather so much, and put her in danger.

Matt worked with another mechanic. There was just the two of them in the little shop the day I stopped in. Matt had to go across the road for parts. After he left, the other mechanic said, "Mrs. Vance, I like your husband. But if you don't stop him from bringing your little girl out here, she is going to get killed."

"What happened?"

"See how busy this highway is? Well, twice today your husband had to go across the street. Your daughter was asleep in the car. When she woke and found her dad gone, she tried to go across the highway to find him. If I hadn't been here, you might not have a daughter. Sometimes she's asleep in a car he is working on, and he will hoist the car in the air with your little girl in it. Sometimes she wakes up, and hangs out of the window. I'm afraid if he continues to bring her here, she is going to get hurt. Not only that, your husband is going to be in big trouble if the boss finds out he is bringing her here."

I was so angry. I didn't know what to say. It was obvious I could not trust Matt with Heather anymore. Things were getting worse at home between us. Just a couple weeks before the mechanic told me about the dangers Matt was exposing our daughter to, strange things began to happen in our house. Chairs would be tipped over in the living room. Closed windows would be opened, allowing the wind to blow the curtains. The televisions in the house would be on when we returned home—the sound turned up so loud it hurt our ears. Every morning something would be in disarray.

Randy had taken off again and was living with friends, but Steven was still living at home, and he was scared. He reached home after school before I did but refused to go inside alone. He would sit on the steps waiting for me to get home. The first two times I called the sheriff. They checked the house and couldn't find any evidence that anyone from the outside was causing these things. The strangest part was that Matt was not concerned at all while Steven, Heather and I were scared to be in the house alone. The third time the sheriff came they suggested I have deadbolts installed on the door and put clear tape around the windows. But strange things continued to happen.

One night when we returned home from Bible study, every light in the house was on. We went through the house turning them off, checking to see that everything was all right. Another time Heather's dolls and little stuffed animals were all lying in front of one of the blaring televisions. They were all covered with a blanket. The lights and blaring television incidents happened repeatedly, making me wonder if we should have the pastor come to banish whatever spirit was tormenting us.

My friends said Matt was doing these things to scare me, but I couldn't think of any reason why he would do something so sick and cruel to his two children and me. I still go to God in prayer asking His forgiveness if the detective and I wrongly accused Matt. The last sheriff who came said the things that were happening were petty stuff, but the person doing it was a very sick person and could be dangerous. He gave me a detective's card and told me to call him the next time something occurred. Heather was so scared she had begun sleeping in bed with us. Matt still acted unconcerned, as if nothing was happening. Everyone I spoke with was convinced Matt was involved. The thought that Matt could be doing this made me angry rather than afraid.

Then one night an incident occurred that made me feel it really was my husband trying to scare me. I woke from a sound sleep feeling as if someone was watching me. Matt was not in bed beside me. I looked toward the bedroom door. When I stirred, he stood frozen in the middle of the doorway. I couldn't think of any reason Matt would want to frighten me, yet everyone kept telling me Matt was behind all the strange happenings.

I was always up at four thirty every morning. Once the strange things started happening, I made a point to check the house. One morning I discovered our two big family Bibles on the floor in front of the door with Donna's picture sitting on them. We had just had new plush carpet installed. In front of the recliner chair it looked like someone had tried to write words on the carpet. Cold chills ran through me when I saw the Bibles and the indentation of the words.

This is going too far, I thought. I found the card with the detective's number and called him.

"Don't touch anything until I get there," he said.

Matt was asleep, as usual. He never knew when I left in the morning. I did not wake him. I watched for the detective and opened the door before he could ring the bell. As he stepped inside he asked, "Where's your husband?"

When I told him, he went straight to the bedroom and woke him. "Get out of bed and come and explain the stuff in the living room."

Matt was in shock. He didn't know what to do or say. The detective made him place his hand over the markings on the rug. His hand fit perfectly.

"Why are you doing this?" the detective asked.

Matt swore it wasn't him.

"Sir, if this happens again, you will be in serious trouble," the detective said.

"How can you prove I did anything?" Matt asked. "This is my house. If you take fingerprints, you will find mine over everything here."

"Whatever problem you and your wife are having, you need to work it out. But, sir, don't let anything like this happen in this house again, or you will go to jail." As the detective walked outside, he asked to speak to me for a minute.

"Mrs. Vance, if your husband is doing this, his mind is sick. If you are having any kind of domestic problem, if I were you, I would get away from this house for a while until you can get help. You need to work things out."

I didn't say anything to Matt, and he didn't say anything to me. I just took Heather and left for work. But from that day forward nothing ever happened in the house again. It was not even mentioned. I wanted to forget all the things that had happened, but every morning when I stepped out of the bedroom, I checked through the house.

One day Matt and I got into an argument. I couldn't help but ask him, "How come the scary stuff stopped after the detective told you that you would go to jail if it didn't stop?"

"It was the devil. The devil wanted you to believe it was me, and that's why he stopped."

I couldn't leave it at that. "The devil, Matt?"

"It's because of your culture, your practice … where you come from." Matt had said many hurtful things to me in the past, but I was stunned at these words. I had lived with him for thirteen years, and it was unbelievable that he could think these things about me and my upbringing in Honduras.

"You are wrong about my culture. We do not practice evil. We are cursed by sin, just as the whole human race is. People choose to do evil, or good. We all have that same choice. I am so thankful I had parents who taught me about good and evil and the consequences we face for whichever one we choose. I have always tried, with God's help, to do unto others as I would have them do unto me—that includes you, too, Matt."

I felt myself being stripped of all the beautiful things I used to believe in. I felt naked and exposed and ashamed. When I had divorced my first husband, I was able to walk away without any strings attached. This time another life was going to be affected. I didn't know which would be worse—my daughter living in an abusive home or being bounced back and forth every weekend from parent to parent. I couldn't bear the thought of her being away from me every other weekend and not knowing what kind of care she would have. In my haste to be free from Matt, I had forgotten the law would require me to share Heather with him. When that thought hit me, I knew I didn't have an option. I couldn't let him have her for a weekend. I knew he cared for her in his own way, but he was not the most responsible dad. I had to put Heather first. The legal separation matter was not brought up again. I knew I would have to try to make the best of things. I could tell Matt was worried because I didn't mention anything about the separation or divorce, and I continued to distance myself from him.

I came home from work one day and found Matt's car in the driveway. It was unusual for him to come home early, and I was surprised to see him. He came home late every day, but I never questioned him. I was only home a short time when someone knocked on the door. Matt was quick to run to the door.

"Come in, pastor," I heard him say. Our pastor didn't live too far from us, and Matt worked on his car many times, so I wasn't surprised to hear his voice. Matt invited him to come in and sit down. Matt came in the kitchen where I was making dinner and said, "The pastor would like to talk to you for a few minutes."

Right away, I figured he must have told the pastor what was happening between us. I realized, too, Matt was worried because I hadn't told him anything more about the lawyer, and he thought I was going through with the divorce. I stopped what I was doing and went into the living room to greet the pastor.

"Esther," he began, "Matt asked me to come by today to speak to you. He tells me you are divorcing him. I would like to know who you think you are? Matt is a good man. Why are you doing this to him? He is a hard-working man. He does not deserve this from you." The pastor said all this in one breath.

I was shocked to think he would talk to me like this. I was at a loss for words. Usually I can defend myself, but this happened so fast, and I was not expecting to hear my pastor insult me this way. I can't describe how disappointed I was in my pastor to attack me this way. He had no idea what had taken place between Matt and me over the years. The pastor acted very angry with me. I felt as if I was standing before a judge and jury. There was nothing I could say to defend myself; I was condemned before the trial even started. The pastor already believed everything Matt must have told him about me. The pastor was convinced I was doing an evil thing to such a good man. I knew in my heart it would be a waste of breath to try to explain anything to the pastor.

Then, out of respect for him, I said, "Pastor, the reason I am divorcing Matt is because he is not a good husband to me."

I didn't want to go into any details with him as he had already passed judgment on me. I just wanted him to get out of my home.

"Pastor," I said, "Matt should have brought you here a long time ago. I begged him many times to get together with you, but he refused. Matt said I was the one who needed help and no pastor needed to know our business."

I was so angry that evening. I felt helpless. I wanted to go back to the lawyer and tell her I wanted to go through with the divorce. The only thing that prevented me from doing this was the thought of how it would affect Heather. I didn't talk to Matt for days. He started coming home on time in the evening and working around the yard doing things that needed to be done.

I take full responsibility for continuing the sick relationship with Matt that had a devastating effect on five children's lives. I think of the saying, "Misery loves company." During that time I found myself seeking out women who were going through similar situations. We would tell one another what was happening, how much we hated it, and what we were going to do about it. None of us ever acted upon anything. For years we continued to feed on each other while our children suffered. I'm so thankful that when God looks down on us He sees all of us alike. We all need Jesus. He is the only one who can keep us from retaliating in anger to those who hurt us. I believe it was a mistake when I decided not to go through with the divorce. I wanted to do what was best for Heather, but five years later I realized I did her more harm by staying with Matt.

I prayed a miracle would change our hearts toward one another, but neither of us seemed capable to change. Matt and I pretended all was well with our marriage when we were with others, and once in a while we managed at home. But the devil kept working to destroy our family.

Matt completely lost interest in doing anything around the house. He was fired from his job, and decided he didn't want to work as a mechanic anymore. He did a few odd jobs, but soon he began spending more of his time at home or in the park. Without his income, it was harder to make ends meet. We fell behind in paying our bills. The roof needed replacing. Just like our marriage, it seemed everything around us was falling apart. Everything I strived to accomplish seemed to fail. I was angry and confused and didn't know what to do. I asked myself where I had gone wrong. I prayed and prayed, asking God to help me not to be the kind of wife and mother Matt accused me of being.

During this time I wasn't aware of what Matt was telling Heather. Later, I learned he was brainwashing Heather against me, exactly as he had done with the boys years before.

"Don't do that. Mommy will be mad."

"Mom says we need to work around the house today. I can't take you to the park."

"No, Daddy can't play with you now. Mommy will get angry. She thinks I play with you too much."

It wasn't any wonder I was looked upon as an evil mother and stepmother. My husband brainwashed the children into thinking I didn't want them to have any fun in their lives. I tried to teach them balance in everyday living. With God's help, I tried to be a good mother and friend to my children. However, in their young critical years when their character was forming, they were told I wanted to be in control of their lives.

My stepdaughter, Stella, was the only child who understood what was going on. She had lived with it for seventeen years. She tried to warn me about her stepdad, but I hadn't listened. I realize now Matt wanted my sympathy, and I refused to give it to him.

He hated me because I wanted him to take responsibility for his life and family and get a job. He couldn't take the pressure of being a full-time employee with a wife and children. The responsibility was too much for him.

Matt refused to go back to work as a mechanic, yet it was the only trade he had. My salary was not enough to cover everything. Our health insurance for the family was a quarter of my pay. We ended up taking out a second mortgage on our home, but this only added another bill to our list of people who needed to be paid each month. We struggled from paycheck to paycheck. I never had money left after paying the bills, and I never asked for any from Matt. Still, I expected him to at least take responsibility for half our expenses.

Matt wasn't a lazy person, but he wanted to choose what he wanted to do whenever he felt like doing it. His inconsistency drove me crazy. He could be working on something important, something that needed to be done, and he would stop and go watch TV or take the kids to the park. When he returned he would discover he needed something from the store, which would be closed. There was always much to be done around the house, and Matt would always promise to do it later. It always had to be an emergency for Matt to do it right away.

On the other hand, I wanted everything done yesterday. I don't think anything upsets me more than seeing things needing to be done that I couldn't do myself, and Matt refusing to do it because I nagged him. Matt didn't like to be told what to do, and that is why he didn't like a regular job. He didn't seem to care if we lost the house. He couldn't understand why I was angry and rarely communicated with him. I knew a marriage without communication was more likely to fail, but I had said everything that could be said and more. I reached the point where I needed to make a decision. I was exhausted, angry, and stressed. It was affecting my health. My life was a mess.

I wanted Matt out of my life, but I didn't want him out of Heather's life. I knew that if I left Matt and he met another woman, he would not have any time for Heather. She loved her dad so much. She would be devastated being rejected by him. Her life would be affected so much more than the other four children, so I kept hanging on. Every time I thought about ending the marriage, I thought about having to share Heather with Matt. I decided I would continue to make the best of it until Heather was old enough to be able to let me know what she did on weekends with her dad.

Six years passed before I found myself walking up the stairs to the office of the divorce lawyer again. "This time, I mean it," I told her. "I'm going through with the divorce."

My file was on her desk. "I want to be honest with Matt. I want the house I'm living in and the car. Matt can have our other house and the truck. We will divide the furniture. I know he wants the dining room set as he had that when we got married. I don't care what furniture he asks for because it's nothing to write home about."

The lawyer asked me all the standard questions a lawyer asks, and then said, "Are you planning to ask for alimony? You can, you know, but it will be up to the judge to decide."

I shook my head. "No, I hadn't planned to ask for alimony."

"What about child support? I have to tell you, that too, will be up to the judge."

"I wasn't going to ask for child support. However, I do want him to pay two hundred and sixty two dollars a month to cover the cost of the second mortgage I had to take out on the house."

"Are you sure you don't want to ask for anything else?" The lawyer asked.

"No, Matt is not a bad man. He loves his daughter, and I think he will always do what is right toward her." I kept giving Matt the benefit of the doubt, but boy, was I wrong about that!

When the lawyer asked about my debts, I explained, "I borrowed money from my credit union to remodel the house Matt will be getting."

"I can ask for that money back for you, but again the judge would decide."

"No, Matt doesn't have a steady job. He won't be able to pay me back."

I was feeling sorry for him. He was calm all through the divorce; it was as if he was blocking it out. He wouldn't talk to me about it. When the divorce became final, I told Matt we were legally divorced, and he needed to leave my house. I showed him the papers.

"We are not divorced. That is just a piece of paper. In God's sight, we are still married," Matt insisted.

I wanted Matt out, but that meant him taking Heather every other weekend. He didn't have a place to live as his house was rented. He had had enough time, but he had made no effort to ask them to find another place to live because Matt didn't have any intention of moving out of my house.

I told Matt I would never take full blame for our divorce. Yes, I chose to divorce him, but divorce was never in my plan when we got married. When I filed for the divorce the first time, and didn't go through with it, Matt thought I was bluffing. In a way I prayed that he would take it seriously and make a change so it would never come to this. Now he was trying to make me feel as if I was the worst woman in the world for divorcing him. I gave him every chance to treat me the way a man should treat his wife, especially a man who professes to know God. Matt would quote Bible verses and tell me I was sinning.

God sees every secret thing that happens. Sometimes we might be able to fool our friends and people around us, but we can't fool God. When I asked Matt to seek professional help with me, he said, "You're the one who needs help." I often responded back, "We both need help if we want to save our marriage."

Matt knew he had no right to demand anything from me. The first couple of months after the divorce, Matt acted as if he had lost everything he owned. He was looking for pity, and I was still giving it to him. One reason I didn't want Matt to be angry with me was because of Heather. His visitation rights were Friday through Sunday.

"When you move out, I will bring Heather to church Saturday mornings, and you can take her after church and bring her back on Sunday."

He agreed, but he didn't have any plans to move out. Around this time I was scheduled for a same-day surgery procedure to remove a lump from my breast and have it biopsied. Two years before the divorce, I had discovered lumps in my breast that turned out to be noncancerous. When additional lumps emerged, the surgeon advised me to have them removed. I was scared I had cancer, but thank God, it was only scar tissue from the biopsy.

Donna offered to take me to the hospital for the procedure, but I told her I'd ask Matt. Donna had just had twins and was nursing them. It would have been a lot for her to bring them along, sit at the hospital, and then pick up Heather from school. Matt didn't have a permanent job, so I asked him if he wouldn't mind dropping me off at the hospital. Donna would pick me up after the biopsy.

"No problem," Matt said. "What time do you have to be there?"

"Ten thirty."

"Would you mind making me a pie and a lima bean casserole? We're having a get-together at work, and I'm supposed to bring something."

I told him I would, but I have to admit I really didn't feel like cooking that night. Matt had no idea how worried I was because I hadn't told him anything about the procedure or what was going on. Matt went to the store for the ingredients, and then joined me in the kitchen to help me prepare the dishes. I remember him thanking me because it was late by the time we finished.

"Tomorrow I need to have the food there by ten o'clock, Esther. I'll drop off the food and be right back to take you to the hospital."

"I need to leave here by nine thirty, Matt. It takes forty-five minutes to an hour to get to the hospital, and I need to be there on time."

"Don't worry. I will be back on time," Matt said.

I had called Donna earlier to let her know that Matt would take me.

"Mom, I got a babysitter. I'll come and take you."

I convinced her Matt would take me.

"Okay, Mom. Call me if you need me."

That night while Matt and I were in the kitchen preparing the food a feeling came over me to say to Matt, *Why don't we try to work things out and start over?* But I was not able to bring myself to say those words to him.

The next morning I waited for Matt to return. Nine thirty came, and there was no sign of him. I knew I wouldn't make it on time if I waited longer.

I called Donna and told her I would drive to her house so I could leave my car there, and she could drop me off at the hospital. I wouldn't be able to drive after the biopsy, and my car would be safe at her house. Donna got me to the hospital on time. As I sat in the waiting room, I kept hoping Matt would walk in the door and tell me traffic or car problems had held him up. I wasn't taken into surgery until twelve thirty, but Matt never showed up. When I came out of recovery, I asked Donna if Matt had come or called.

"No, Mom, I haven't heard a word from him."

Eight hours after the procedure I was released, but I was very ill after the biopsy. The nurses helped me outside and into Donna's car. A friend of mine came to the hospital to see how I was doing. When he saw how sick I was, he offered to drive to my home to help Donna get me out of the car. I didn't have enough strength to walk alone; it took the two of them to get me inside my house.

Matt got home around six o'clock that Friday evening. He was in the house about ten minutes before he came down the hall to the bedroom. He stood by the door and looked in at me.

"Donna said you are not feeling too good."

I was too sick to respond. Thank God I was because what I wanted to say to him would not have been what he wanted to hear. That night Matt came and lay in bed beside me. He was asleep in seconds. I couldn't get out of bed to use the bathroom. I had to use the bedpan. Then I got extremely nauseated, and I vomited for four days. Donna moved in and stayed for a week to help me until I was well enough to take care of myself.

I'd had the surgery on Friday. Saturday morning as Matt was dressing for church, Donna said to him, "Matt, will you take the two girls to church with you?" The girls were up and getting dressed. They loved to go places with him. He always made it fun for them.

I heard Matt respond, "Isn't your mother going to church today?"

"Matt, my mother is sick. She can't even go to the bathroom on her own."

"Sometimes we think we are too sick to get out of bed, but if we get up and move around, we find out that we are not as sick as we think we are," Matt said.

I laid in bed listening to his comments. I got sicker just thinking about the fact that on Thursday night I had almost asked him to work on our relationship. What a fool I was to think he could ever change. Each time he did something like this, I came one more step to telling him to get out of the house. My only fear was that he would tell Heather I had kicked him out.

The people renting his house finally left in disgust when Matt refused to repair a large hole in the roof that allowed gallons of water to pool on the floor when it rained. With his house free, Matt finally moved out of my house, which was a very happy day for me. With every fiber in my body, I knew I couldn't go on living like I had been. After Matt left, I realized I had grieved and healed with him living right in the home with me. It was a relief to have him gone. The feeling that came over me was the same as when I left Mrs. Camille after twelve years. I didn't realize how in bondage I had been those fourteen years with Matt.

The other thing that worried me about Matt leaving was the dark. I didn't know how Heather and I were going to make it at night. We were both afraid of the dark. Ever since those "weird" things occurred, I was afraid to come out of my bedroom at night. I knew I had to trust God to protect us, but we lived on five acres of land, and it was a bit secluded. Nelly tried to assure me that everything was going to be okay, that God would watch over Heather and me. I couldn't let Heather know how scared I was. I had to be brave for her, so I slept with the house lit up like a Christmas tree, and we both slept through the nights without any problem.

I considered moving, but I loved living in the country and couldn't afford to move anyway. I prayed many times and asked God to take the fear away from Heather and me, so I couldn't understand why God wasn't answering my prayer. Why wasn't He taking this fear away? Nelly kept reminding me to read Psalm 23 as it tells us to fear no evil as God is with us always. The Bible also tells us He will keep in perfect peace those whose minds stay on Him.

I kept praying, and one night sweet relief came. My air conditioner unit is beside my bedroom door. Sometimes when the back door is open, the air seems to get into that closet, and it makes it seem as if the door opens and closes by itself. I've seen and heard it happen many times during the day. One night I was asleep, and the air conditioner kicked on. The door did its thing, and the noise scared me badly. I jumped out of bed; then I realized right away what had caused it as I could hear the unit running.

"Thank God," I said. If I hadn't heard it running, I would have thought someone was in the house. I dropped to my knees and prayed for God to send angels to protect us. A comforting feeling swept over me. I felt the presence of angels by our front door protecting us.

"Dear Jesus, I am so tired of being afraid. Please send two of the biggest and bravest angels from heaven to my house to protect Heather and me. We are so afraid to live in our own house. Please put one by my back door and one near the front door." I was very specific and I prayed that prayer from the depth of my heart.

That night my prayer was answered. Praise God. I always woke at five o'clock in the morning. The first thing that usually would pop into my mind was to check to see if anything strange had happened while I was asleep. That morning when I awoke, I remained in bed for a few minutes with my eyes closed. I had no urge to get up and look around, and I didn't feel afraid. In my mind I imagined two big angels standing on either side of my front door. They were dressed in camouflaged outfits and wore a sword at their side. Their shorts reached below their knees. I lay there and kept repeating out loud to myself, "Jesus, You answered my prayer." It was so very real to me.

When I got up, I felt a peace come over me. The urge to go and peek out my front door made the hair stand up on my arms. A chill ran through me, but it didn't scare me. I was filled with a happy feeling. I felt free from the fear of the unknown. For years afterwards I could close my eyes at night and see the angels faithfully standing by my front door. Then one night when my eyes and thoughts took me to the front door, only one angel was there. Right away my eyes and mind went to the back door, but there wasn't an angel there. But I was still at peace. To this day I can close my eyes and see my beautiful guardian angel standing beside my front door.

Chapter 26

Matt saw Heather every other weekend, and they had fun together. Which meant that I became the most boring mother in the world. Heather couldn't wait for her weekends with her daddy, but one day she admitted to me that she didn't like being with him at night.

"At night Daddy goes to his friend's house to play cards and whatever else they do, and I have to go with him. Mommy, I hate going there with Daddy. He stays there too long, and I go under the table by his feet and go to sleep. I'm afraid of the man there because he looks at me."

I told Matt what Heather told me.

"I'd never put Heather in any danger," Matt said. He even mentioned the names of the guys he visited. I knew all of them and believed they were all gentlemen.

"Matt, if Heather feels uncomfortable around them, maybe you shouldn't take her there."

The fact of the matter was that I didn't trust Matt. I had a very negative feeling about him. Heather was too young to understand, and she thought I was being mean to her dad. To top it off, I was the one who disciplined her, took away privileges when it was necessary, made her practice the piano, told her "no," and heard Matt tell her, "Mama will get mad if you do that."

He would never say "no" to her. I always had to take the blame, so he could look good to his children. Little did I know that Matt was poisoning the children's minds with lies about me. He even told Heather and Alexis, my granddaughter, that if they were left alone with me I could get angry enough to kill them. He brainwashed the children into thinking I was a bad mother.

Sadly, I knew Matt would eventually reject Heather when he got a girlfriend and moved on with his life, and I hated him for it already. I knew she would be devastated because he was her idol, and somehow I figured she would blame me for the rest of her life.

Sure enough it didn't take long for Matt to find someone to marry. Heather came home all excited. "Daddy is getting married. He's buying a very expensive home in a prestigious neighborhood, and I'm going to live with him and his new wife."

It broke my heart when Heather told me she wanted to live with her father. It was a shock. I couldn't believe my daughter would leave me this way. I guess I was being selfish as Matt had just as much right to her as I did. But I knew she was being brainwashed about living in a beautiful home. When she came home from her weekends with her father, she would happily tell me about the parties they talked about and the expensive stores where he promised they would shop.

I was so angry I would tell her it was a lie and that those things would never happen. She was just a little girl and believed in her father. She thought I was a jealous mother who didn't want her daddy to remarry. She thought I was being mean for not wanting her to live with her dad where she would have fun. I tried to explain to her that I wasn't jealous. I told Heather I loved her and didn't want to see her hurt, but she was too young to see it.

"Don't do this to my little girl," I begged Matt.

He laughed in my face. "My fiancée will make Heather a good mother." He even had Heather believing this.

I'd always heard, "Don't put your spouse down in front of your children." This is easier said than done. I tried to explain to Heather why I had to leave her dad. She loved her father so much she believed everything he said. He told her when she was a baby I used to pick her up and throw her against the wall. He told her I threw her off the counter. Matt twisted every word I said to the children. He made them believe my discipline was bad for them and that I was evil.

Heather was convinced her daddy loved her more than I did. When she returned home from her weekend visits, she would tell me the things she did. It wasn't anything bad, but I was surprised at the freedom he gave her. What he had considered wrong for Donna and Stella wasn't wrong for Heather.

Whenever I saw Randy, he would tell me Matt was allowing Heather to do things he used to forbid him and Steven to do. He never allowed the girls to paint their nails or put on a little eye shadow. Movies were taboo when the other four children were growing up. They were not allowed to go even once in all those years of our marriage. I went along with Matt. He made the rules, and I tried to help the children abide by them. They hated some of the rules, especially the girls. Worst of all was when Matt accused them of doing things they didn't do. I thought he was trying to protect them at first, but he went about it the wrong way. When they became teenagers, he didn't allow them the freedom to make choices.

When Heather came home wearing makeup and with her nails painted, I couldn't believe Matt was the same man I had been married to for fourteen years. He had changed so much. I asked him what made him change.

"The woman I'm dating and planning to marry has different views," he told me. "She'll make Heather a good mother."

Basically, Heather was tricked into believing life was going to be all fun and games living with her father and his new wife. I begged Matt not to confuse our daughter this way. I tried to explain we both had already done enough damage to her. She had so much faith in what her father said. I tried to prepare Heather, but she built up a wall and refused to listen to anything

I had to say.

"You're jealous," she would cry. "You don't want Daddy to get married!"

Once Matt was married, Heather couldn't wait until he came back from his honeymoon. She was so excited. He had promised her she could come and live with them just as soon as they returned. She counted the days. I didn't think his new wife would want Heather to move in that quickly, but Heather was convinced they wanted her.

Heather had become very disrespectful to me. Already she felt she didn't have to obey me any longer because she was going to live with her daddy. In her eyes I was an old, mean, jealous mother. I was shocked to think my twelve-year-old daughter could turn against me and say the things she did.

Heather moved in with her father and new stepmother the day they returned from their honeymoon. That night when my daughter walked out of my house, she took a part of my heart with her—a part that has never been able to heal. Maybe, if Heather had been older, I would have been able to deal with her rejection. There was nothing I could do but cry.

Chapter 27

I felt like the woman in the Bible who woke up in the morning and found another woman's dead baby lying beside her. She knew someone had switched the babies and her baby was alive. The two women were taken before King Solomon. Both swore the baby belonged to them. King Solomon, who the Bible says was the wisest man who ever lived, went to his secret chamber to seek wisdom from God. I can imagine the silence in the courtroom as everyone waited to learn of the king's decision. The life of an innocent child was at stake. How I wish Matt and I had sought God's wisdom in Heather's case instead of allowing bitterness and strife to come between us.

The Bible speaks of a record book in heaven where all of our deeds, good and bad, are listed. We may be able to hide things from our friends and other people, but we cannot hide anything from God. One day we will all have to stand before Him, and the book will be opened. I pray when Matt and I face God concerning Heather, we find that God saw we were simply ignorant of the love each of us had for her. I pray he will write "forgiven" beside both our names, knowing how much we loved her.

Not only did Matt hurt Heather, but he turned his back on his grandchildren. Although not biological, Donna's children considered Matt to be their grandpa. He did fun things with them, and they thought he was the greatest grandpa in the world. Sadly, after he remarried, he rejected them as he did Heather. When my grandchildren would see him at church, they would run to him with their arms in the air so he could pick them up. But he would completely ignore them. It broke my heart to see how he treated them. They couldn't understand why their grandpa wouldn't have anything to do with them anymore.

"Grandpa has another family and needs to spend time with them now," I told the children. They heard my words, but their hearts couldn't understand. When he continued to ignore them, they no longer ran to him, and he faded out of their lives.

I suspected the same thing would happen between him and Heather, but I thought there was a bond between them, and I hoped he wouldn't break her heart. Heather soon discovered that daddy wasn't in control of anything. His promises were soon forgotten. It took only a few days for Heather to discover the fun times were over. Weeks passed, and she was still sleeping on a mattress on the floor in her stepsister's bedroom. She wasn't wanted there. Her stepsister was older and wanted her privacy.

Matt's new wife had to go away for a couple weeks. This left Heather, her father, and a stepbrother home alone. It was summer. Heather was not in school, and her father had to go to work. Heather was left home alone with her stepbrother, whose friends were in and out of the house. She smelled beer and marijuana smoke frequently. She knew what it was because of her experience with Randy smoking it at home.

"Mom," Heather told me one day, "Daddy bought me doughnuts and chocolate candies, and I stayed locked in the bedroom all day. I was afraid to come out while Daddy wasn't home."

Heather thought she was going to be part of the family and have freedom like she was used to at our home. I tried to prepare her for what I feared was going to happen, but she believed I was just being mean. However, she soon learned the truth.

Six weeks after the wedding, while I was out, Heather left a frantic message on my answering machine. "Mommy, Mommy, where are you? I'm coming home tonight! Daddy's wife is coming home from her trip, and she says Daddy needs to bring me back home. She said the best place for me is home with my mother. She said you have to take responsibility and take care of me."

When I heard that message, I had all kinds of mixed feelings. Anger was one of them. I felt degraded. Both Matt and his wife knew I was a responsible mother. But they had lured my daughter away with false promises. At eleven-thirty that evening, I answered the phone. Again, I listened to the desperate voice on the other end of the phone.

"Mommy, I have to come home. Daddy's wife is coming back tomorrow, and Daddy needs to bring me home tonight."

Heather had already been through more than she should have. She was ready to come home, and I was happy. I left the front door unlocked and went to my bedroom and closed the door. I didn't want to have any kind of confrontation with Matt when he dropped Heather off. I was afraid I would say something I would regret. I didn't even want to hear his voice.

I heard the car door close, and moments later the front door opened. I heard Heather open her bedroom door, and then, everything was quiet. I looked through my bedroom window. Matt's car was gone. My heart was so sad; it didn't matter anymore what Matt and Heather thought of me. I felt as if I had lost her. I had lost that beautiful warm feeling when my precious little girl would hug me and say, "I love you, Mommy." I would pick her up and swing her around and say, "I love you, too." I felt I would never be able to get that close to Heather again. I knew if she would let me, we could start all over again. I had never stopped loving her, not for one second.

When we talked, I let her know I was disappointed in the way she had turned on me, but there was nothing she could do that would ever stop me from loving her. I stressed this love to her, Donna, and Stella. How very much I loved them and would give my life for any one of them.

Heather stayed locked in her bedroom for days. She would come out to call her daddy, but he never answered the phone. She left message after message, but he never returned her calls. I saw her crying and knew how much she was hurting. But she refused to let me help her as she had built up an even stronger wall between us. She wouldn't let me in.

God forgive me, but I began to hate Matt more and more every day for what he did to our daughter and what he was still doing. He was caught up in his new life with his new family, and there was nothing wrong with that. However, he also had a responsibility to Heather. She was his very own daughter. She loved him so much that she turned against me for him. I never will be able to understand how Matt could reject Heather. Right before my eyes, I witnessed the devastation of a father's rejection on a child. I had seen it with the other children, but they had each other. Heather was alone. I watched her turn from a trusting little girl who used to pray to Jesus not to let it rain when she wanted her birthday party outside to a sad and withdrawn child.

When Jesus was hanging on the cross, it hurt God the Father to see His precious Son suffering for our sins; it hurt Him so badly He turned His back for just a moment. Jesus felt as if His Father had rejected Him, and He cried, "Father, Father, why have You forsaken me?"

If Jesus felt rejected by His heavenly Father, we can feel the same from our earthly father.

Heather eventually stopped calling her dad. Yet she saw him every Sabbath at church. Of course, although she saw him, she really didn't know what how to act around him. "Mama," she said, "I don't know what to say to Daddy when I see him."

For my own sanity, I tried to avoid coming in contact with him because when I did I walked away hurt and frustrated. Satan was working hard on me to reap the seeds of hate. Every time I saw Matt my heart despised him more for what he had done and was doing to Heather. It got so that whenever I went to church and saw his name in the bulletin I wanted to leave. It was hard sitting in church having to listen to Matt pray those long beautiful prayers knowing how he treated his daughter.

The relationship between Heather and me began to get a little better. She still blamed me one hundred percent for leaving her father, even though he ignored her and sometimes treated her like a stranger.

Matt paid the child support each month ordered by the court, and he saw her every Saturday. But he did nothing more for her. I wished Heather could see him like he was, but her love was so strong she couldn't bear the thought of her daddy not being a part of her life.

"Please consider what you are doing to your daughter," I said to Matt one day. "I tried to explain to her the way you treated me, but she didn't want to hear it. She said, 'That's between you and him.' When she discovers who you are for herself, it will be worse than anything I could ever tell her. May God forgive you for what you have done to all of your children."

I knew I was wrong for trying to tell my daughter about her father, but I was tired of him hurting her. Time did not heal Heather's pain. Her hurt grew deep inside her heart. As she became a teenager, it was even harder for her to accept her father's rejection. She needed her dad's love and affection.

As the years went by, she finally accepted that he didn't care about her. I had to be mother and father to Heather, just as any other single mother does. It's not an easy job. God certainly didn't plan it to be this way. Our selfish desires to please ourselves cause so many divorces and ruin the lives of our children. Whatever mistakes I made while raising the five children God placed in my care, I know I did my best with the knowledge I had. I wanted what was best for them. God knows I didn't want them to experience some of the things I had lived through by making hasty and unwise choices. What came across as control to them was my attempt to try and lead them in the right direction so that they would avoid the mistakes I had made throughout my life.

I struggled to keep things running smoothly for Heather and me. Stella came to our rescue with monetary assistance and made it possible for Heather to do and have many things I would not have been able to provide on my salary. Heather went from grade school to high school. She kept her grades up and became involved in school activities. She was on the gymnastic team and traveled different places with them. She was a cheerleader, played the piano, had fun with friends, and participated in church activities. Still, none of this filled the place caused by the loss of her father.

Chapter 28

My favorite author has a book on raising children in which she says that we, as parents, sometimes think we own our children. The children are really individuals with minds of their own. God loans each child to us. Parents have a responsibility to teach their children right from wrong and to bring them up in the admonition of God. We are to teach by example. Some of us fail because of the way we were brought up. No one is perfect, and no one wants to be blamed. From the beginning of time, humans have blamed others. Adam blamed Eve, and Eve blamed the devil. We want someone else to carry the guilt so we can be free, but someone always has to pay sooner or later.

Many children pay the price when there is a divorce. I have come into contact with so many hurting and angry children in my work. I wish that people would seek God's guidance if they are contemplating a divorce and there are children involved. Children don't need material things. They need a mom and a dad who love and respect one another. In our society today, parents tend to buy children more things than they need. And then, in order to make ends meet, both parents work long hours on multiple jobs.

I was no exception when it came to filling some of my daughters' needs with stuff. I tried to make sure they fit in with their friends. I made many sacrifices thinking I was doing what every good mother should do. I sent them to church school. I took them to church every week, but I failed to faithfully spend those precious moments with Jesus and my children, like my parents did with me.

The most important thing in my life when I was a child was the time I spent with my parents. My mom would sit all of us children down—boys and girls—and give each one of us a needle, thread, thimble, and piece of cloth. That's how we learned to patch our dresses and pants. We would often sing and learn Bible verses while we worked. My mother used every opportunity to teach us about Jesus. As hard as life was living on the island with my family, I cherish the times we spent together. Most of the time, we didn't know where our next meal would come from, but God always seemed to provide what we needed just in time.

I truly believe God honored my parents' faithfulness. I feel we were the luckiest ten children to have them as our mom and dad because they taught us about God.

Among the many Bible principles my parents taught me, they urged me to love and forgive those who hurt me. The more I thought about forgiveness, the more I realized how much I needed to become like a little child in order to forgive Matt. I remember falling on my knees and crying out to God that I could never forgive Matt because he had severed the relationship between Heather and me. But not forgiving someone can destroy your health and affect those around you.

When the disciples asked Jesus to teach them how to pray, He told them to first ask for forgiveness of their sins, then to forgive those who trespassed against them. I still don't understand God's forgiveness and mercy. When you are unforgiving, it is like a cancer. Peter asked Jesus how many times we should forgive someone, and Jesus said seventy times seven.

"Jesus, you know I don't want to forgive Matt, but You forgave me of my sins. Please teach me how to forgive Matt." It was a struggle to pray that prayer, but I was tired of carrying that awful load. I wanted to give it to Jesus and let Him bear it for me. I had prayed many, many times before asking God to help me not to despise Matt. It seemed the more I prayed, the worse it became. I finally dropped to my knees before God and told him I was helpless and needed His forgiveness. I told him how hard I had tried over the years, but it hadn't worked. Now, I was ready for Him to teach me how to let go and surrender everything to Him. I believe Jesus is waiting with open arms when we are truly ready for Him to cleanse us from our sins and make us pure and clean within.

There is a story in the Bible about a woman Jesus met at Jacob's well. She didn't know it was Jesus. The culture of her day looked down on her. She was surprised that Jesus, a Jew, would stoop low and ask her for a drink of water. I believe Jesus looked in this woman's heart and saw she was broken from all of the bad choices she had made. It wasn't a coincidence that she came to the well that day. I believe the Holy Spirit drew her there so she could come in contact with Jesus. I believe there is a time, like Solomon said, for everything, including accepting Jesus as our personal Savior. We cannot do it on our own. The Holy Spirit has to draw us to Jesus, and then we have to be willing for Him to do His work in us. The woman at the well was willing. She recognized that Jesus was like no one she had ever met, so she ran to get her friends to come and meet Him. She said, "He told me everything I ever did. He knows all about me, and He is not ashamed to be seen talking to me."

What a relief it was the day Jesus set me free. I understand now why I have had so many disappointments in my life. Instead of looking to God to fill my needs, I looked to my husbands. They were insecure, and neither was capable of caring for a family. I was desperate for love and someone to fill the voids in my life, and I became blinded by my needs.

In writing this book, I have experienced the joy and peace that forgiveness brings. When I started writing, hurt and anger controlled my life. Praise God for His forgiveness. As He helped me heal, I came to the place where I could stand before Mrs. Camille, Phillip, and Matt and, with an honest heart, say to them, "I forgive you for the pain and hurt you caused me. I ask your forgiveness for anything I did to cause you to treat me the way you did. May God forgive us all."

I am now able to move on with my life and live it to the fullest because I have become acquainted with the One who is able to forgive and cleanse me from all of my sins and unrighteousness. The night I completed this book, I felt a sense of relief, and I knew I was forgiven.

If someone has treated you wrong, God knows about it. He never left your side, not for one moment. He carried you in His arms when you felt you didn't have the strength to go on. He felt the pain of every blow. He heard every unkind word and saw every tear you shed.

Jesus suffered at the hands of men. He was ridiculed and beaten. He committed no sin, yet He was willing to be abused and mistreated because of His unconditional love for us. I can testify to the world that He lives. Jesus lives in me. I feel clean inside. I can say the names of the people I thought wronged me now. Praise God there is no animosity in my heart toward them anymore. My prayer is that they, too, might seek to make things right with God and discover the forgiveness, joy, and peace that comes with repentance.

I shed many tears in writing this book. I had tried to forget some of the terrible experiences I had lived through. Some of them happened from my bad choices and wanting to please myself. But there were other circumstances that I had no control over. The Bible says in this world we will have trials and tribulations. It doesn't say we "might" have them, it says we "will" have them. But Jesus says, "Be of good cheer. I have overcome the world." I thank God He was able to make something of me. I am thankful God looks at us through His Son. He sees what we can become through Him.

When I was a child, I thought my life was the most horrible life a child could live. As I grew older, I realized my suffering was nothing compared to what some people go through, including my Savior who humbled Himself and became a servant to us.

I do not understand why God has led me through so many storms. Then I feel so unworthy and ashamed for complaining, and I look to the Bible for guidance. I read the story of Peter, Paul, and Jonah. They were in literal storms when they called out for Jesus to save them. He didn't prevent them from going through the storms. He went through their storms with them.

I want to be like Job. He couldn't understand why so many awful things happened to him. Even his wife asked him why he didn't curse God and die. Job told her, "You speak like a foolish woman." I think he meant to say, "Where will I go if I turn away from my Maker?" When Job's friends forsook him, he felt as if God had forsaken him, too. He cried out, "God, even if You kill me, I will serve you until my last breath."

These are some of the stories my mom and dad used to tell us again and again. I never liked the beginning of these stories as they made me sad. My mom was always able to tell these stories as if she was right there and saw it happen. As I got to know Jesus better, I prayed He would become as real to me as he was to my mom and dad. I know today that He is real, and like Job, I can say, "God, even if You kill me, I will serve you until my last breath."

As a small child, I'd dreamed of coming to America. Listening to stories, I created my own dreams of life in America and what it had to offer. America does have opportunities, but many people come with hopes and dreams they are unable to fulfill. I've had many setbacks since I came to the United States, but I feel very fortunate for the opportunities many still long for. This land lets you enjoy the freedom to work and worship as your own heart dictates.

I have spent most of my life in America, and I love this country. I was lonely and discouraged my first year. Life here has its ups and downs, just as it does in other places. But with God's help, I was able to pick up the broken pieces. He placed many loving friends in my life. They were there to encourage me. I am grateful to Mrs. Adela for giving me a place to live. I was a stranger, and she took me in. She gave me shelter and food and asked nothing in return.

When I look back now, I often wonder what my life would have been like if I had not come to America. But then I think about God's guidance through the years, and I realize that I'm where God wants me to be. I can testify that Jesus is who He says He is. He is real in my life, and He was there all the time. He was there the day my mom took me to Mrs. Ethelle, and He there was when Udeen stole me away and took me home. God had other plans for me. For many years, I wished I had stayed with Mrs. Ethelle. I choose to believe that was not the place God wanted me to be. I don't know why He would allow me to leave someone so kind and gentle and go to work for someone who treated me like a slave, but I choose to trust Him.

God saw my future and tried to prepare me for it. It's unlikely I would have learned some of the hard lessons living with Mrs. Ethelle. With Mrs. Camille I learned responsibility. I also learned to obey and please her. She did not allow mistakes. I had to learn to live with rejection, which was the hardest thing for me to accept. At age seven, I couldn't understand why I had to have my own plate, spoon, and fork. I was slapped and called names if I was caught using a different glass. I couldn't understand but had to accept the fact that I had to wait outside while they were eating. The person I worked so hard to please told me many times that I was no good. The one thing that saved me was seeing my mom and dad and having them remind me that Jesus loved me. My parents had no idea how Mrs. Camille treated me. They told me to be obedient and respectful.

Whenever Mrs. Camille called me names, I wanted to call her one back, but I didn't dare. I sure did a lot of name calling in my mind, along with many other thoughts of things I wished I could have done to her. She continued to abuse me until the day I left. When she hit me that final day and I hit her back, I didn't feel at all proud of myself. I wasn't sorry, but I was ashamed of myself.

I was nurtured and loved at home those first critical seven years of my life. My parents' teachings were so valuable; I'm sure they saved my life. I'm sure, too, that God worked through my parents to prepare me for those twelve years. I was a slow learner. Sometimes it seemed as if I was regressing instead of progressing. Every time I felt trampled down, I thought of my parents and how good they were to me.

My heavenly Father brought me from a land where I felt there was no future to a land where I was able to give my daughter opportunities I never had. I have been able to achieve many of the dreams I shared with my father.

I thank God every day for His blessings and for the journey I have been through. I'm so thankful God gave me a heart that can love and forgive. He blessed me with so much that I have been able to help take care of my mother, father, brothers, and sisters whenever there is a need. My dad always believed in me. My mom said if I put my hope and trust in Jesus He would never let me down. When I was growing up, I could never understand how they could feel that way about God. It seemed as if He didn't know we existed because we were so poor, but Mom and Dad both discovered the peace that comes from trusting and believing God is who He says He is. They tried to teach us that happiness does not come from what we have, or who we know. Instead, happiness comes from knowing God. He transformed their lives and gave them the peace than many in the world do not understand.

Time has healed many of my scars now that I've learned to forgive. I don't know if I can forget, but I don't think God expects us to. He healed my wounds and is teaching me how to love one day at a time. He tells me to cast all my cares on Him because He cares about me. He tells me I can come to Him whenever I mess up, and He will never call me an ugly name. He'll whisper gentle words to my heart, just like my dad used to do. I've discovered that everything my dad told me about Him is true.

One beautiful thing I finally accepted and believe is that I am a child of God. I am made in His image. I'm not here by chance; I was made for a reason and that is to love and worship Him. All I wanted was to be loved and accepted, but I always looked for it in the wrong places and from people unable to love themselves. It has taken me my whole life to figure out why things didn't go right for me. I tried to show the people I loved that all I wanted was their happiness. What I failed to understand was I was trying to do everything on my own instead of allowing God to work through me. My good intentions were my idea. After being hurt, I realized my ideas and thoughts meant something only to me. I felt as if I wasted my entire life with good intentions for the people I loved.

Now that I've met Jesus and made Him Lord of my life, I know I can do nothing on my own. In Him, and through Him, I can do all things because He truly lives in me. Now and then I may look sad and worn out, but deep inside I know I am a daughter of the King. No power on earth can touch the joy and peace I feel when I, like Mary who was condemned to die, can sit at Jesus' feet and weep and hear Him say to me, "I don't condemn you;. Your sins are forgiven; go and sin no more."

God allowed me to go through many trials—childhood slavery, abuse, ridicule, low self-esteem, two abusive husbands, and an abusive stepson. I'm so thankful I can tell Jesus how much I was hurt. I can now say with a thankful heart I have found forgiveness in Jesus. With a truthful heart I can shout to the world that I have forgiven those who were unfair to me. I have asked God to forgive me for anything I have done to cause anyone to sin against Him. Thanks be to God that where there was hate, there is now love and forgiveness.

Jesus sees everything that is happening. He sees every tear that falls, every hand raised in anger, every hurtful word spoken. He sees when one is left to raise little children alone. Jesus will never leave us. When we truly surrender ourselves to Him, Jesus heals our broken hearts and mends our wounds. He then guides us in His ways, which are much higher than our ways.

Chapter 29

I would like to relate a story I learned long ago.

A man was walking along a road. He could see other travelers moving slowly ahead of him. He was relieved to see them, as he was lonely walking the road by himself. He was hungry and thirsty, as he had walked a long way already. He was not carrying a load, so he was able to catch up to them. He was surprised to see that each of the travelers was carrying a long, heavy log. They were moving very slowly and appeared tired and worn. When he asked why they were carrying the logs, they seemed unable to see or hear him. They stared straight ahead, almost as if they were being led. As they passed intersecting roads, other weary travelers joined them. They would stop only long enough to pick up a log from beside the road. Some of the more weary travelers began to fall by the wayside. Immediately another traveler would stop and put down his log while he helped the fallen traveler to his feet. Both would pick up their heavy logs and continue on the road.

"Maybe it's because I'm not carrying a log that they won't talk to me," the man decided. "I hope we don't have to go much further. I'll wait a little longer before I pick up a log; then I won't have to carry it so far."

Soon the man saw a log that looked to be the perfect size for him to carry. He stopped, bent over, and started to pick up the log. *Oh, no*, the man thought. *This log is too long and too heavy. I don't want to carry this one*. He continued to walk empty-handed beside the log-carrying travelers. Still, he felt all alone. He wanted them to talk to him. He needed their companionship. The original travelers had accepted all the others who had joined them. *Why won't they accept me? It has to be the log*, he thought. Soon the man saw another log, but as he picked it up, he realized it was much longer and heavier than his original log. Now, however, as he walked along, the log-bearing travelers smiled and nodded their heads at him, as if to say, "Now you are one of us."

Soon the man's steps grew slower, and he began to fall behind. "No, I cannot let this happen. Maybe I can find a shorter log." He looked and looked, but there were no more logs to be found. Tired and weary, he fell further and further behind. "This log is too long." As the man was about to drop the log, he noticed a saw beside the road. He couldn't believe his eyes. Without hesitation, he cut off a section of the log. It was so much shorter and lighter he soon caught up with the travelers, only to find them laying down their logs. The road had dipped down to a river. He stood and watched as one by one the weary travelers pushed their log into the water and used it to make their way across. Each one had carried their heavy load without complaining, willingly bearing their burden, knowing the reward waiting at the end of their journey. Only the long heavy logs could carry the traveler across the river. The man's gaze focused on a tall man standing on the other side of the river. It was Jesus. He was waiting patiently with open arms for each of the travelers.

The man saw that he would be unable to cross the river with his shortened log. He cried out, "Jesus, if I knew You were waiting there, I would have been willing to carry my heavy burden."

Like the story, I believe we have a certain number of trials and crossroads to travel. Some of us shun our responsibilities, expecting others to carry our load. Many times my burdens were heavy. I wanted to lay them down and run away, but there was nowhere to run. This story encouraged me to go on. I carried my heavy burdens until one day I fell beneath them. Then Jesus reached out and said, "My child, if you would let me, I will carry that load for you."

I gave them all to Jesus, and praise God, He set me free.

We invite you to view the complete
selection of titles we publish at:

www.TEACHServices.com

Scan with your mobile
device to go directly
to our website.

Please write or email us your praises, reactions, or
thoughts about this or any other book we publish at:

P.O. Box 954
Ringgold, GA 30736

info@TEACHServices.com

TEACH Services, Inc., titles may be purchased in bulk for
educational, business, fund-raising, or sales promotional use.
For information, please e-mail:

BulkSales@TEACHServices.com

Finally, if you are interested in seeing
your own book in print, please contact us at

publishing@TEACHServices.com

We would be happy to review your manuscript for free.

www.ingramcontent.com/pod-product-compliance
Lightning Source LLC
Chambersburg PA
CBHW081837170426
43199CB00017B/2761